S0-BFE-041

THE INCOME-TAX BURDEN
ON STOCKHOLDERS

NATIONAL BUREAU OF ECONOMIC RESEARCH
. . .

FISCAL STUDIES

The Income-Tax Burden
on Stockholders

DANIEL M. HOLLAND

NEW YORK UNIVERSITY

A STUDY BY THE

NATIONAL BUREAU OF ECONOMIC RESEARCH, NEW YORK

PUBLISHED BY

PRINCETON UNIVERSITY PRESS, PRINCETON

1958

Printed in the United States of America

by Princeton University Press, Princeton, New Jersey

TO MY MOTHER AND FATHER

Preface

THE existence of two income taxes on corporate earnings—a tax at the corporate level and another at the personal level when earnings are distributed—has long been a sore spot in our income tax structure. It is generally agreed that this leads to a rate of taxation for stockholders different from the rate for other income recipients.

But the extent of difference and even its direction—whether "overtaxation" or "undertaxation"—have been matters of controversy. By pointing to the distributed segment of corporate earnings it is a simple matter to demonstrate overtaxation.[1] By considering only the undistributed portion, undertaxation can be shown.

What is the net result when both distributed and undistributed corporate earnings are considered? This is our problem.

The attempt was made to measure the differential taxation of stockholders for 1940-1952 (excluding 1942 and 1943 because the necessary data are lacking). Most of the principles relevant to this problem have been developed by other investigators. The main concern here has been to provide quantitative evidence consistent with these principles, in order to show how heavy this overtaxation or undertaxation was, what factors determined its magnitude, and how much of a net difference it made to federal revenues in the years studied. The answers are not always entirely satisfactory, for the results are only as valid as the assumptions used in their derivation. One could, indeed, say that a major contribution of this study is to show the kinds of assumptions that must be made to solve the problem, and the quantitative effect of the choice of one set of assumptions rather than another. In particular, while most of these findings are based on the assumption that the corporation income tax rests on profits, others have been developed to show what happens to the estimates when it is assumed that half the tax is shifted, i.e. not borne by stockholders. Another test analyzes the effect of modifying the tax law definition of net income to take account of current costs of replacing inventory and depreciable assets. These are only two of a number of tests and alternative calculations that were made. But the results rest on many other assumptions which are spelled out in the body of the report. The reader should keep them in mind.

[1] Some words used repeatedly in the text are heavily laden with inferences which are highly controversial. "Overtaxation," "undertaxation," and related words are written with quotes only occasionally to remind the reader that they express allegations and not the views or opinions of the author. The reader is asked to "see" these terms in quotes when the marks are omitted in favor of appearance and readability.

The conclusions are, therefore, tentative at best. Certainly all questions are not answered, and the answers provided are subject to qualification. Yet headway has been made with the problem. The results should be useful to anyone who must grapple with the complexities of our tax system and is concerned with its effects and with distributive justice.

The findings are summarized in Chapter 8. It is desirable at the outset, however, to provide a general idea of what the reader may expect to find in the study. Here, then, are examples of conclusions that the reader will encounter below in more elaborate and quantitatively buttressed form.

1. Not all stockholders were overtaxed. Despite the double taxation to which they were subject, some stockholders were undertaxed. If their pro rata share of corporate earnings had been taxed promptly and in full as part of personal income, their tax liability would have been larger than it was under both the corporation and personal income taxes. This is because a sizable proportion of corporate earnings are not distributed, and for some stockholders the personal tax rate on such earnings if distributed would have exceeded the rate of corporation income tax.

Overtaxation was at its heaviest at the bottom of the income scale, dwindled as stockholder income rose, and turned into undertaxation at the top of the income range. The income level at which the change from overtaxation to undertaxation occurred varied from year to year, influenced by significant yearly variations in a number of factors. Among these are the height and progressivity of the personal income tax, the rate of corporate tax, the amount of corporate earnings, and the allocation of corporate earnings between dividends and retentions.

2. The revenue that would be yielded if all corporate earnings were taxed as part of personal income (an assumption treating stockholders as "partners" in corporate enterprise) has been compared with the combined yield from the existing corporation tax and the personal income tax on stockholders. The difference between the two proved to be surprisingly small. As of 1955, for example, the current net revenue contribution of the corporation income tax came to a sum that could also have been obtained from a 3 percentage point hike in the personal income tax rate (with stockholders' pro rata share of corporate earnings included in income). In another year, 1947, no increase in personal income tax rates would have been necessary to maintain federal revenues, for either tax structure—the existing two taxes on corporate earnings or the hypothetical taxation of all corporate earnings under the personal income tax alone—would have brought approximately

the same amount of revenue. (See Chapter 6 for a qualification of these revenue estimates.)

3. If the corporate tax is actually shifted in whole or in part, the observations on over- and undertaxation need to be modified, not in general pattern but in magnitude. Overtaxation would be a less severe problem, undertaxation would be more important.

4. On the other hand, if corporate earnings were measured with reference to the current rather than the historical costs of maintaining inventory and replacing depreciable assets, then overtaxation is more severe than our usual method would indicate, and undertaxation is not as widespread.

5. Much has been made of the progressivity effect of the corporation income tax, since, if it is not shifted, its weight falls on a source of income highly concentrated in its distribution. But the analysis indicates this effect is uneven and indiscriminate at best. Stockholders with essentially similar taxable incomes were found subject to widely varying effective rates of tax because some had invested heavily and others lightly in corporate stocks. But even for "average" stockholders in each income class, the progressivity effect of the corporate tax is equivocal. The findings are to some degree dependent on the definition of progressivity used. Under one definition stockholders in lower income brackets were taxed more progressively because of the corporate levy. Under two other definitions, less progressive taxation of stockholders was the general rule.

6. Only a slight degree of relief is afforded most stockholders by the dividend exclusion and tax credit incorporated in the Internal Revenue Code of 1954. These provisions are designed to reduce somewhat the double taxation of distributed earnings. The extent to which such earnings are overtaxed varies inversely with the stockholder's income level, but the relief provisions are not directly geared to this relation. Therefore, considered in relation to the condition they are designed to alleviate, the credit and exclusion operate in somewhat capricious fashion.

The numerous qualifications to which this study's findings are subject are noted in the text. Some general omissions or noteworthy features of the study's approach should be mentioned here.

The investigation was limited to double taxation, without taking account of the possibility of triple taxation because of inclusion of 15 per cent of dividends received by corporations in the corporate income tax base. This omission, however, is not serious. Our basic measures would be changed very slightly by an adjustment on this score.

The study adopts one point of view. There are, of course, others.

Double taxation, under- or overtaxation pose no problem for those who believe that the corporation as such is a proper subject for taxation.[2] (But even proponents of this point of view would probably recognize the problem raised by deliberate use of the corporation to avoid personal taxation.)

In general, the published statistics and the categories under which various items reported on tax forms are tabulated have been accepted. Except for a test calculation (see Chapter 4) no adjustments are made for underreporting of dividends or other sources of income. Moreover, no allowance is made for the fact that in some closely held corporations income tends to be paid out as officers' compensation, rather than as dividends, and therefore, free of corporate tax.

The note of caution sounded earlier bears repeating. The conclusions should not be accepted uncritically. The conceptual framework and statistical procedures, set forth in the first chapter and developed in concrete detail in the next two chapters, were selected from a number of possibilities. This must be considered in evaluating the findings and in using them properly.

Acknowledgments

THIS study was initiated while I was a Carnegie Research Associate at the National Bureau of Economic Research. Of the many people who have generously provided help and critical advice in the course of the work I am particularly indebted to: the late Robert Murray Haig for his aid and encouragement in the early stages of the investigation; Lawrence H. Seltzer for his continuing interest and suggestions from start to finish of the project; Arthur F. Burns who spelled out for me in a searching reading of an earlier draft what is involved in economic research; Richard B. Goode and W. Leonard Crum, for both the guidance and insights provided by their published work and the comments they made in critically reviewing an earlier draft of the manuscript.

In addition, at one stage of its development or another, I have benefited from a careful reading of the manuscript by Solomon Fabricant, Harold M. Groves, Clarence Heer, Thor Hultgren, Geoffrey H. Moore, Beardsley Ruml, Carl S. Shoup, and Richard Slitor. Helpful comments and suggestions were made by Percival F. Brundage, Gerhard Colm, Marius Farioletti, Michael Gort, C. Lowell Harris, A. G. Hart, C. Harry Kahn, Simon S. Kuznets, Eugene Lerner, George Lent, Maurice E. Peloubet, Marshall Robinson, Dan T. Smith, William S. Vickrey,

---

[2] See, for example, Gerhard Colm, "The Corporation and the Corporate Income Tax in the American Economy," *American Economic Review*, May, 1954, pp. 486-503.

and Leo Wolman. I wish to thank Thomas R. Atkinson of the Federal Reserve Board of Atlanta who made unpublished materials available to me.

In the early stage of the project, Bella Kobocow helped me with the intricacies of *Statistics of Income*, and Gloria Moskowitz and Fred Stuart rendered computational assistance. Doris Eiseman and Mary Anne Crossot were responsible for most of the heavy burden of statistical work and helped me clarify a number of conceptual problems. Near the completion of the project Juanita Johnson with great ability and diligence took the data in hand, checked all the computations, and generally helped to put the pieces together. In this difficult task, her "strength was as the strength of ten."

Louise Cooper improved the language of an earlier draft. To Margaret T. Edgar who painstakingly edited a later version and whipped the manuscript into final shape, I am particularly grateful. H. Irving Forman, with characteristic skill, drew the charts. Dorothy Chesterton and her typing staff met the challenge of my handwriting with dignity and perseverance.

While all those cited helped to shape the study, this does not mean that they are to be identified with either its point of view or its procedures. Quite the contrary is true in a number of cases. For the study's conclusions and errors I alone am responsible.

Daniel M. Holland

Contents

Tables

Appendix Tables

Charts

THE INCOME-TAX BURDEN
ON STOCKHOLDERS

Introduction

STATEMENT OF THE PROBLEM

OUR composite system of corporate and personal taxation has been for some years the target of criticism from opposite directions. Some critics contend that it results in excessively heavy "double taxation;"* others argue that it enables the rich, by corporate retention of earnings, to avoid high upper-bracket personal tax rates and thereby to lower their tax burden. This study attempts to assess the quantitative evidence that bears on these contentions.

Such questions of equity inevitably arise from differences in tax treatment, and it is a fact that the federal tax laws treat a stockholder's corporate earnings differently from other sources of income. A brief historical review will clarify the problem.

At no time since 1913 has our income tax structure (corporate and personal combined) provided for complete equivalence of tax liability between corporate earnings and other categories of income. But an initial attempt at income tax equivalence was made for the distributed component of corporate earnings. The personal income tax act of 1913 exempted dividends from normal tax. Both the tax rate on corporate income and the normal tax rate on personal income were set at 1 per cent; thus for distributed earnings the corporate tax operated as a withholding feature of the personal levy. This treatment continued through 1918, as increases in the personal normal rate were matched by increases in the corporate rate,[1] with these exceptions: a corporate rate greater than the personal normal rate in 1917, and on the first $4,000 of normal tax income in 1918. But from 1919 on, the corporate rate exceeded the personal normal rate and thus the corporate tax became, in part, a separate and distinct levy on distributed corporate earnings.[2] The rate gap widened gradually until 1936 when the bridge

---

* See footnote 1, page xi of Preface.

[1] But even during this period, failure to include the corporate tax payment as part of the personal income surtax base led to a slight measure of differential taxation of distributed corporate earnings. For example, in 1916, corporate earnings of $1,000 were subject to a 2 per cent corporate tax and when the remaining $980 was received by a taxpayer in the 5 per cent surtax bracket, a personal income tax of $49 was due, making a total tax liability of $69. Coming from another source, the same sum would have been subject to $70 of personal income tax (2 per cent normal and 5 per cent surtax). Again, in this same year, corporate earnings of $1,000 in the 10 per cent surtax bracket were subject to a corporate tax of $20 and a personal tax of $98 (i.e. 10 per cent of the $980 distributed as dividends), or $118 in all. On the same amount from other sources the levy was $120 ($20 of normal tax and $100 of surtax).

[2] In some years between 1919 and 1936, at the higher income levels this led, how-

between the two taxes was removed completely by the abolition of the dividend exemption. A return to something like the 1919-1936 procedure was instituted by the Internal Revenue Code of 1954 in the form of a tax credit based on dividends received.[3] But, here too, a substantial gap exists between the personal income tax credit and the rate of corporate tax. Therefore, since 1919 the distributed earnings of corporate enterprises have been treated differently from the other sources of income for federal income tax purposes:[4] from 1919 to 1936, because the corporate rate was higher than the personal normal rate; from 1936 through 1953, because corporate earnings were taxed at the corporate level when earned with no allowance at the personal level when distributed; and from 1954 on, because the personal income tax relief accorded distributed earnings falls short of the corporate tax rate.

As for the undistributed component, non-equivalence has always been the rule. The personal marginal rates that would have applied if retained earnings had been distributed were progressive, and the corporate rate actually levied on retained earnings was, in general, proportional, so that at all but one particular level of stockholder income they were dissimilar. In addition, capital gains taxation tended either to aggravate this discrepancy at the lower income levels or to moderate it, albeit very imperfectly, for stockholders with high taxable incomes. The adjustment on this score was at best very loosely geared to the stockholder's personal income status. For retentions do not show up systematically in share prices; not all such increments are realized in taxable form; and even when so realized, they have been subject, over the period of the income tax, to a variety of special rate provisions.

The present study is an attempt to develop a measure of the "unequal" burden on stockholders caused by the different tax treatment accorded the net corporate earnings component of their incomes.

---

ever, to undertaxation of distributed corporate earnings. Because the corporate tax liability was not included in the personal surtax base, ". . . the deduction of the corporation tax from the reportable dividends reduced the surtax payable below what it would be were no tax collected at source. The corporation income tax rates were usually somewhat higher than the top normal tax rates, so that this advantage was usually offset; nevertheless, in some years the net result was still that in the highest brackets the dividend recipient was more lightly taxed than the salary or interest recipient, even including the burden of the corporation income tax and assuming all earnings to be currently distributed" (William Vickrey, *Agenda for Progressive Taxation*, Ronald, 1947, p. 153).

[3] The Internal Revenue Code of 1954 established an exclusion from taxable income of the first $50 of dividends ($100 for joint returns) and a credit against personal income tax of 4 per cent of dividends in excess of the excluded amount.

[4] Differential taxation before 1918, because of the failure to include the corporate tax in the personal income tax base, was very small.

Its purpose is not to examine all the features of our tax system that may lead to differential levies on various sources of personal income, such as, for example, the social security taxes which are levied on wages and salaries, or tax-exempt interest. The study is limited to the analysis of the differential burden on stockholders caused by the existence of one income tax at the corporate level and another at the personal level. (But it leaves out of account the tax on intercorporate dividends.) The magnitudes here are large, and thus a matter of continuing concern in tax policy. While concentrating on the period 1940-1952 (primarily because it is the most recent for which data are available), the relevant changes made by the Internal Revenue Code of 1954 will be examined in Chapter 7.

Statistical measurement of the differential rates involved is a formidable enterprise and can be ventured only with the aid of assumptions whose relevance and reliability must be examined in detail later. The main aim can be put very simply by two questions: How heavily, compared with other sources of income, have corporate earnings been taxed? How heavily, compared with other taxpayers, have stockholders been taxed? These questions may be put in a somewhat different way: How much greater (or less) was the tax liability on the stockholder's share of corporate earnings and his total income than the tax that would have been due had his pro rata portion of net corporate earnings been reached fully and promptly by the personal income tax alone?

We shall find, for example, using one possible measure (the measure that, despite many qualifications to be considered in the chapters that follow, was judged most appropriate to the problem at hand) that, in 1950, a married stockholder with an income of $5,000 from all sources, of which $975 was from corporate earnings,[5] had a combined corporate-personal income tax liability $304 greater than he would have paid had the $975 been income from other sources subject only to the personal income tax. This differentially heavier tax load represented 31.2 per cent of the corporate earnings component of his income and 6.1 per cent of his total income. So at this income level, on average, corporate earnings were taxed almost one-third more heavily than income from other sources; and the income tax for stockholders was six percentage points heavier than it would have been had their pro rata share of net corporate earnings been subject in full to the personal income tax alone.

In the same year, but at the $500,000 stockholder income level, the

[5] Defined as his pro rata share of pre-tax corporate net income, i.e. the sum of corporate tax, dividends, and retained earnings.

findings are very different. Here the typical married stockholder paid a tax $70,055 *lower* than he would have paid had an increment to his income the size of his pro rata share of corporate earnings ($440,500) been subject to the personal income tax alone. He received a differential tax advantage equal to about 16 per cent of the corporate earnings component of his income and about 14 per cent of his total income.

These results are cited here to show the type of measures used rather than as representative of the findings. Nor should they be accepted without an examination of the qualifications discussed in Chapters 2 and 4, and Appendix B. If the corporate income tax is shifted, wholly or in part, the extra burdens just cited are too high. If corporate income is defined to allow for current costs of maintaining inventories and replacing depreciable assets, they are too low. How accurately the underlying basic assumptions of this study reflect the complex nature of our tax system is, of course, a matter each reader will wish to assess for himself. These assumptions and a number of alternatives which would change the findings are examined in Chapter 4.

In deriving the basic measures it is assumed that corporation income taxes are not shifted but constitute a burden on the stockholders, i.e., that the corporate income tax reduces by an equivalent amount what could otherwise have been distributed to stockholders. There is, of course, no unanimity of opinion about where the corporation income tax falls. If shifted, it rests on the purchasers of finished commodities, or the suppliers of raw materials and productive services, or both, rather than on corporate earnings. That the corporate income tax rests on profits is probably still the most prevalent view among students of public finance (though other opinions are also strongly held). It is, of course, the incidence assumption usually implicit in the contention that corporate earnings are overtaxed or differentially taxed.

So, at best, this study is a partial job. In the main it is based on that assumption about incidence which, if valid, makes either double- or overtaxation a meaningful charge. While the results under an alternative shifting assumption are also investigated, most of the study's findings must be interpreted in the light of the non-shifting assumption. The complex problem of incidence is examined in greater detail in Chapter 4.

The study is shaped by the view that any evaluation of the relative tax load on net corporate earnings must take into account both the distributed and undistributed portions of these earnings. Investigations of the weight of the corporate-personal tax system have usually been focused upon one or the other, with different conclusions resulting.

Those who focus on distributed earnings (dividends) argue that because such income is subject to two sets of income taxes it is taxed more heavily than income from other sources. For example, only one tax is assessed on the interest paid to owners of corporate bonds—the tax paid by the owner himself; the corporation is permitted to deduct the interest payments from its income tax base; but no such deduction is permitted for dividend payments.[6] This is the reasoning behind the charge phrased variously as the double-taxation of dividends, distributed earnings, or corporate earnings. It was one of the reasons for the relief provisions recently incorporated in the Internal Revenue Code of 1954. As President Eisenhower summarized it in his Budget Message to Congress for the fiscal year 1955: "At present, business income is taxed to both the corporation as it is earned and to the millions of stockholders as it is paid out in dividends. This double taxation is bad from two standpoints. It is unfair and it discourages investment."[7]

Those who concentrate on the undistributed part of corporate earnings argue differently. They contend that because the corporate rate is below the personal rate at high income levels, upper-bracket taxpayers can, through corporate retention of earnings, avoid high personal surtax rates (paying, at most, only the lower capital gains tax). Such was the emphasis behind President Roosevelt's initial proposal of an undistributed profits tax in 1936: "The accumulation of surplus in corporations controlled by taxpayers with large incomes is encouraged by the present freedom of undistributed corporate income from surtaxes. Since stockholders are the beneficial owners of both distributed and undistributed corporate income, the aim, as a matter of fundamental equity, should be to seek equality of tax burden on all corporate income, whether distributed or withheld from the beneficial owners."[8]

To remedy the omissions inevitable in either of these points of view, the position is adopted, for purposes of this tax burden comparison, that earnings, both distributed and undistributed, should be considered as allocable to the individual taxpayers in the various income brackets who actually own the stock of United States corporations, in proportion to their holdings as measured by their dividend receipts.

[6] Exceptions: Dividends paid out of capital (i.e. disbursements in excess of accumulated profits and earnings) are not taxed as income to the stockholder. Dividends paid on the preferred stock of public utilities issued prior to 1942 are exempt from a portion of the corporate tax.

[7] *The Budget of the United States Government for the Fiscal Year Ending June 30, 1955*, 1954, p. M18.

[8] *Congressional Record*, 74th Cong., 2d sess., 1936, p. 3146.

It follows that the tax which these corporations pay on their earnings should also be considered as a part of the tax burden of the individual stockholders. These are the assumptions behind the basic method employed, which imputes all corporate earnings (dividends, corporate savings, and corporate taxes) to individual stockholders, and correlatively adds corporate taxes to their income tax liability. Use of that method for analytical purposes carries no implication as to the desirability or feasibility of treating the owners of corporations as members of a partnership and imputing both corporate earnings and corporate taxes to them annually as part of their taxable personal income. The sole reason for using the device of imputation is the belief that the quantitative weight of the special tax treatment of corporate earnings can best be measured by relating this income share to the income level of its claimants.

A number of factors—particularly legislated tax rates, variations in the ebb and flow of economic fortune, and corporate distribution practices—enter into the determination of the differential tax load on stockholders. By an appropriately judicious choice of illustrative data, either over- or undertaxation can be demonstrated. This being the case, it seemed sensible to use the most realistic data available, the annual Internal Revenue Service tabulations from tax returns as published in *Statistics of Income.*

The measures developed in this study are directed to a comparison of the combined federal corporate-personal income tax on the net corporate earnings component of stockholders' income with the tax that would have been due if this income share had been subject promptly and in full to the personal income tax alone. If the sum of the personal income tax on dividends and the corporate tax on net corporate earnings exceeds the potential personal income tax on an increment of taxable income the size of net corporate earnings, the conclusion is that the stockholder was overtaxed. The findings do not refer to specific stockholders but to typical stockholders representing the aggregate experience at a number of income levels, 19 in all, ranging from $1,000 to $500,000.

To take account of the wide variability in the important underlying factors—tax rates, profit levels, and dividend pay-out ratios—comparisons were made for every one of the years in the period 1940 through 1952 (except 1942 and 1943 as noted previously). This period covers the years from the earliest to the most recent (at the time of writing) for which sufficiently detailed data were available. Wide differences encountered over the period of the study include: effective rates of corporate tax (calculated on a net basis for the earnings of

8

income and deficit corporations combined) varying from about 37 per cent in 1947 to around 60 per cent in 1944; net corporate earnings (before corporation income taxes) imputable to taxable stockholders ranging from about $5 billion in 1940 to $31 billion in 1951; dividends reported by personal income taxpayers of $3.1 billion in 1940 and $6.8 billion in 1950; dividends as a per cent of net corporate earnings (before corporation income taxes) of 19 per cent in 1944 to 59 per cent in 1940; personal income tax rates starting at 4 per cent at the first bracket and reaching 79 per cent at the top in 1940 compared with the 1944 (and 1945) rate schedule which spanned a range from 23 per cent to 94 per cent.

But the values for these years do not, in some cases, reach the extremes of earlier years. In particular, there is nothing in the years 1940-1952 like the corporate earnings experience of the early thirties. In 1930, 1931, and 1932, corporate earnings as a whole were negative, but taxes were levied on the income of net income corporations and the dividend receipts of individuals. Without performing any elaborate calculations, it can be concluded that in those three years the differentially heavier taxation of stockholders was more severe than in any of the years covered by this study. About its comparative level in other years not covered by our study no simple a priori statement can be made.

WHAT ARE THE MAGNITUDES INVOLVED?

The aggregate data that follow cast little light on the issues of tax liability equality that arise from the existence of the corporation income tax. Findings germane to such issues will be examined in the chapters that follow. But the data in Tables 1 and 2 provide background information on the magnitudes involved in the problem to be studied.[9]

Typically, for the period covered by the study, about three million dividend recipients annually were subject to personal income tax, and therefore, in some sense, double taxed.[10] These are the stockholders enumerated in Table 1, line 1. Crediting to them their pro rata share

[9] The entries in these tables are estimates for the "double-taxed" segment, i.e., stockholders who paid personal income taxes. More precisely, these "stockholders" are taxpayers who receive some or all of their income from dividends; throughout, the phrases "dividend recipients" and "stockholders" are used synonymously (see Appendix B for an explanation of the methods used in estimating the entries in the tables).

[10] The data on this score are not completely homogeneous. Starting in 1948 with the introduction of permissive income splitting for joint returns, a number of married dividend recipients who had filed separately to minimize liabilities now filed jointly, thus reducing the number of stockholders (as the term is here used). This is apparent from a comparison of 1947 and 1948, lines 1 and 14.

TABLE 1

Basic Data on Taxable Stockholders, 1940 through 1952

	1940	1941	1944	1945	1946	1947	1948	1949	1950	1951	1952
1. Number of dividend returns (*thousands*)	2,015	2,889	3,048	3,114	3,156	3,245	2,925	3,175	3,297	3,681	3,862
Adjusted gross income of stockholders:											
2. Total (*$ in millions*)	$11,495	$14,779	$17,516	$19,778	$22,486	$23,885	$27,360	$27,684	$32,628	$36,143	$37,435
3. Average (2) ÷ (1)	5,705	5,116	5,747	6,351	7,125	7,361	9,354	8,719	9,896	9,819	9,693
Imputed gross income of stockholders:[a]											
4. Total (*$ in millions*)	$13,654	$22,534	$32,239	$30,654	$34,963	$40,953	$45,931	$41,924	$55,992	$60,598	$57,398
5. Average (4) ÷ (1)	6,776	7,800	10,577	9,844	11,078	12,620	15,703	13,204	16,983	16,462	14,862
Tax on stockholders (*$ in millions*):											
6. Personal[b]	1,164	2,310	4,898	5,455	5,693	5,935	5,543	5,249	7,012	8,286	8,754
7. Corporate[c]	1,959	5,721	10,822	7,796	6,068	8,129	8,841	7,506	13,025	16,746	14,057
8. Combined corporate personal tax (6) + (7)	3,123	8,031	15,720	13,251	11,761	14,064	14,384	12,755	20,037	25,032	22,811
Effective tax rates (*per cent*):											
9. Personal income tax (6) ÷ (2)	10.1%	15.6%	28.0%	27.6%	25.3%	24.8%	20.3%	19.0%	21.5%	22.9%	23.4%

Table 1, concluded

	1940	1941	1944	1945	1946	1947	1948	1949	1950	1951	1952
10. Combined corporate personal tax (8) ÷ (3)	22.9%	35.6%	48.8%	43.2%	33.6%	34.3%	31.3%	30.4%	35.8%	41.3%	39.7%
11. Total corporate earnings of stockholders[d] ($ in millions)	$5,302	$11,302	$18,087	$14,243	$16,555	$21,867	$23,906	$19,903	$30,202	$31,220	$26,506
Corporate earnings ($ in millions):											
12. For distribution	4,289	6,454	7,922	6,905	6,183	7,323	8,167	8,593	11,655	13,843	13,073
13. For retention	1,013	4,848	10,165	7,338	10,372	14,544	15,739	11,310	18,547	17,377	13,433
14. Taxable dividends[e] ($ in millions)	3,127	3,565	3,368	3,367	4,078	4,793	5,405	5,778	6,840	6,766	6,543

Source: Estimated from data in *Statistics of Income for 1940* through *for 1952*, Part 1, Bureau of Internal Revenue.

[a] Equals line 2 plus the excess of corporate earnings (before tax) over dividends.

[b] Estimated by assuming in each adjusted gross income class that the personal income tax liability of dividend recipients is the same as the average taxpayer's in that class.

[c] Equals that proportion of corporate income taxes allocated to personal income taxpayers on the basis of their proportion of total net dividend payments of all corporations.

[d] Equals that proportion of net corporate earnings imputed to personal income taxpayers on the basis of their proportion of total net dividend payments of all corporations.

[e] Includes dividends reported as such plus an estimate of the dividend component of income from estates and trusts.

of net corporate earnings leads to a considerable increase in income.[11] This is demonstrated by the aggregate figures (lines 2 and 4) and by the derived averages (lines 3 and 5). In 1950, for example, the average income as reported for personal income tax (adjusted gross income) of stockholders was $9,896; after full imputation of net corporate earnings the average was $16,983.

Not only were net corporate earnings a much larger total than dividends; they were also considerably more volatile. Dividends received by taxable stockholders ranged from $3.1 to $6.8 billion; net corporate earnings from $5.3 to $31.2 billion; between 1948 and 1949 dividends went up by around 7 per cent, but net corporate earnings fell by over 17 per cent (lines 11 and 14).

For analytical purposes net corporate earnings have been broken down into two components—earnings for distribution and earnings for retention. Earnings for distribution are defined here as the amount of pre-corporate tax earnings required for payment of dividends. For example, with the corporate rate at 50 per cent, two dollars must be earned for every dollar of dividends paid. Similarly, earnings for retention are the pretax counterpart of retained earnings. Earnings for distribution are clearly double–taxed (but, of course, not twice as heavily)—once at the corporate level and again when received as dividends. Earnings for retention, while not double taxed, may be over- or undertaxed depending on what would have been the rate applicable to this income share had it been taxed as part of the personal income of stockholders. Both earnings for distribution and earnings for retention represent sizeable additions to stockholders' income. (With dividends already included in stockholders' income, only the corporate tax on earnings for distribution constituted a net addition.) It is apparent, however, that the latter constituted (in all but the earliest two years of our period) a larger sum annually (compare lines 12 and 13). This suggests that simple, a priori conclusions about the overtaxation of stockholders are not easily drawn. Different results will characterize stockholders at various income levels. Careful analysis is in order.

Crediting stockholders with their full pro rata share of net corporate earnings also calls for inclusion of the corporate tax in their income

---

11 While in every year covered by the study there were net retained earnings (after corporation income taxes), for imputed gross income to be greater than adjusted gross income it is necessary, merely, that the algebraic sum of retained earnings and corporation income taxes be positive. For, as the term is here used, net corporate earnings equal the sum of dividends, undistributed earnings, and corporate income taxes. This usage, though it departs from the customary definition, is the most logical and useful for the present purposes.

tax load. The corporate income tax is significant, involving a considerable adjustment. In all the years investigated, the total imputed corporate tax outweighs the personal income tax for stockholders (see lines 6 and 7). Thus, assuming the incidence of the corporate income tax to be on shareholders, it appears that when full account is taken of corporate earnings and federal income taxes thereon, stockholders, in the aggregate, were subject to effective rates of income taxation considerably higher than those of the personal income tax (compare lines 9 and 10). Indeed, in some years the combined corporate-personal rate was more than twice the personal rate and it never was less than 30 per cent greater.

But useful as they are for indicating that ours is no insignificant question, these aggregate data do not get at the heart of the problem. For assessing the equality or inequality of the income tax load on stockholders and other taxpayers with similar incomes, the aggregate data of Table 1 have two primary faults. They fail to make allowance for the progressive nature of the personal income tax structure, and they overstate the burden of the corporate income tax.

We should expect larger incomes, i.e., those which include fully imputed net corporate earnings as part of personal income, to be taxed at higher rates than those which include only dividends, for the standard of comparison—the personal income tax—is progressive. Thus the question as to whether (and, if so, to what extent) stockholders are overtaxed is not answered by the statistics in Table 1. To answer this question the aggregates must be broken down and the tax burden on stockholders at specific income levels analyzed. More particularly, to determine the difference in burden (positive or negative) on stockholders, their actual tax liability under the combined corporate-personal income tax is compared with the tax they would have been liable for had their pro rata share of net corporate earnings, along with the rest of their income, been subject promptly and in full to the personal income tax alone.

In this procedure it is recognized that the corporate tax constitutes a net levy on stockholders smaller than its face amount. If it is assumed to rest on profits, shareholders are deprived of income (either actual or potential). But if no such tax existed, and instead all of corporate earnings were includible in the personal income of stockholders for tax purposes, there would be an increase in personal income tax liability due to the inclusion in the personal income tax base of that portion of net corporate earnings that presently goes to meet corporate tax payments.[12] Similarly, personal income tax liability would increase

[12] The interrelation of the corporate and personal income tax has been lucidly

because of the imputation of retained earnings. Therefore, in deriving the measures of the differential tax burden on stockholders, the potential personal income tax on retained earnings is also taken into account.

Further information on the significant changes in incomes of stockholders that follow from considering all of corporate earnings and not merely the distributed portion is furnished in Table 2. The year 1950 was chosen as the most recent for which data were available when this analysis was made. The data for stockholders have been classified and worked up on two bases: first, in terms of the personal income tax income concept, adjusted gross income, which includes dividends reported on personal returns as the measure of personal income from

TABLE 2

Distribution of Adjusted Gross Income and Imputed Gross Income, Dividend Returns, Dividends, and Net Corporate Earnings, 1950

ADJUSTED GROSS INCOME CLASS ($000's)	ADJUSTED GROSS INCOME BASIS				
	Total number taxable returns (1)	Number taxable returns reporting dividends (2)	Dividend returns as % of all returns (3)	Per cent of dividend returns (4)	Cumulative % of dividend returns (5)
Under 1	1,570,113	29,419	1.9	0.89	0.89
1 and under 2	5,996,778	211,605	3.5	6.42	7.31
2 and under 3	8,717,908	351,286	4.0	10.66	17.97
3 and under 4	8,668,606	437,463	5.0	13.27	31.24
4 and under 5	5,740,400	428,272	7.5	12.99	44.23
5 and under 10	6,114,699	1,055,136	17.3	32.01	76.24
10 and under 25	1,074,970	550,460	51.2	16.70	92.94
25 and under 50	220,107	159,918	72.7	4.85	97.79
50 and under 500	82,259	72,127	87.7	2.19	99.98
500 and over	842	838	99.5	0.03	100.00
Total	38,186,682	3,296,524	8.6	100.00	100.00

For source, see below.

corporate activity; and secondly, in terms of an income concept, imputed gross income, in which the full pro rata share of net corporate earnings, instead of dividends,[13] is used as a measure of personal income from corporate activity and as the basis for classification.

Note how the center of gravity of the whole distribution moves

demonstrated by Richard B. Goode in *The Corporation Income Tax* (Wiley, 1951, pp. 90-91).

[13] This procedure is explained in Chapter 2 and in Appendix B.

Table 2, *continued*

ADJUSTED GROSS INCOME BASIS, *continued*

ADJUSTED GROSS INCOME CLASS ($000's)	Amount of dividends ($000's) (6)	Per cent of total dividends (7)	Cumulative % of total dividends (8)	Adjusted gross income of stockholders ($000's) (9)	Per cent of AGIª of stockholders (10)	Cumulative % of AGI of stockholders (11)
Under 1	10,232	0.15	0.15	24,565	0.08	0.08
1 and under 2	90,837	1.33	1.48	331,448	1.02	1.09
2 and under 3	180,943	2.65	4.12	887,481	2.72	3.81
3 and under 4	216,677	3.13	7.29	1,521,934	4.66	8.48
4 and under 5	224,822	3.29	10.58	1,906,667	5.84	14.32
5 and under 10	877,308	12.83	23.41	7,076,665	21.69	36.01
10 and under 25	1,445,631	21.14	44.55	8,017,450	24.57	60.58
25 and under 50	1,180,820	17.26	61.81	5,394,994	16.53	77.12
50 and under 500	2,184,657	31.94	93.75	6,621,792	20.29	97.41
00 and over	427,587	6.25	100.00	844,953	2.59	100.00
Total	6,839,514	100.00	100.00	32,627,949	100.00	100.00

ª Adjusted gross income.
For source, see below.

Table 2, *continued*

ADJUSTED GROSS INCOME BASIS, *concluded*

ADJUSTED GROSS INCOME CLASS ($000's)	Dividends as % of AGIª (12)	Average AGIª of stockholders (13)	Average imputed gross income per AGI class (14)
Under 1	41.7	$ 835	$ 2,023
1 and under 2	27.4	1,566	3,033
2 and under 3	20.4	2,526	4,286
3 and under 4	14.2	3,479	5,171
4 and under 5	11.8	4,452	6,245
5 and under 10	12.4	6,707	9,547
10 and under 25	18.0	14.565	23,536
25 and under 50	21.9	33,736	58,959
50 and under 500	33.0	91,807	195,280
500 and over	50.6	1,008,297	2,751,206

ª Adjusted gross income.
For source, see below.

Table 2, *continued*

IMPUTED GROSS INCOME BASIS			
IMPUTED GROSS INCOME CLASS ($000's)	*Number taxable returns reporting dividends* (15)	*Per cent of dividend returns* (16)	*Cumulative % of dividend returns* (17)
Under 1	9,766	0.30	0.30
1 and under 2	93,379	2.83	3.13
2 and under 3	224,976	6.82	9.95
3 and under 4	279,278	8.47	18.43
4 and under 5	438,489	13.30	31.73
5 and under 10	1,100,845	33.39	65.12
10 and under 25	745,337	22.61	87.73
25 and under 50	235,316	7.14	94.87
50 and under 500	164,773	5.00	99.87
500 and over	4,362	0.13	100.00
Total	3,296,521a	100.00	100.00

a Differs from Column 2 because of rounding.
For source, see below.

Table 2, *continued*

IMPUTED GROSS INCOME BASIS, *continued*			
IMPUTED GROSS INCOME CLASS ($000's)	*Amount of corporate earnings* ($000's) (18)	*Per cent of net corporate earnings* (19)	*Cumulative % of net corporate earnings* (20)
Under 1	1,709	0.06	0.01
1 and under 2	31,312	0.10	0.11
2 and under 3	128,982	0.43	0.54
3 and under 4	183,620	0.61	1.15
4 and under 5	389,636	1.29	2.44
5 and under 10	1,945,637	6.44	8.88
10 and under 25	4,395,388	14.55	23.43
25 and under 50	4,417,861	14.63	38.06
50 and under 500	13,614,454	45.08	83.14
500 and over	5,093,281	16.86	100.00
Total	30,201,880	100.00	100.00

For source, see below.

Table 2, *concluded*

IMPUTED GROSS INCOME BASIS, *concluded*

IMPUTED GROSS INCOME CLASS ($000's)		IGI[b] of stockholders ($000's) (21)	Per cent of IGI (22)	Cumulative % of IGI (23)
Under	1	9,483	0.02	0.02
1 and under	2	161,448	0.29	0.31
2 and under	3	599,478	1.07	1.38
3 and under	4	1,001,241	1.79	3.16
4 and under	5	1,987,254	3.55	6.71
5 and under	10	7,692,079	13.74	20.45
10 and under	25	11,582,389	20.69	41.14
25 and under	50	8,422,958	15.04	56.18
50 and under	500	19,179,004	34.25	90.43
500 and over		5,356,544	9.57	100.00
Total		55,991,878	100.00	100.00

b Imputed gross income.

Source: Columns 1-14, except columns 2 and 9, *Statistics of Income for 1950* Part I, Bureau of Internal Revenue; Column 2 figures are the numbers of returns reporting dividends plus estimated numbers reporting income from estates and trusts derived in part from dividends; Column 9 is computed with the assumption that, in each income class, stockholders (dividend recipients) and other taxpayers have the same average income; Columns 15-23 are derived from *Statistics of Income, op. cit.*, by a series of procedures explained in Chapter 2, and Appendix B.

upward when all of corporate earnings are included. (Compare columns 2 and 15, 8 and 20, and 11 and 23.) The distributions arrayed by imputed gross income are considerably more concentrated than the adjusted gross income distributions. Interesting too is the wide gap between the average imputed gross income and the average adjusted gross income in each adjusted gross income class (see columns 13 and 14). The figures in column 14 are not rearrayed by imputed gross income classes but are listed according to the adjusted gross income classes from which they were derived. The imputed gross income counterpart is, of course, higher in every adjusted gross income class, but the differences become increasingly pronounced as adjusted gross income increases. This is a reflection of the fact that, except for the four lowest income classes, dividends account for a constantly increasing proportion of adjusted gross income as that income rises.[14]

One further point stands out from the data of Table 2. For 1950 (and there is nothing unusual about this year), over half of all divi-

[14] At the lower income levels there are relatively few dividend returns. The high proportion of dividends to total income in these classes may be explained by the high proportion of pensioners and other non-working persons for whom property income, including dividends, would be a major source of income.

dends and over three quarters of corporate earnings fall in the income classes over $25,000. Likewise, about 40 per cent of adjusted gross income and nearly 60 per cent of imputed gross income is found in the $25,000 and over segment of the income array. The number of stockholders here, however, is small—7 per cent on an adjusted gross and 12 per cent on an imputed gross income basis. This means that we shall have to pay more attention to the upper income ranges and examine the upper tail of this distribution more thoroughly and with more detailed income class breakdowns than is either usual or necessary in more general studies of income distribution or tax burden.

As noted earlier, this introductory section was not designed to discuss the findings of the study. It proposes merely to set forth the problem and suggest the framework in which it will be analyzed. In view of disparate opinions regarding the equity of the income tax structure as it bears on stockholders, because of the complexities underlying the concepts of overtaxation and undertaxation, and because the magnitudes involved are large, it is clear the problem is significant. Answers to the questions formulated here are needed.

CHAPTER 1

Conceptual Framework and Plan of the Book

FOR understanding the results of this study and appreciation of the qualifications attached to the findings, the reader needs at the outset a brief explanation of the statistical procedures used and of the conceptual framework which underlies the whole report. In this chapter a brief explanation of methods and concepts is developed to show how the findings were derived, while the discussion of the findings in the next two chapters will serve to elaborate the bare structure and emphasize its limitations. A detailed exposition of the sources and procedures appears in Appendix B.

INITIAL STATISTICAL PROCEDURES

All the data are from *Statistics of Income,* the annual Internal Revenue Service (formerly Bureau of Internal Revenue) tabulations from federal income tax returns—Part 1 for individuals, Part 2 for corporations.

The calculations are limited to double-taxed stockholders, i.e., dividend recipients who had some personal income tax liability. They do not cover, therefore, dividend recipients who were not subject to the personal income tax because of income below the minimum or specifically exempt (e.g. non-profit organizations); nor do they include stockholders who did not receive dividends in a particular year. Moreover the investigation is concerned only with individuals, and omits fiduciaries (trusts and estates) subject to personal income tax.

The initial objective of the statistical procedures was the development of a distribution of stockholders' income, including in income their full pro rata share of pre-tax corporate earnings.

The starting point was the *Statistics of Income* tabulation that cross-classifies dividend recipients by the size of their adjusted gross income and their dividend receipts.[1] In this array, for example, appears

[1] Adjusted gross income is picked off tax returns for tabulation in *Statistics of Income.* Bear in mind that throughout the book this term connotes a specific definition of income. The "gross" in its title is misleading since it is essentially a net income concept. In general it is defined as the sum of net income from all sources (including only 50 per cent of long-term capital gains and excluding interest on state and local securities and certain other types of income) before personal deductions and exemptions. More particularly, it is defined "as gross income *minus* allowable trade and business deductions, expenses of travel and lodging in connection with employment, reimbursed expenses in connection with employment, de-

19

one entry for stockholders (dividend recipients) with adjusted gross income of $4,000 and under $5,000 of which up to $100 is dividends, another for those in this same income class with dividend receipts of $100 and under $200, etc. In all, there are 225 such cells. For each cell the average adjusted gross income was obtained by assuming it to be the same for dividend recipients as for all taxpayers; dividends per stockholder were estimated in each cell by using the mid-point as a first approximation and then adjusting for consistency with the total reported for each income class in *Statistics of Income*.[2]

Next aggregate net earnings and dividends for all corporations were computed, and the difference between earnings and dividends determined.[3] The ratio of this difference to total dividends was used as a "blow-up" factor which, when applied to dividends, provided the necessary addition to the average adjusted gross income in each stockholder cell to arrive at imputed gross income, i.e., stockholders' income defined to include their full pro rata share of net corporate earnings.[4]

Then, the income data were rearrayed in 15 imputed gross income classes. For each class the average imputed gross income and the fraction representing net corporate earnings were computed. From a plot of these values we read off the proportion represented by net corporate earnings at selected imputed gross income levels, some 19 in all, ranging from $1,000 to $500,000.

---

ductions attributable to rents and royalties, deductions for depreciation and depletion allowable to life tenants or to income beneficiaries of property held in trust, and allowable losses from sales of property." (*Statistics of Income for 1950*, Part I, p. 7.)

[2] In this brief description a number of specific features of the method are not spelled out. For example, the dividend component of income reported by individuals as income from estates and trusts was estimated. Details of the procedure will be found in Appendix B.

[3] Aggregate net earnings (generally called net corporate earnings in this study) is the algebraic sum of the net income of income corporations and the deficits of loss corporations. It is the sum, therefore, of dividends, net retained earnings and corporate taxes (normal and surtax and excess profits tax where applicable).

[4] The excess of net corporate earnings over dividends was used in deriving this multiplier because dividends are already included in adjusted gross income. Implicit in the procedure is the assumption that, on average, for stockholders in every one of our income-dividend size cells the pay-out ratio (i.e., the ratio of their dividend receipts to the earnings of the corporations which paid them) was the same. For an explanation of why this seemingly strong assumption may be reasonably accurate see W. L. Crum, "The Taxation of Stockholders," *Quarterly Journal of Economics*, February 1950, p. 26. As Crum points out, in the lower income-dividend size cells, the few securities held by each of the large number of dividend recipients would, for the group as a whole, average out to a "representative" portfolio; despite the small number of stockholders in the upper income-dividend cells, the same result would be likely because most would possess portfolios of wide variety and coverage.

CONCEPTUAL FRAMEWORK[5]

These data provided the basic material for investigation of our problem—the extent to which stockholders were differentially taxed during the period under study. Four measures, each focusing on a particular aspect of the problem, were used.

Differential against Earnings for Distribution

First to be examined is the alleged double taxation of distributed earnings. In this connection the relevant component of stockholder income is not dividends which are net of the corporate tax. Rather, in estimating the reduction in potentially disposable income caused by this tax, we must work with the pre-tax equivalent of distributed earnings, to which we give the title of earnings for distribution. Assuming for simplicity a corporate tax rate of 50 per cent, then for every dollar of dividends paid out, corporations must earn two dollars. If a given "average" stockholder, therefore, has $100 of dividends, the earnings for distribution component of his income will be $200. The difference between earnings for distribution and dividends measures the corporate tax on the distributed segment of net corporate earnings. To this is added the personal income tax on dividends (considered an increment to the stockholder's taxable income from other sources) to obtain the total income tax actually levied on earnings for distribution.

But this does not measure the differential tax load. For, relating the corporate tax to the income status of the taxpayer means that the personal income taxpayer is not deprived of an amount of potential income equal to the corporate tax payment on earnings for distribution. Had this sum been paid to him instead of to the government, it would have been taxable as personal income. So it is only the difference between the corporate tax and the product of the corporate tax multiplied by the marginal rate of personal income tax that represents the extra burden on stockholders' earnings for distribution.[6] For example, with the corporate rate at 50 per cent, every dollar of

[5] The main outlines of this conceptual framework are not novel. In setting it up, I have drawn on the work of previous investigators, in particular Richard B. Goode and W. Leonard Crum:

Richard B. Goode, *The Corporation Income Tax* (Wiley, 1951) and *The Postwar Corporation Tax Structure*, (Treasury Dept., Division of Tax Research, 1946).

W. L. Crum, "The Taxation of Stockholders" (*Quarterly Journal of Economics*, February 1950).

In addition, I have benefited greatly from the comments of both Goode and Crum on an earlier draft of this manuscript.

[6] Goode, 1951, *op. cit.*

earnings for distribution bears a 50 cent corporate tax, but had this 50 cents been paid to stockholders it would have represented something less than a 50 cent addition to their personal income after tax. If the relevant marginal rate is 20 per cent, the deprivation due to the corporate tax will be 40 cents; if the potential marginal rate is 90 per cent, the corporate tax causes a loss of potential disposable income of only 5 cents. So the potential personal income tax on earnings for distribution is computed and subtracted from the actual combined corporate-personal income tax on that component of stockholder income to find the net extra burden on the distributed portion of net corporate earnings. For comparison among income levels and between years, the absolute extra burden was converted to an incremental effective rate by taking it as a percentage of the earnings for distribution component. We call this measure the differential against earnings for distribution.

The derivation of the measure may be summarized symbolically as follows. (For simplicity, all rates and differentials are expressed as ratios.)

$C_e{}^7$ = effective rate of corporate tax on earnings for distribution
D = dividends received
E = earnings for distribution; $E - C_e E = D$
P = applicable marginal rate of personal income tax
N_e = absolute extra burden on earnings for distribution
$\dfrac{N_e}{E}$ = differential against earnings for distribution

Then

$$
\begin{aligned}
N_e &= PD + C_e E - PE \\
&= PD + C_e E - (PD + PC_e E) \\
&= C_e E - PC_e E \\
&= C_e E\,(1 - P) \\
\frac{N_e}{E} &= C_e\,(1 - P)
\end{aligned}
$$

Since P rises as stockholder income rises but never reaches 100 per cent, the differential against earnings for distribution is a declining function of stockholders' income, but always positive. In relation to the distributed segment of net corporate earnings, then, the corporate tax constitutes a burden that is always smaller than its face amount, a burden that varies inversely with the level of stockholders' income. But this is only part of the story.

[7] The lower case form of the symbol is used to designate the particular tax rates and liabilities associated with corporate earnings and each of its components.

Differential against Earnings for Retention

There still remains for consideration the undistributed segment of net corporate earnings—earnings for retention, or the remainder of net corporate earnings after subtraction of earnings for distribution. Following the logic of the procedure in connection with the distributed portion, we compute the corporate tax on earnings for retention and compare it with the hypothetical personal income tax on that component of corporate earnings. The difference between these two tax liabilities is the measure of the net extra burden. This extra burden, taken as a percentage of earnings for retention, is designated the differential against earnings for retention.

Add to the symbols listed above:

R = earnings for retention *pre tax*

C_r = effective rate of corporate income tax on earnings for retention
(This is higher than C_e because earnings for retention are net of deficits reported by loss corporations.)

N_r = absolute extra burden on earnings for retention

$\dfrac{N_r}{R}$ = differential against earnings for retention

Then

$$N_r = C_r R - PR$$
$$= R\,(C_r - P)$$
$$\frac{N_r}{R} = C_r - P$$

It is apparent that the differential against earnings for retention can be positive, zero, or negative depending on the relative heights of C_r and P. With C_r invariant on stockholders' income and P a rising function thereof, the differential will be a declining function of stockholders' income, and at some point in the income scale, if P is high enough, the differential will become negative. (Note that because the personal income tax rate schedule is progressive, the P that applies here is higher than the one in the differential against earnings for distribution formula.)

Differential against Net Corporate Earnings

The combination of the two measures just discussed provides us with the composite or net result—the differential against net corporate earnings which, with corporate earnings equal to the sum of earnings for distribution and earnings for retention, is a weighted average of the differential against each of these components of net corporate earnings.

Add to the symbols listed above:

T = net corporate earnings = $E + R$

N_t = the absolute extra burden on net corporate earnings

$\dfrac{N_t}{T}$ = the differential against net corporate earnings

Then

$$N_t = N_e + N_r$$
$$= C_e E (1 - P) + R (C_r - P)$$

Since

$$T = E + R$$

$$\frac{N_t}{T} = \frac{N_t}{E + R}$$

$$= \frac{C_e E (1 - P) + R (C_r - P)}{E + R}$$

$$= C_e (1 - P)\left(\frac{E}{E + R}\right) + C_r - P\left(\frac{R}{E + R}\right)$$

The differential against net corporate earnings will, of course, have the same characteristics as its components. The higher the proportion of earnings for retention to total corporate earnings, the closer N_t/T lies to N_r/R. Further since both its components behave in the same way on this score, it will be a declining function of stockholders income. Also, after a point N_r/R can (and in most years of this study did) weigh so heavily that N_t will turn negative—i.e., an income tax differential in favor of net corporate earnings will exist at the higher income levels.

With this differential we can answer the question: how much more (or less) heavily were corporate earnings actually taxed than they would have been if subject in full to the personal income tax alone?

Differential against Stockholders' Income

One more measure has been used in our analysis. By relating the extra burden to the total income of stockholders, we obtain the differential against (or in favor of) stockholders. It enables us to answer the question: how much more heavily, measured in terms of effective rates, were stockholders actually taxed on the whole of their income from all sources by the combined corporate-personal income tax system than they would have been with the corporate tax abolished and their pro rata share of net corporate earnings subject fully and promptly to the personal income tax?

Add to the symbols listed above:

S = imputed gross income of stockholders

O = stockholders' income from sources other than net corporate earnings $= S - T$

$\dfrac{N_t}{S}$ = differential against stockholders

$S = T + O$

N_t — the extra burden on net corporate earnings—is also the extra burden on stockholders, since it is only on the corporate earnings component of their income that stockholders are differentially taxed. Therefore:

$$\frac{N_t}{S} = \frac{N_t}{T + O}$$

With O positive, the differential against stockholders lies below that against net corporate earnings.[8] But, since the only difference is in the denominator, the smaller the value for O, i.e., the larger the proportion of T in S, the closer N_t/S to N_t/T. Thus, as we shall see, at the lower stockholder income levels, the two measures diverge considerably; near the top of the income scale, however, they lie very close together. This is a reflection of the fact that, except for the lower portion of the income range, the proportion of T to S is a rising fraction reading up the array of stockholder incomes.

Three Variants

One problem in our conceptual framework still remains for consideration. As described, the actual tax load on earnings for retention consists simply of the corporation income tax, and the extra burden on this segment of corporate earnings is measured as the difference between the corporate tax and the hypothetical personal tax. This measure is designed variant 1 of our standard method. Values of the differentials against earnings for retention (and of the differentials against net corporate earnings and stockholders, in whose derivation this measure of the extra tax burden on earnings for retention is employed) we call variant 1 values. Variant 1 is a clear-cut measure that tells us for a given year how much more (or less) income tax stockholders paid on their pro rata share of earnings for retention than would have been due if this income share had been subject promptly and in full to the personal income tax alone. But it leaves out something.

---

[8] Of course, when the differentials have negative values this means that the absolute value of the former is the lower, i.e., the differential against stockholders is less negative.

For it can be argued that some portion, at least, of retained earnings would show up as capital gains, and that some of these capital gains would be realized by stockholders in taxable form. Thus, because of current retentions, sometime in the future an additional tax liability would be incurred. Therefore variant 2 was developed. Under variant 2, in measuring the tax load on earnings for retention a term, explained below, was added to represent the present value of the future capital gains tax on the undistributed earnings of a given year. Unless otherwise specified it is the variant 2 values that are used throughout this study.

To make such an adjustment with precision is impossible, however. Too many factors about which little is known are involved. To what extent do retained earnings show up in share prices? What proportion of resulting capital gains is realized, and of this what fraction shows up in taxable form? Our adjustment, therefore, is arbitrary but reasonable in the sense that it is in the right direction, and that substantial changes in the assumptions used in its derivation would lead to only slight changes in the size of the estimated additional tax liability on earnings for retention.

Briefly, variant 2 incorporates an additional tax liability on stockholders—a capital gains tax—determined on the assumptions that for each dollar of retained earnings share prices rose by 72 cents, and that two-thirds of these increments in the value of stock were realized in taxable form at an even rate over a five year period. The adjustment for the future capital gains tax liability enters as an additive term in N_r/R, N_t/T, and N_t/S.

But it might be argued that this adjustment does not go far enough. For one assumption used in the variant 2 estimate is that stock prices rose by only 72 per cent of reinvested earnings, or that 28 cents of every dollar of retained earnings failed to show up in enhanced stock values. Apparently, then, when earnings are reinvested rather than paid out, stockholders lose 28 cents per dollar of such earnings. Should not this be considered a deprivation and, while not a formal tax, should it not be taken into account in estimating the extra tax load on earnings for retention? Despite good grounds for answering this question in the negative, and because the matter is debatable, variant 3 was developed. Very simply, in addition to the corporate tax and the present value of the future capital gains tax due to reinvested earnings, variant 3 includes the present value of this 28 cent loss as part of the tax on earnings for retention. This adjustment affects N_r/R, N_t/T, and N_t/S, making them higher than the variant 2 values which, in turn, of course, exceed the variant 1 values of the differentials. (An amplified description of the procedures used under each of the variants and an indication of how much the values differ will be found in Chapter 2.)

But variant 3 seems to cover too much. For there is a difference between a tax and the reduction in potentially disposable income caused by the failure of corporations to distribute fully. The latter lacks the strong element of compulsion that characterizes a federal tax levy. Stockholders are not forced to acquiesce in corporate distribution policies. They can press for fuller distribution by the companies whose shares they hold; or acquire shares in corporations whose policy it is to distribute most of their earnings; or make other kinds of investments. On this reasoning variant 2 was selected as superior. Variant 3 goes too far; variant 1 not far enough.

There are additional grounds for doubting the relevance for our study of the adjustment that distinguishes variant 3. While an attempt to explain the failure of reinvested earnings to be reflected fully in share prices lies beyond the scope of this study, grounds for considering the variant 3 adjustment unwarranted are suggested by several plausible explanations. To William Vickrey the failure "argues either that the directors of the corporation have disposed of the undistributed earnings adversely to the interests of the stockholders or that the reinvestment has been made on the basis of information not shared by investors in general."[9] In either event, it appears that the loss may not be properly considered as an additional levy on stockholders. It seems more appropriate to attribute the loss to errors in judgment on the part of management. Such errors affect the income of shareholders in corporations that distribute earnings in full and also of those who, as owners of noncorporate business enterprises, are subject to the personal income tax. These taxpayers do not profit from any special tax law solicitude, except that because of their losses the capital gains they report may be smaller or the capital losses they deduct may be larger. An estimated overall loss on this account is taken into account by the variant 2 adjustment which reckons the future capital gains as 28 per cent less than they might have been.

Another possible explanation of the 28 cent attrition in capital value for every dollar of reinvestment may be the fact that standard accounting or tax law determinations of net income regularly result in overstatement. These determinations may fail to allow for competitive obsolescence, i.e. the degree of capital destruction caused by shifts in demand and changes in techniques of production, and do not, as a rule, take account of the higher cost of maintaining inven-

[9] William Vickrey, *Agenda for Progressive Taxation*, Ronald, 1947, p. 150.

tories and replacing depreciable assets when price levels rise (except in the case of inventories for those corporations that use Lifo). Considerations of this sort, however, do not validate the variant 3 adjustment for our purposes, for the definition of income in our benchmark, the personal income tax system, is similarly "shortsighted," also failing to take account of these factors. So it may be concluded that on this score no special adjustment is required in the method.

While, for the reasons cited, variant 2 is preferable and is generally used in the text discussion, in recognition that, to some extent at least, the matters at issue are fuzzy enough to give rise to questions of taste as well as of logic, the differentials based on all three variant measures of the extra burden on earnings for retention have been computed for every year of the study and are tabulated in Appendix A. It will be noted, however, from an examination of these data that our argument remains basically the same no matter which variant is judged to be most appropriate; the pattern of the differentials is the same for all three variants.

ORGANIZATION OF THE BOOK

It is hoped that the description of the procedures and concepts which underlie the whole study will serve for quick reference as the reader follows the detailed findings presented and discussed in the chapters that follow. In each, the limitations of the available data and the shortcomings of the findings are made explicit.

Chapters 2 and 3 approach the problem by discussing detailed quantitative findings. Chapter 4 examines the effects on the findings of some assumptions and procedures alternative to those used in our standard method.

The scene shifts in Chapter 5 to a consideration of the question of the progressivity effect of the corporation income tax. Chapter 6 is concerned with the effects on federal tax revenue and on distribution of stockholder income of the two types of tax structure which have been compared at other points in the study. Aggregate rather than average differential taxation of stockholders is computed by the existing system of corporate taxation and by a system which would extend to stockholders the tax treatment now applied to members of a partnership.

Chapter 7, on the basis of our findings, analyzes the provisions of the Internal Revenue Code of 1954 designed for relief of stockholders from double taxation. A brief summary of the findings is given in Chapter 8. Appendix A contains tabular summaries of the differentials; Appendix B sets forth particular features of the method in detail.

CHAPTER 2

The Findings for 1950

THIS chapter presents and analyzes the findings for 1950 in terms of the previously described measures related to the differential income tax on net corporate earnings and the total income of stockholders. With the findings for this one year the broad pattern of the differentials can be laid out, and, in conjunction with this, a detailed explanation of the methods used in the study illustrated by reference to a particular body of data can be developed. Moreover, since the study covers a number of years, estimates of the differential tax burden for one of them will serve as a basis for comparative study of the period as a whole and of selected years, and for an analysis of the effect of changes in the variables that determine the degree of over- or undertaxation. The year chosen, 1950, is the most recent for which complete data were available when this analysis was in work. Chapter 3 deals with variations in the differentials and their characteristics in several other years, and over the period 1940 through 1952 as a whole. Chapter 7 analyzes the effect of the relief provisions introduced in 1954.

DIFFERENTIALS FOR 1950

How heavy was the differential taxation of net corporate earnings and of stockholder income? What did the picture look like in 1950? Chart 1 summarizes the answer in terms of the four selected measures. The reader is reminded that the results are for "average" stockholders representing the aggregate experience in each stockholder income class, that the values plotted are those obtained from variant 2 of our standard measures, and that the income of stockholders includes their pro rata share of pre-tax corporate earnings. The marginal rate schedules for joint and separate returns showed substantial differences, except at the two extremes of the income range, because of the income splitting permitted married stockholders. Therefore, the differentials for each type of return were computed separately, and weighted averages were struck for plotting the chart.

Examination of line 1—*the differential against earnings for distribution*—reveals that the double taxation of distributed earnings was substantial but became steadily less severe as stockholder income rose. At the bottom of the taxable stockholder income scale, earnings made for distribution to stockholders were subject to a tax more than 34 percentage points higher than would have been due under the personal income tax alone. At the $25,000 stockholder income level the net extra burden averaged about 29 percentage points, and at the top of the stockholder income range plotted on the chart ($500,000) it was only 10 per cent. The higher the stockholder income level the lower the differential against earnings for distribution.

CHART 1—Differentials, 1950

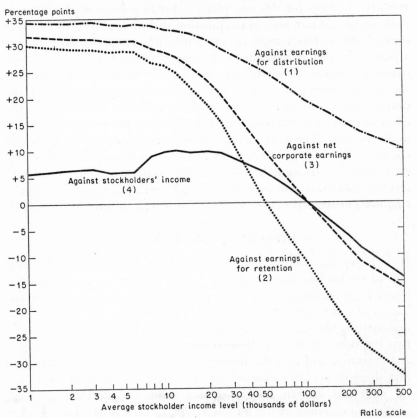

Percentage points

Against earnings for distribution (1)

Against net corporate earnings (3)

Against stockholders' income (4)

Against earnings for retention (2)

Average stockholder income level (thousands of dollars)

Ratio scale

While *the differential against earnings for retention* (line 2) follows the same general pattern, it is lower at all income levels, the difference becoming very marked over the upper portion of the stockholder income array. Starting at 30 per cent for the lowest income class, it falls rapidly to only 15 per cent at the $25,000 mark, above which the burden changes to a benefit increasing to a differential of −33 per cent at the top of the stockholder income scale. At this level ($500,000) the earnings for retention component of stockholders' income was subject to a tax liability 33 percentage points *less* than would have been the case had it been reached promptly and in full by the personal income tax alone. It appears then, that on their share of earnings for retention some stockholders were overtaxed and others were undertaxed to significant degrees. The inversion from over- to undertaxation occurred, on average, at just over the $50,000 stockholder income.

The weighted average of these two measures, *the differential against net corporate earnings,* traces the same general path over the income range as the differentials that comprise it, and falls between them (line 3). Reflecting the greater absolute magnitude of earnings for retention, it lies closer to line 2 than line 1.[1] Over most of the income scale the net corporate earnings component of stockholders' income was overtaxed, but for stockholders higher up the income pyramid undertaxation occurred. The heaviest extra burden lies on the lower stockholder income levels ($1,000 to $10,000)—between 32 and 29 percentage points. Above $10,000 the differential falls rapidly, reaching 0 at about $100,000 and a low point of −16 per cent at $500,000. Thus the substantial over- or undertaxation found on net corporate earnings depends on the stockholder's income level.

So far, by use of the first three measures, our inquiry has disclosed that the net corporate earnings component of stockholder income was subject to a tax differential, which means that total stockholder income was either over- or undertaxed. How much heavier or lighter was the effective tax rate for stockholders than the rate would have been if their income (including their full pro rata share of net corporate earnings) had been reached by the personal income tax alone?[2] (The personal income tax is used as the benchmark in this connection and for determining the other differentials also because it presumably measures the community's consensus as to the rates of income taxation appropriate at different income levels.)

The answer is provided by *the differential against stockholders' income,* line 4 on the chart. It appears that the majority of stockholders, having incomes ranging from $1,000 to $50,000, were liable to an appreciable extra income tax of from 6 to 10 percentage points. Those most severely affected were in the income range between $10,000 and $25,000 with a maximum differential of 10 points. But near the top of the income scale a different picture emerges, with the differential de-

---

[1] In 1950, earnings for distribution totaled $11 billion, earnings for retention $19 billion. (These figures are the totals for taxable stockholders only.)

[2] Another way of putting the question is this: How much heavier (or less onerous) is the combined corporate-personal income tax rate on stockholders at a given income level than the personal income tax on nonstockholders with a similar amount of income?

clining very rapidly after the $50,000 point and reaching 0 at a little over $100,000. Stockholders with incomes above this point enjoyed a tax benefit that became relatively more important as income increased. Thus, at the $500,000 imputed gross income level we find the combined corporate-personal income tax liability to be 14 percentage points lower than would have been the case without the corporate tax and with stockholders' full pro rata share of net corporate earnings subject only to the personal income tax.

Instead of falling constantly, as income rises, the differential against stockholders tends first to increase over a portion of the income range and then, after reaching a maximum between the $10,000 to $20,000 level, to fall constantly thereafter. Why this difference in behavior compared with the other three differentials? It occurs because of uneven variations in the proportion of imputed gross income that is derived from corporate earnings. For the value of the differential against stockholders is equal to that fraction of the differential against net corporate earnings that net corporate earnings represent of imputed gross income. In general this fraction tends to rise with income. (This is why we find the solid line on the chart lying closer to the dashed line at the higher income levels.) Over the stockholder income span from $6,000 to $20,000, the rise in the proportion of net corporate earnings to imputed gross income more than compensates for the fall in the differential against net corporate earnings, thereby causing the product—the differential against stockholders—to rise over this range.

The findings apply to average stockholders and figures on how many fell in the over- and undertaxed categories cannot be obtained directly from these data. However, from a closely related set of procedures (discussed in Chapter 6) we can get some idea of the number of stockholders in each of these categories. For 1950 the estimate is about 3.3 million double-taxed stockholders. Slightly under 3.2 million paid a higher combined corporate-personal income tax than would have been due under the personal income tax alone and were, in the sense adopted here, overtaxed. On the other hand, some 4 per cent, about 130,000 were undertaxed.[3] For the latter, a higher tax liability would have occurred if the corporate tax had been eliminated and their share of corporate earnings had been taxed in full as personal income. While small as a proportion of all stockholders, the undertaxed group

3 These estimates, while germane, are not strictly comparable with the variant 2 values of the differentials that have been used in discussing the findings for 1950. For in deriving the number of over- and undertaxed stockholders, no account was taken of the future capital gains tax liability on reinvested earnings of 1950. An adjustment on this score would lead to somewhat larger overtaxed and smaller undertaxed totals than those given in the text.

assumes greater importance when its share of all double-taxed net corporate earnings is measured. Forty four per cent of net corporate earnings was undertaxed.

The findings plotted in Chart 1 are the averages for joint and separate returns taken together. Table 3 shows how the differentials varied with the type of return filed by stockholders at the same income level. The differentials are higher for joint returns than for separate returns, because the marginal rate schedule applying to married persons who file jointly was lower than for separate returns over most of the taxable income scale. For 1950, assuming the proportion of separate to joint returns to be the same for stockholders as for all taxpayers, it is estimated that about 786,000 taxable dividend recipients filed separate returns, and about 2,511,000 filed joint returns.

The findings for 1950 are based on the tax treatment of corporate earnings then in effect. With the Internal Revenue Code of 1954 modifications of the procedure for taxing dividends were introduced —an exclusion of the first $50 of dividends ($100 for joint returns) and a personal income tax credit equal to 4 per cent of dividends over and above the amount excluded. How this dividend tax relief would have changed the results for 1950 is considered in Chapter 7.

THE FINDINGS IN DETAIL

Up to this point the discussion has dealt with the findings, presented directly with little elaboration. But the results are the offspring of a long line of assumptions and choices between possible procedures. A detailed discussion of how the findings were derived will serve to point up the specific features of the selected method and to provide a sense of the magnitudes involved. But it will do more. It will also help the reader to a fuller understanding of our measures and their limitations. The derivation of the differentials on joint returns for 1950 (which were over three-fourths of the total number of taxable returns filed by stockholders) will be discussed with reference to the data of Table 4.[4]

In column 1 are listed the nineteen "average" stockholder income levels selected as representing the whole range of stockholder income.[5]

[4] A similar set of computations was undertaken for separate returns in arriving at the differentials discussed earlier in this chapter.

[5] These same nineteen levels were used for every year in the period 1940-1952 (except 1942 and 1943 for which the data necessary for our calculations were not tabulated). Of course, there were stockholders with over $500,000 of imputed gross income, but little would have been gained by adding several more income levels. What happens at the top of the income range is indicated adequately by the $500,000 stockholder income.

TABLE 3

Comparison of Differentials for Separate and Joint Returns, Variant 2 Values, 1950

(per cent)

AVERAGE STOCKHOLDER IMPUTED GROSS INCOME ($000's)	DIFFERENTIAL AGAINST:							
	Earnings for distribution		Earnings for retention		Net corporate earnings		Stockholder imputed gross income	
	Separate	Joint	Separate	Joint	Separate	Joint	Separate	Joint
1	34.3	a	30.0	a	31.7	a	5.7	a
3	34.3	34.3	29.1	29.1	31.1	31.1	6.5	6.5
5	33.0	34.0	26.9	29.4	29.2	31.2	5.7	6.1
8	31.6	34.1	23.4	27.1	26.5	29.8	8.2	9.2
10	31.6	33.1	20.9	27.0	25.1	29.3	8.6	10.2
15	28.5	32.7	13.5	23.3	19.3	26.9	7.3	10.1
25	23.9	30.0	1.2	17.2	10.0	22.2	4.6	10.2
50	18.7	25.8	—10.3	1.9	1.2	11.2	0.5	6.7
100	14.8	19.8	—22.7	—9.7	—8.2	1.7	—5.8	1.2
250	8.6	14.0	—32.9	—25.9	—16.9	—10.5	—12.8	—8.0
500	7.1	10.6	—34.2	—32.6	—18.2	—15.9	—15.9	—14.0

a No joint returns at this income level.

TABLE 4

Derivation of the Differentials, 1950

(joint returns)

DERIVATION OF THE TAXABLE INCOME EQUIVALENT OF ADJUSTED GROSS INCOME

AVERAGE STOCK-HOLDER IMPUTED GROSS INCOME $000's) (1)	Corporate earnings as a per cent of imputed gross income (2)	Net corporate earnings component (1) × (2) (3)	Other income (1) — (3) (4)	Dividends[a] (3) ÷ 4.4158 (5)	Adjusted gross income component (4) + (5) (6)	Taxable income equivalent[b] (7)
1	18.0%	$ 180	$ 820	$ 41	$ 861	
2	20.2	404	1,596	91	1,687	$ 304
3	20.9	627	2,373	142	2,515	601
4	18.9	756	3,244	171	3,415	1,124
5	19.5	975	4,025	221	4,246	1,711
6	19.4	1,164	4,836	264	5,100	2,438
8	30.9	2,472	5,528	560	6,088	3,330
10	34.8	3,480	6,520	788	7,308	4,348
12	36.0	4,320	7,680	978	8,658	5,532
15	37.6	5,640	9,360	1,277	10,637	7,308
20	42.3	8,460	11,540	1,916	13,456	9,890
25	46.2	11,550	13,450	2,616	16,066	12,403
50	59.7	29,850	20,150	6,760	26,910	22,281
75	68.2	51,150	23,850	11,583	35,433	30,189
100	70.0	70,000	30,000	15,852	45,852	38,837
150	71.6	107,400	42,600	24,322	66,922	56,214
200	72.8	145,600	54,400	32,973	87,373	70,772
250	76.1	190,250	59,750	43,084	102,834	81,959
500	88.1	440,500	59,500	99,755	159,255	118,963

Source: Basic data used for computations from *Statistics of Income for 1950*, Parts 1 and 2.
a Dividends for each income level were obtained by dividing the net corporate earnings component by 4.4158 which is the 1950 ratio of net corporate earnings to dividends.
b The taxable income equivalent is derived by interpolation from a plot of the relation of taxable income to adjusted gross income, both as tabulated in *Statistics of Income*. There is no entry in this column (and in the rest of the table) for the $1,000 average stockholder imputed gross income because it had no taxable income equivalent. (*Table continues on next pages*)

In this connection, all of net corporate earnings is taken to be the measure of personal income from corporate activity. To obtain imputed gross income their pro rata share of corporate income taxes and undistributed profits was added to stockholders' adjusted gross income (which includes dividends), and stockholders were rearrayed in the income classes in which they fell on imputation. The proportion of imputed gross income accounted for by net corporate earnings was computed, class averages were struck, and by interpolation the values in column 2 were obtained. These percentages apply to the average

Table 4, *continued*

DIFFERENTIAL AGAINST EARNINGS FOR DISTRIBUTION

AVERAGE STOCK-HOLDER IMPUTED GROSS INCOME ($000's) (1)	Corporation income tax on earnings for distribution[c] (2) × 0.1594 (8)	Complement of marginal rate of personal income tax applicable to corporate tax payment (9)	Net extra burden on earnings for distribution[d] (8) × (9) (10)	Earnings for distribution[e] (5) + (8) (11)	Differential against earnings for distribution[f] [(10)÷(11)]×10 (12)
1					
2	$ 64	82.60%	$ 53	$ 155	34.2%
3	100	82.60	83	242	34.3
4	121	82.60	100	292	34.2
5	155	82.60	128	376	34.0
6	186	82.60	154	450	34.2
8	394	82.60	325	954	34.1
10	555	79.98	444	1,343	33.1
12	689	79.98	551	1,667	33.1
15	899	79.09	711	2,176	32.7
20	1,349	76.34	1,030	3,265	31.5
25	1,842	72.70	1,339	4,458	30.0
50	4,759	62.51	2,975	11,519	25.8
75	8,155	54.32	4,430	19,738	22.4
100	11,161	47.85	5,341	27,013	19.8
150	17,124	42.09	7,208	41,446	17.4
200	23,215	37.33	8,665	56,188	15.4
250	30,334	33.92	10,288	73,418	14.0
500	70,234	25.66	18,019	169,989	10.6

c The multiplier was derived as follows: the dividend ratio of 0.369702 of after-tax earnings of net income corporations multiplied by the tax proportion of 0.431270 of the income of deficit and income corporations combined equals 0.1594, more precisely, 0.159441. Corporate income tax on earnings for distribution, column 8, is the product of net corporate earnings (column 3) and 0.159441. Seemingly roundabout, this procedure was more convenient in computation. It is equivalent to applying a tax rate of 41.317 per cent to earnings for distribution.

d The extra burden on earnings for distribution is derived by multiplying the corporate tax on earnings for distribution (column 8) by the complement of the relevant marginal rate (or weighted average of marginal rates) of personal income tax at each income level (column 9). The rates used in deriving column 9 are those that would apply to an increment of the amount in column 8 to a taxable income of the size given in column 7.

e The amount of earnings for distribution at each stockholder income level (column 11) can be computed from the data in a number of ways, but most simply by adding dividends (column 5) and the corporate tax paid on this portion of corporate earnings (column 8).

f The differential against earnings for distribution is derived by computing column 10 as a per cent of column 11.

stockholder at each income level, and, therefore, represent the composite of experience. In each imputed income class we have stockholders with varying amounts of adjusted gross income. For example, in the imputed income class $5,000 and under $7,000, are stockholders

Table 4, continued

DIFFERENTIAL AGAINST EARNINGS FOR RETENTION, VARIANT 2

AVERAGE STOCK-HOLDER IMPUTED GROSS INCOME ($000's) (1)	Earnings for retention (3) — (11) (13)	Corporation income tax on earnings for retention (3) × 0.2718 (14)	Taxable income plus corporate tax on earnings for distribution (7) + (8) (15)	Marginal rate of personal income tax applicable to earnings for retention (16)	Potential personal income tax on earnings for retention (13) × (16) (17)	Current extra burden on earnings for retention (14) — (17) (18)
1						
2	$ 249	$ 110	$ 368	17.40%	$ 43	$ 67
3	385	170	701	17.40	67	103
4	464	206	1,245	17.40	81	125
5	599	265	1,866	17.40	104	161
6	714	316	2,624	17.40	124	192
8	1,518	672	3,724	19.57	297	375
10	2,137	946	4,903	20.02	428	518
12	2,653	1,174	6,221	21.22	563	611
15	3,464	1,533	8,207	23.66	820	713
20	5,195	2,300	11,239	27.06	1,406	894
25	7,092	3,140	14,245	30.72	2,179	961
50	18,331	8,114	27,040	46.97	8,610	—496
75	31,412	13,904	38,344	55.10	17,307	—3,403
100	42,987	19,028	49,998	59.89	25,744	—6,716
150	65,954	29,194	73,338	67.19	44,315	—15,121
200	89,412	39,577	93,987	72.15	64,507	—24,930
250	116,832	51,715	112,293	76.09	88,892	—37,177
500	270,511	119,739	189,197	82.74	223,815	—104,074

g The corporate tax on earnings for retention was obtained by multiplying column 3 by 0.2718, or, more precisely, 0.271829. This multiplier is the product of the ratio of retained earnings to the after tax income of net income corporations—0.630298—and the proportion—0.431270—that taxes represented of the net corporate earnings of income and deficit corporations combined. This was the simplest method for computing column 14. It is equivalent to applying a rate of 44.264 per cent to earnings for retention.

h The extra burden on earnings for retention equals the differences between the actual corporate tax liability and the liability that would apply under the personal income tax.

Table 4, continued

DIFFERENTIAL AGAINST EARNINGS FOR RETENTION, VARIANT 2, continued

AVERAGE STOCK-HOLDER IMPUTED GROSS INCOME ($000's) (1)	Retained corporate earnings (13) − (14) (19)	Annual present value of taxable realized capital gains¹ (19) × 0.04178 (20)	Marginal rate assumed applicable in					Present value of future capital gains tax on retained earnings of 1950 20[(21) + (22) + (23) + (24) + (25)] (26)	Total extra burden on earnings for retention (18) + (26) (27)	Differential against earnings for retention [(27) ÷ (13)] × 100 (28)
			1951 (21)	1952 (22)	1953 (23)	1954 (24)	1955 (25)			
1										
2	$ 139	$ 6	20.4	22.2	22.2	20.0	20.0%	$ 6	$ 73	29.3%
3	215	9	20.4	22.2	22.2	20.0	20.0	9	112	29.1
4	258	11	20.4	22.2	22.2	20.0	20.0	12	137	29.5
5	334	14	20.4	22.2	22.2	20.0	20.0	15	176	29.4
6	398	17	20.4	22.2	22.2	20.0	20.0	18	210	29.4
8	846	35	20.4	22.2	22.2	20.0	20.0	37	412	27.1
10	1,191	50	22.4	24.6	24.6	22.0	22.0	58	576	27.0
12	1,479	62	22.4	24.6	24.6	22.0	22.0	72	683	25.7
15	1,931	81	22.4	24.6	24.6	22.0	22.0	94	807	23.3
20	2,895	121	27.0	29.0	29.0	26.0	26.0	166	1,060	20.4
25	3,952	165	30.0	34.0	34.0	30.0	30.0	261	1,222	17.2
50	10,217	427	39.0	42.0	42.0	38.0	38.0	850	354	1.9
75	17,508	731	48.0	52.0	52.0	47.0	47.0	1,798	−1,605	−5.1
100	23,959	1,001	50.0	52.0	52.0	50.0	50.0	2,542	−4,174	−9.7
150	36,760	1,536	50.0	52.0	52.0	50.0	50.0	3,901	−11,220	−17.0
200	49,835	2,082	50.0	52.0	52.0	50.0	50.0	5,288	−19,641	−22.0
250	65,117	2,721	50.0	52.0	52.0	50.0	50.0	6,911	−30,266	−25.9
500	150,772	6,299	50.0	52.0	52.0	50.0	50.0	16,000	−88,074	−32.6

¹ Explanation of the derivation of this multiplier is given in detail in the text. Briefly it is: 0.2412 (the relevant proportion of realized capital gains reported as taxable) × 0.866 (the present value of the future value of capital gains) = 0.2089 ÷ 5 (years over which the gains would be realized) = 0.04178.

Table 4, *continued*

DIFFERENTIALS AGAINST NET CORPORATE EARNINGS
AND STOCKHOLDER IMPUTED GROSS INCOME

AVERAGE STOCK-HOLDER IMPUTED GROSS INCOME ($000's) (1)	Extra burden on net corporate earnings (10) + (27) (29)	Differential against net corporate earnings [(29) ÷ (3)] × 100 (30)	Differential against stockholder imputed gross income [(29) ÷ (1)] × 100 (31)
1			
2	$ 126	31.2%	6.3%
3	195	31.1	6.5
4	237	31.3	5.9
5	304	31.2	6.1
6	364	31.3	6.1
8	737	29.8	9.2
10	1,020	29.3	10.2
12	1,234	28.6	10.3
15	1,518	26.9	10.1
20	2,090	24.7	10.4
25	2,561	22.2	10.2
50	3,329	11.2	6.7
75	2,825	5.5	3.8
100	1,167	1.7	1.2
150	−4,012	−3.7	−2.7
200	−10,976	−7.5	−5.5
250	−19,978	−10.5	−8.0
500	−70,055	−15.9	−14.0

who formerly fell in adjusted gross income classes $600 and under $1,000, $1,000 and under $1,500, $1,500 and under $2,000, $2,000 and under $2,500, $2,500 and under $3,000, $3,000 and under $4,000, $4,000 and under $5,000, $5,000 and under $7,000. After imputation they are all in the same income class, but their imputed gross income contains very different proportions of net corporate earnings. The entries in column 2 come from interpolations based on the average value in each class. Note that at the lower income levels the ratio of net corporate earnings to imputed gross income is fairly constant, hovering around 20 per cent. From about $8,000 on up, however, it becomes a rapidly rising function of income size. At the top of the income scale, on average, close to 90 per cent of stockholder total income comes from this one source.

Columns 3 and 4 are obtained simply as indicated in the table. Net corporate earnings were 4.4158 as large as dividends in 1950. The entries in column 3 were divided by this figure to obtain the dividend

Table 4, *continued*

			NET CORPORATE TAX			
AVERAGE STOCK-HOLDER IMPUTED GROSS INCOME ($000's) (1)	Base for net corporate tax on earnings for retention¹ (15) + (19) (32)	Complement of marginal rate of personal income tax applicable to corporate tax payment^k (33)	Net corporate tax on earnings for retention¹ (14) × (33) (34)	Net corporate tax on net corporate earnings (10) + (34) (35)	Net corporate tax as a per cent of net corporate earnings [(35) ÷ (3)] × 100 (36)	Net corporate tax as a per cent of stockholder income [(35) ÷ (1)] × 100 (37)
1						
2	$ 507	82.60%	$ 91	$ 144	35.6	7.2
3	916	82.60	140	223	35.6	7.4
4	1,503	82.60	170	270	35.7	6.8
5	2,200	82.60	219	347	35.6	6.9
6	3,022	82.60	261	415	35.7	6.9
8	4,570	79.98	537	862	34.9	10.8
10	6,094	79.98	757	1,201	34.5	12.0
12	7,700	77.26	907	1,458	33.8	12.2
15	10,188	76.34	1,170	1,881	33.4	12.5
20	14,134	72.00	1,656	2,686	31.7	13.4
25	18,197	67.52	2,120	3,459	29.9	13.8
50	37,257	49.51	4,017	6,992	23.4	14.0
75	55,852	42.45	5,902	10,332	20.2	13.8
100	73,957	36.99	7,039	12,380	17.7	12.4
150	110,098	29.94	8,742	15,950	14.9	10.6
200	143,822	24.44	9,673	18,338	12.6	9.2
250	177,410	19.94	10,313	20,601	10.8	8.2
500	339,969	16.11	19,285	37,304	8.5	7.5

j This tax base is the sum of stockholder taxable income plus the corporate tax on earnings for distribution (column 15) and retained corporate earnings (column 19).

k The rates in this column are the complements of the personal rates that would apply to the corporate tax on earnings for retention (column 14).

l Column 34 (column 14 × column 33) represents the excess of the actual corporate tax payment over the personal tax that would have been due on an increment to stockholder income (column 32) equal in size to the corporate tax on earnings for retention.

Table 4, *c o n c l u d e d*

NET INCOME TAX SAVING

VERAGE STOCK- HOLDER MPUTED GROSS INCOME ($000's) (1)	Marginal rate of personal income tax applicable to retained earnings$m$ (38)	Potential personal income tax on retained earnings$n$ (19) × (38) (39)	Net income tax saving on retained earnings$o$ (39) — (26) (40)	Net tax saving as a per cent of net corporate earnings [(40) ÷ (3)] × 100 (41)	Net tax saving as a per cent of stockholder income [(40) ÷ (1)] × 100 (42)
1					
2	17.40%	$ 24	$ 18	4.5	0.9
3	17.40	37	28	4.5	0.9
4	17.40	45	33	4.4	0.8
5	17.40	58	43	4.4	0.9
6	17.40	69	51	4.4	0.9
8	19.15	162	125	5.1	1.6
10	20.02	238	180	5.2	1.8
12	20.02	296	224	5.2	1.9
15	23.66	457	363	6.4	2.4
20	26.36	763	597	7.1	3.0
25	29.33	1,159	898	7.8	3.6
50	44.17	4,513	3,663	12.3	7.3
75	53.15	9,306	7,508	14.7	10.0
100	57.33	13,735	11,193	16.0	11.2
150	64.92	23,864	19,963	18.6	13.3
200	69.44	34,603	29,315	20.1	14.7
250	72.95	47,506	40,595	21.3	16.2
500	81.82	123,362	107,362	24.4	21.5

m The marginal rates of personal income tax that would be applicable (column 38) to retained orporate earnings (column 19) considered as an increment to taxable income plus the corporate ax on earnings for distribution (column 15).

n The potential personal income tax liability on retained earnings was computed (column 39) by multiplying retained corporate earnings (column 19) by the marginal rates of personal income tax (column 38).

o From the potential personal income tax liability on retained earnings (column 39) was subracted the present value of the future capital gains tax liability on retained earnings (column 6) to arrive at the net income tax saving on reinvested earnings (column 40).

component of stockholders' income, column 5. Adding columns 4 and 5 furnishes column 6—the adjusted gross income component at each average stockholder income level.

From the relation that obtained for all personal income taxpayers was estimated the taxable income equivalent (for normal and surtax) of stockholders' adjusted gross income (column 7). This furnished the base from which to pick off the relevant marginal rates of personal income tax. For, at every step we compare the actual tax liability with the potential personal income tax liability, and this latter involves increments to taxable income and the tax rates applicable to them.

Differential against Earnings for Distribution

In the first chapter the extra burden on earnings for distribution was defined as the amount by which the corporate tax on earnings for distribution exceeds the personal tax that would have been due on an increment to taxable income equal in size to the corporate tax. Tabulated in column 8 is the corporate tax on earnings for distribution, obtained by multiplying column 2 by 0.159441. This is a roundabout method that minimized computing. Dividends comprised 0.369702 of after-tax earnings of net income corporations, while corporate tax liability came to 0.431270 of the income of deficit and income corporations combined. The product of these two ratios is 0.159441, which was applied directly to net corporate earnings to get the corporate tax on earnings for distribution.

In effect, the corporate tax was allocated between dividends and retained earnings to arrive at earnings for distribution and earnings for retention on the basis of the relative weights of dividends and retained earnings in the after-tax net income of income corporations. But this procedure, which implicitly assumes that all earnings out of which dividends were paid were subject to this year's corporate income tax, appears open to question since some dividends were distributed by deficit corporations, and, quite obviously out of earnings made in prior years. Little distortion is introduced on this score, however, for in 1950 less than 1 per cent of dividend payments were made by deficit corporations. (Comparable percentages characterize the other years of our study. In no case does the figure reach 3 per cent.) Therefore, even with large variations in effective rates of income tax from year to year, the earnings for distribution figure will be off to an insignificant degree. For example, from 1949 to 1950 the effective rate of corporate tax on earnings of income corporations rose by 7 percentage points—from 34.5 to 41.5. Yet if earnings for distribution had been computed on the assumption that all dividends of deficit corporations had been distributed from earnings taxed at the 1949 rate (a more refined method) the estimate would differ from that of earnings for distribution under the usual procedure by less than one-tenth of one per cent. Not a very serious matter.

The extra burden on earnings for distribution can be written as $C_eE - PC_eE$ (where C_eE equals the corporate tax and P the relevant marginal rate of personal income tax) or $C_eE \ (1 - P)$. In column 9 are listed the relevant $1 - P$ for increments the size of column 8 to each of the taxable incomes of column 7. The extra burden on earnings for distribution appears in column 10. It is obtained by multiplying column 8 by column 9. The entries in column 10 indicate how much more was taken from earnings made for distribution to stockholders because they were double taxed, than would have been due if these earnings had been subject in full to the personal income tax alone.

For a measure that permits comparability among income levels, the absolute extra burden has been taken as a percentage of earnings for distribution. The amount of earnings for distribution at each stockholder income level is found in column 11. It can be computed in a number of ways, but most simply by adding columns 5 and 8.

Column 12—the differential against earnings for distribution—is derived by dividing column 10 by column 11 and then multiplying by 100. The evidence of column 12 is clear cut and unequivocal. At every level of stockholder imputed gross income we find overtaxation of earnings for distribution due to double taxation. Most worthy of note is that, taken as an incremental effective rate (here called the differential), the extra tax burden is a decreasing function of the size of stockholder income. *The higher the stockholder's income level, the lower the additional effective rate of tax.* In the discussion of the conceptual framework of this analysis (see Chapter 1), the reason for this relationship was given. In developing our formulas, it was shown that the differential against the earnings for distribution component of the income of stockholders is equal to C_e $(1 - P)$, where C_e is equal to the effective rate of corporate tax and P the marginal rate of personal income tax that would have applied to a personal income increment equal to the corporate tax on earnings for distribution. Since C_e is the same at all stockholder income levels and P rises with income, C_e $(1 - P)$, the differential against earnings for distribution, is a declining function of stockholder income. The corporation income tax on the distributed portion of net corporate earnings was most burdensome for those at the lower income levels, least burdensome for those at the top of the income scale. (Stockholders with income below the taxable minimum are omitted, but they would be subject to the heaviest extra burden).

So much for the distributed segment of net corporate earnings. What about the undistributed part?

Differential against Earnings for Retention

The earnings for retention component of net corporate earnings is defined as the difference between net corporate earnings (column 3) and earnings for distribution (column 11). Tabulated in column 13, earnings for retention equal net corporate savings plus that portion of the corporate tax not allocated to dividends. In determining net corporate saving, the losses of deficit corporations were subtracted from the undistributed profits of net income corporations. In other words, for purposes of our investigation, not only the pro rata share of the earnings of corporations but also the proportionate share of deficits is imputed to stockholders in determining the amount of personal income derived from corporate activity. In 1950, earnings for retention were considerably greater than earnings for distribution; the ratio of the former to the latter came to about 1.7.[6]

The corporate tax on earnings for retention, column 14, was obtained by multiplying net corporate earnings (column 3) by 0.2718. Use of this multiplier minimized the necessary calculations, and is equivalent to applying a rate of 44.264 per cent to earnings for distribution. (See the explanation below the table.) This is higher than the effective rate of 41.317 per cent that was used in connection with earnings for distribution.[7] But this is as it should be. For the fraction of the total corporate tax to be allocated to undistributed earnings was determined on the basis of the data for net income corporations. But in computing net undistributed earnings, which together with the corporate tax component constitutes earnings for retention, the losses of deficit corporations are subtracted from the retained earnings of income corporations.

So far the actual corporate tax liability on earnings for retention has been measured. To determine the extra burden the benchmark figure—the potential personal income tax liability—must be computed. Column 15 lists for each class the base from which to start this computation—taxable income as defined for the personal income tax plus the corporate tax on earnings for distribution. Then, considering earnings for retention an addition to taxable income as tabulated in column 15, the marginal rates of personal income tax that would have applied are determined (column 16). Column 17, the potential personal income tax on earnings for retention, is the product of columns 13 and 16. If the full amount of earnings for retention had been distributed (or imputed to stockholders for personal income tax purposes) these figures show the ensuing increase in personal income tax liability.

[6] In every year of our study except 1940 and 1941, earnings for retention exceeded earnings for distribution.

[7] Use of rounded figures causes the values in column 14 to diverge slightly from those that would have been obtained by use of exact figures.

The difference between the actual corporate tax liability (column 14) and what would have been due under the personal income tax (column 17) constitutes the current extra burden on earnings for retention (column 18). This extra burden can be (and in most years of the study was) either positive or negative. For, depending on the stockholder's income level, the corporate rate will exceed the relevant personal marginal rate as in 1950 at incomes below $50,000, or fall short of it as at higher income levels.[8] Note that this is referred to as the current extra burden, but there is an additional consideration concerning the tax on earnings for retention.

INCREASED STOCK PRICES AND CAPITAL GAINS TAX ON STOCKHOLDERS RESULTING FROM RETENTION OF EARNINGS

When corporations retain earnings and share prices rise as a result, realization of this increment in value will lead to an increased capital gains tax. Should this not be included in the tax load on earnings for retention? The belief that it should leads to the question: how to compute it? Merely to raise some of the more relevant questions indicates the impossibility of arriving at even a fairly accurate answer. By how much do share prices rise? To what extent are the gains realized? How much of this realization is covered by taxable transactions? Over how long a period do the gains accrue? With all these imponderables involved, it should be clear that the figures in column 26 that constitute the estimated additional capital gains tax liability are not precise. They are no more than illustrative. But they are not misleading, for, while a number of arbitrary assumptions were made in their derivation, none of the assumptions seems unreasonable. If, at various points, a number of alternative assumptions had been chosen, the same general picture would have emerged.[9]

More specifically, starting with undistributed earnings (after corporation income taxes), the attempt was made to estimate: (1) to what extent these retentions could be expected to increase the price of stock; and (2) to what degree the personal income tax of stockholders would be increased because of the resulting realized capital gains. To estimate (1), findings of the Cowles Commission study of stock prices were used as the basis for assuming that 72 per cent of such reinvestment would be reflected in share values.[10] The procedures

8 The exception is the one particular income level at which rates are equal.
9 A test incorporating a number of alternative assumptions is reported on below.
10 The 72 cents comes from a finding for the period 1870-1937 "that every $2.50 of earnings retained by a corporation has, on the average, been associated with an increase of $1.80 in the value of its stock." (Alfred Cowles 3rd and Associates, *Common Stock, Indexes 1871-1937*, Principia, 1938, p. 42.)

45

for arriving at (2) were more complicated. Since not all of capital gains are realized, and some realized gains are not taxable, it seemed reasonable to suppose that only two-thirds of the potential gains would show up on tax returns. It was assumed further that their realization would not begin until under the tax law they would be considered long-term gains, only half of which would be includible in taxable income. Therefore 0.2412 (i.e., the product of 0.72 $\times$ 0.67 $\times$ 0.5) of retained earnings after corporation income tax was considered to be the relevant proportion of realized capital gains that would show up on stockholders' tax returns. Further, it was supposed that these gains would be realized over a period of five years, representing for each year increments to stockholder taxable income (personal income tax definition) assumed to be the same as in 1950. This provided the basis for computing the future increment to personal income tax liability attributable to the reinvested earnings of 1950. Then, with 5 per cent as a reasonable rate of return on alternative investment opportunities open to stockholders and as the relevant rate for discounting, the present value of this future increment to personal income tax liability was estimated.

For convenience in computation this present value correction (i.e., the present value would be 0.866 of the future value) was applied to the proportion of realized capital gains estimated above as reported for tax purposes—0.2412. The result, 0.2089, was divided by 5, to cover the assumed realization of these capital gains evenly over a 5 year period. This provided the multiplier—0.04178—used in deriving column 20 from the figures in column 19 which are the undistributed (reinvested) earnings, obtained by subtracting column 14 from column 13. To these values was applied the multiplier 0.04178 to obtain the annual present value of taxable realized capital gains (under our assumptions) from 1951 through 1955. These figures comprise column 20.

On a further assumption—that stockholder taxable income from all other sources (personal income tax definition) in all of these years would be the same as in 1950—the marginal rate applicable in each of these years to the capital gains increment was determined. These rates are listed in columns 21 through 25. (The 50 per cent ceiling in 1951, 1954, and 1955, and the 52 per cent maximum in 1952 and 1953 stem from the alternative tax option, open to taxpayers who had net long-term capital gains.)

By multiplying the annual present value of taxable capital gains (column 20) successively by the marginal rate for each of the next five years (columns 21 through 25) and summing up the products, estimates were obtained of the present value of the increased future capital gains tax liability attributable to the reinvested earnings of 1950. This item, entered in column 26, constitutes an addition to the income tax load on earnings for retention.

Addition of columns 18 (the current extra burden) and 26 (the present value of the additional future extra burden) furnishes the total extra burden on earnings for retention (column 27). The future capital gains tax liability adjustment does not change the pattern; our conclusion stands, viz., the total extra burden on earnings for retention can be positive or negative depending on the income level of the stockholder. The higher the income level and the potential marginal rate of personal income tax, the more likely a negative extra burden. Thus, on average in 1950, the earnings for retention component of incomes of married stockholders with over $50,000 of imputed gross income was subject to a lower income tax liability than would have been the case had it been reached by the personal income tax alone. Below this income level the reverse was true.

Again, for purposes of comparability among income classes the extra burden was computed relative to its base. The differential against earnings for retention, entered in column 28 (equals the division of column 27 by column 13 expressed as a percent), is an inverse function of stockholder income: the lower the income of stockholders, the higher the differential; after $50,000 for married taxpayers, the higher the income of stockholders, the more strongly negative the relative extra burden on earnings for retention.[11] Comparison of the results

[11] In connection with the future capital gains tax liability adjustment, the reader's suspicions are almost certain to be aroused by the number and breadth of the underlying assumptions. Choice of other assumptions, however, would have made little difference in the findings.

The extent of such changes was tested by sample calculations using different ratios for the proportion of capital gains realized in taxable form, and assuming differing lengths of time over which they were realized. The results of the test, showing the net extra burden on earnings for retention for the weighted average of joint and separate returns, 1950, are summarized in the table below:

	Standard assumption	Alternative assumption			
	Two-thirds of gain realized in taxable form	One-third of gain realized in taxable form		Three-fourths of gain realized in taxable form	
Imputed gross income level ($000's)	over 5 years	over 1 year	over 10 years	over 1 year	over 10 years
3	29.1%	28.1%	27.8%	29.6%	28.8%
6	29.4	28.2	28.0	29.8	29.1
12	25.7	24.5	24.2	26.2	25.7
20	20.4	18.9	18.6	21.1	20.3
200	−22.0	−24.7	−25.3	−20.7	−22.0

Changing the assumptions would, of course, change the results. But even strongly

at the extremes of the stockholder income scale shows that, whereas the average stockholder with $2,000 was subject to a tax liability on the earnings for retention component of his income more than two and one-half times the liability calculated by applying the rates of the personal income tax alone, the actual corporate-personal tax at the $500,000 average stockholder income level was about three-fifths as high as the potential personal income tax liability on earnings for retention. (Remember these data apply to stockholders who filed joint returns.)

One further point will be mentioned now and elaborated later. The findings just presented are a composite result influenced by both corporation distribution policy and the corporation income tax. For in determining the extra burden (or benefit) on earnings for retention there are two factors at work: (1) the tax saving due to non-distribution; (2) the net burden of the corporation income tax. By the tax saving due to nondistribution is meant the difference between the personal income tax that would have been due had retained earnings (column 19) been fully distributed and the present value of the future capital gains tax on reinvested earnings (column 26). Even at the lowest marginal rate bracket, the potential personal income tax exceeds the future capital gains tax so there is always a tax saving, and it becomes increasingly important as the marginal personal rate that would have applied to retained earnings rises. The net corporate tax burden, on the other hand, is always positive, but it declines in degree as the level of stockholder income rises. For it is the amount by which the actual corporate tax on earnings for retention exceeds the personal tax that would have been due if stockholders had received as personal income the sum paid as corporation income tax. With (1) increasingly negative (i.e., if measured as a burden) and (2) decreasingly positive as income rises, the extra burden on earnings for retention inevitably falls as average stockholder income rises and, after a point, the burden usually turns to a tax saving.

Differential against Net Corporate Earnings

The extra burden on net corporate earnings tabulated in column 29 is the sum of the extra burden on each of the components of this income share (column 10 plus column 27). Not all stockholders were put at an income tax disadvantage because they were double-taxed.

---

different assumptions about the proportion of total gain realized in taxable form, and the period over which the realization would take place, lead to very slight changes in the value of the differential, while the conclusions relating to the income level pattern of the extra burden are not changed at all.

On average, if the corporate tax were abolished and each stockholder's pro rata share of corporate earnings were called fully and promptly to account as part of personal income, those filing joint returns in 1950 would have been affected in either of two ways: stockholders with imputed gross incomes below approximately $150,000 would have paid lower taxes on their share of net corporate earnings; those with incomes above $150,000 would have paid higher taxes on their share of net corporate earnings.

How important was the extra burden or tax saving? It has been measured as a proportion of both the net corporate earnings component and stockholders' imputed gross income. In column 30 the extra burden is tabulated as a percentage of stockholders' pro rata share of net corporate earnings. The differential in this connection is a weighted average of the differentials against earnings for retention and earnings for distribution. Like each of its components, the differential against net corporate earnings is a declining function of the stockholder's income level. Further, after a point, the positive differential against earnings for distribution is outweighed by the negative differential against earnings for retention, leading to a differential in favor of net corporate earnings. Where along the income scale this will occur depends on the relative weights of earnings for retention and earnings for distribution. The heavier the weight of earnings for retention, the more closely will the configurations of the differential against net corporate earnings conform to the differential against earnings for retention, bringing closer their turning points. Because, however, the differential against earnings for distribution is always positive, the turning point for net corporate earnings will come at a higher income level than that for earnings for retention.

In summary, we find a substantial additional tax on the net corporate earnings component of the majority of average stockholder income levels, but near the top of the income range it is replaced by a sizeable tax saving. Our method of taxing corporate earnings—at the corporate level when earned and at the personal level when distributed —led to a declining extra burden as the income level of stockholders rose and at around $150,000 of imputed gross income it became a benefit which continued to rise with income level.

Differential against Stockholders' Income

Column 31 presents the net extra burden as a rate on stockholders' imputed gross income [(column 29 ÷ column 1) × 100], in effect, this is a measure of the incremental tax rate to which stockholders were subject. It shows us how much more heavily, in terms of effective rates, stockholders were taxed than would have been the case if, with the corporate tax abolished, all their income including their full pro rata share of net corporate earnings had been subject in full to the personal income tax. By use of the personal income tax as the benchmark we find, for example, that because of tax rates actually in effect on corporate earnings the average married stockholder with $3,000 of imputed gross income was subject to a tax six and one-half percentage points *higher,* and the average stockholder with $500,000 was taxed at a rate some fourteen percentage points *lower* than the personal income tax alone would have demanded.

How heavy the income tax differential against (or in favor of) stockholders will be depends on two things: (1) the differential against net corporate earnings and; (2) the proportion of corporate earnings to imputed gross income. In specific terms, the values in column 31 are the product of the differential against net corporate earnings (column 30) and the percentage that net corporate earnings constitute of imputed gross income (column 2); the values in column 31 are, therefore, always lower than those in column 30. Moreover, the differential against stockholders does not trace out precisely the same pattern as the differential against their pro rata share of net corporate earnings. The latter declines continually as stockholder income rises; the former, however, reading up the income scale, tends to rise up to a point ($12,000) and then falls quite steadily. This difference in behavior is a matter of weighting, which requires brief explanation.

The differential against net corporate earnings, as previously noted, is a weighted average of the differentials against earnings for distribution and earnings for retention. Because it was assumed that the same dividends-to-corporate-earnings ratio applied in every one of our stockholder cells, the proportionate weights of earnings for dividends and earnings for retention in net corporate earnings are the same at every average stockholder income level. Since both component differentials are declining functions of income, their weighted average will likewise fall as income levels rise.

The same is not true, however, in the case of the differential against stockholders, which is the differential against net corporate earnings weighted by the proportion of corporate earnings to the whole of stockholder income. For here the weights vary from one average stockholder income to another. The differential against net corporate earnings falls continuously as income rises (with only minor exceptions), while the ratio of net corporate earnings to imputed income behaves irregularly up to the $6,000 stockholder income level and then rises as income increases. Over the lower part of the income range up to

$12,000, the fall in the differential against net corporate earnings is less rapid than the rise in ratio of net corporate earnings to imputed gross income; consequently, the differential against stockholders increases from income level to income level. (Exceptions are from $3,000 to $4,000 where the ratio of net corporate earnings to imputed gross income falls, and $5,000 to $6,000, where there is no change.) From $12,000 up, the direction is reversed to a continuous fall in the differential (except the slight rise between $15,000 and $20,000).

Three Variants of the Differentials

Table 4 is designed to set forth in detail the procedures used in obtaining the values of the differentials that seem most relevant for analyzing the problem of the relative tax burden on stockholders. Therefore it develops the derivation of what were designated in Chapter 1 as the variant 2 values. However, by reference to the table, the differences between our preferred measure and the two other possibilities, i.e. variants 1 and 3, can be made explicit. In what follows, familiarity with the discussion of the variants in Chapter 1 is assumed.

In arriving at the variant 1 values we use the current extra burden on earnings for retention (column 18) instead of the total extra burden as listed in column 27. This leads to lower values for the differentials against earnings for retention, net corporate earnings, and stockholders than those under variant 2. (It would also cause the entries in column 40—the net income tax saving on corporate earnings—to be higher than those tabulated, but calculations of variant values for this measure were not undertaken.)

In computing variant 3, it will be recalled, an adjustment was made for the failure of 28 cents of each reinvested dollar to show up as capital gains. The present value of the addition to the "tax liability" of stockholders in this connection comes to 0.2425 of the entries in column 19—retained corporate earnings. In deriving the differentials under variant 3, values this much higher than those in column 27— total extra burden on earnings for retention—are used. Consequently the variant 3 differentials against earnings for retention, net corporate earnings, and stockholders are higher than as measured by our usual procedure.

How different the values are under each of these variants can be judged from the annual tables in Appendix A, and from Chart 2 which plots the 1950 data for joint and separate returns combined. While differences do, of course, show up, the main conclusion is that the basic income class pattern of all three variants is the same. Therefore, although specific magnitudes would differ, the conclusions

CHART 2—Three Variant Measures of the Differentials for 1950

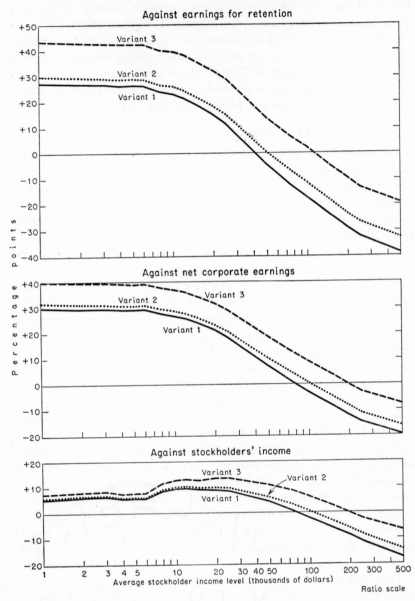

Against earnings for retention

Against net corporate earnings

Against stockholders' income

Average stockholder income level (thousands of dollars)

Ratio scale

reached earlier by reference to variant 2 values would still be valid no matter which of the variants was chosen.

Weighted Averages of Joint and Separate Returns

Separate calculations for stockholders filing joint returns and those filing separate returns were necessary because different personal income tax rates applied for each type of return. To arrive at a single measure, averages were struck for the joint and separate return differentials. The procedure here was straightforward. On the assumption that the same proportion of joint to separate returns holds for stockholders as for all taxpayers, the proper weights were obtained for application at each imputed gross income level. The weighted averages, plotted on Chart 1, are listed in Table 5.

TABLE 5

Derivation of the Weighted Average Differentials, 1950

AVERAGE STOCK-HOLDER IMPUTED GROSS INCOME LEVEL ($000's) (1)	Joint returns as % of total returns (2)	WEIGHTED AVERAGE DIFFERENTIALS[a] AGAINST:			
		Earnings for distribution (3)[a]	Earnings for retention (4)[a]	Net corporate earnings (5)[a]	Stockholder imputed gross income (6)[a]
1	0.0	34.3%	30.0%	31.7%	5.7%
2	19.1	34.2	29.3	31.2	6.3
3	44.6	34.3	29.1	31.1	6.5
4	66.1	33.9	28.7	30.7	5.8
5	76.9	33.8	28.8	30.7	6.0
6	83.2	34.0	28.7	30.8	6.0
8	83.9	33.7	26.5	29.3	9.0
10	84.3	32.9	26.0	28.6	9.9
12	85.1	32.7	24.6	27.7	10.0
15	86.4	32.1	22.0	25.9	9.7
20	86.9	30.8	18.5	23.3	9.8
25	87.2	29.2	15.2	20.6	9.5
50	87.6	24.9	0.4	10.0	5.9
75	87.1	21.7	−6.7	4.2	2.9
100	86.8	19.1	−11.4	0.4	0.3
150	86.2	16.7	−18.7	−5.0	−3.6
200	85.6	14.6	−23.4	−8.7	−6.3
250	85.2	13.2	−26.9	−11.4	−8.7
500	83.8	10.0	−32.9	−16.3	−14.3

[a] Derivation: column 2 × differential for joint returns + (100 − column 2) × differential for separate returns.

The Net Corporate Tax[12] Distinguished from Other Factors

Up to now the objective of our analysis by a variety of measures based on particular assumptions has been to pin point the results of our system of taxing corporate earnings that involves an income tax on the corporate level when earned and a tax on the personal level when distributed in terms of the differential tax liability of stockholders.[13] In the procedure described above two factors influencing the results —the corporate tax and corporate distribution policy—were not treated separately. The findings so far are composite results in which the effects of both factors are merged. It is useful for analytical purposes to separate these two determinants to delineate more specifically the net corporate tax and the personal income tax saving due to the failure of corporations to distribute the whole of their annual earnings, and analyze the role each plays in this set of interrelated factors. For this purpose the net corporate tax has been measured very simply: it is the difference between the corporate tax actually paid and the liability of stockholders if the sum paid as corporate income tax had been subject instead to the personal income tax.

The computation of the net corporate tax on earnings for distribution has already been explained and appears as the extra burden on income from this source (column 10 of Table 4). The derivation of the rest of the net corporate tax is set forth in columns 32 through 35 of Table 4 with explanatory notes below the table. Had there been either full distribution of corporate earnings or the requirement that they be imputed fully to stockholders for personal income tax purposes, that portion of earnings for retention which was paid as corporate income tax would have served instead to enlarge the personal tax base consisting of the stockholder's taxable adjusted gross income, plus the corporate tax on earnings for distribution, plus net corporate saving (retained earnings). This base appears in column 32, as the sum of columns 15 and 19. Column 14 lists the corporate tax on earnings for retention, and column 33 tabulates the complement of the personal marginal rate that would apply to an increment (corporate tax on earnings for retention) the size of column 14 to the tax base in column 32. Column 34 (column 14 $\times$ column 33) is the net corporate tax on earnings for retention—the excess of the actual corporate tax payment over what would have been due under the personal income tax had the corporate tax been included as part of

12 This phrase is taken from Goode, *op. cit.*, p. 92. Our measure, however, differs in several respects from his.

13 How our findings are affected by the dividend relief provisions introduced in the Internal Revenue Code of 1954 is considered in Chapter 7.

the stockholder's taxable income. Addition of the net corporate tax on each of its components—earnings for distribution column 10, and earnings for retention, column 34—furnishes the net corporate tax on net corporate earnings, presented in column 35. The net corporate tax has been converted to an effective rate on net corporate earnings (column 36) and on all of stockholder income (column 37). Weighted averages of these data for joint and separate returns are plotted on Chart 3.

CHART 3—Net Corporate Tax and Net Personal Income Tax Saving, 1950

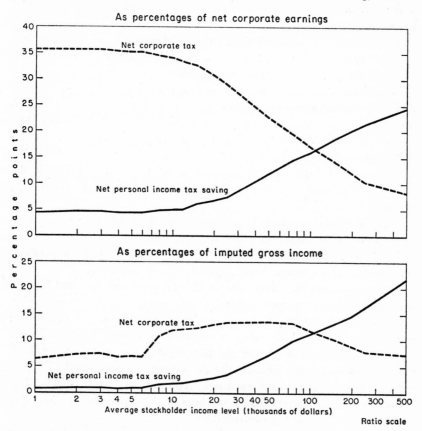

Viewed in this light, the corporate tax, per se, constituted a substantial additional levy on stockholders' net corporate earnings—ranging for joint returns from an extra tax of nearly 36 percentage points at the lower income levels to over 8 points at the $500,000 level. A declining function of income, it fell steadily between these two extremes. Considered in relation to all of a stockholder's income, the net corporate tax, of course, represented a smaller but not an inconsiderable increase in effective rates. The corporate tax raised the rate of income taxation between 7 and 14 points higher than the rates at the same income levels of the personal income tax alone. Here, however, no steady decline is seen reading from low to high incomes, but rather a pattern of rise followed by fall, with the values at the two extremes of the income array about equal. The reasons for this pattern—variations in the rate of fall in net corporate tax on corporate earnings, and in rise of corporate earnings as a per cent of imputed gross income —were discussed in connection with data in column 31, the differential against stockholders.

The reader is reminded that the net corporate tax neglects one salient feature of the taxation of stockholders—their immunity from the current personal income tax liability on earnings retained by corporations. This results in a tax saving, even when the present value of future capital gains tax liability on retained earnings is taken into account. The net tax saving is estimated for 1950, in column 40. The procedure consists of computing the potential personal income tax on retained earnings (net of corporate income tax) and subtracting from it the future capital gains tax adjustment, previously described. Individual steps in the procedure are set forth in columns 38 through 40.

Considering retained corporate earnings (column 19) as an increment to taxable adjusted gross income plus the corporate tax on earnings for distribution (column 15), the marginal rate of personal income tax that would have applied was determined. These rates appear in column 38. Then column 39—the potential personal income tax liability on retained earnings—was computed by multiplying column 19 by column 38. From this the present value of the future capital gains tax liability due to reinvested earnings was subtracted (column 26), the result being the net income tax saving on retained earnings (column 40). Finally, the tax saving was converted to a percentage of net corporate earnings (column 41) and stockholders income (column 42). Weighted averages of these percentages for joint and separate returns are plotted on Chart 3.

For both measures, it is no surprise to find the tax saving increasing · in relative importance as stockholder income rises. For example, the estimated tax saving on this score increases from under 5 per cent of corporate earnings and 1 per cent of stockholder income near the bottom of the income scale, to 24 per cent of net corporate earnings and 22 per cent of imputed gross income at the $500,000 income level.

Now we come up against an old friend in a somewhat different guise: addition of the percentages for the net corporate tax and the tax saving (with its sign taken as negative) furnishes the differential. The net corporate tax falls as income rises; the tax saving increases in relative importance with income. Hence our finding that, after a point (on the chart where the tax saving and net corporate tax lines intersect) the tax saving outweighs the corporate tax—stockholders are undertaxed.

Specifically with reference to the data of Table 4, the reader will note that the algebraic sum of the net corporate tax percentage (column 36) and the tax saving on net corporate earnings percentage (column 41) equals the differential against net corporate earnings (column 30). Also, the differential against stockholders (column 31) is equal to the sum of the net corporate tax on stockholders percentage (column 37) and the net tax saving percentage of stockholder income (column 42).[14] (There will, of course, be slight differences due to rounding.)

[14] As mentioned earlier, in these summations the sign of the tax saving is negative.

CHAPTER 3

Changes in the Differential Tax Burden, 1940-1952

THE procedures described in the preceding chapters were undertaken for each of the years in the period 1940-1952, with the exception of 1942 and 1943 for which years the data required in our calculations were not published. Having examined the findings for 1950 in detail, we can go on to discuss in more summary fashion the results for the other years covered by the study.

That there should be sizeable differences among years is hardly surprising. The results are the outcome of interaction of a number of factors which varied significantly in level and relative weight from year to year (see Table 6). The primary direct determinants of the value of the differentials are:

1. The level of corporate tax rates (columns 4 and 6)
2. The level of personal income tax rates (column 1), and the slope of the rate schedule, i.e., the rapidity with which the effective rate rises
3. The amount and relative importance of earnings for distribution and for retention (columns 3 and 5, and 7 and 8)
4. The amount of net corporate earnings (columns 2 and 9)

1. With everything else equal, the higher the corporate tax rate, the greater the extra burden against earnings for distribution, earnings for retention, corporate earnings and stockholders.

2. Conversely, with other factors unchanged, the higher the personal income tax rate, the lower the extra burden in all these connections. Similarly, the more progressive the rate schedule, i.e., the more rapidly the marginal rate increases, the less onerous these extra burdens become as stockholder income rises.

3. The extra burden (or benefit) on net corporate earnings is a weighted average of (a) the extra burden on earnings for distribution and of (b) the extra burden or benefit on earnings for retention. Therefore, the higher the proportion of earnings for distribution, the greater the weight of (a) in the determination of the extra burden (or benefit) on net corporate earnings. The importance of these proportionate interrelations is particularly apparent at those income levels where we find an extra burden on earnings for distribution and a net tax saving on earnings for retention; but their importance is also obvious at all stockholder income levels.

4. With other factors unchanged, the proportion of income derived

TABLE 6

Summary Information on Taxable Stockholders, 1940-1941 and 1944-1952

(dollars in millions)

YEAR	Effective rate of personal income tax for all taxpayers[a] (1)	Net corporate earnings (2)	Earnings for distribution (3)	Effective rate on earnings for distribution[b] (4)	Earnings for retention (5)	Effective rate on earnings for retention[c] (6)	Earnings for distribution as % of net corporate earnings (7)	Earnings for retention as % of net corporate earnings (8)	Net corporate earnings as % of stockholder income (9)
1940	5.8%	$ 5,302	$ 4,289	27.1%	$ 1,013	78.6%	80.9%	19.1%	38.8%
1941	7.9	11,302	6,454	44.5	4,848	59.3	57.1	42.9	50.2
1944	14.1	18,087	7,922	57.5	10,165	61.6	43.8	56.2	56.1
1945	14.5	14,243	6,905	51.2	7,338	58.0	48.5	51.5	56.1
1946	13.6	16,555	6,183	34.0	10,372	40.0	37.3	62.7	47.4
1947	13.4	21,867	7,323	34.5	14,544	38.5	33.5	66.5	53.4
1948	10.9	23,906	8,167	34.7	15,739	38.2	34.2	65.8	52.0
1949	10.5	19,903	8,593	34.1	11,310	40.5	43.2	56.8	47.5
1950	11.6	30,202	11,655	41.3	18,547	44.3	43.2	61.4	53.9
1951	13.2	31,220	13,843	51.1	17,377	55.6	44.3	55.7	51.5
1952	14.1	26,506	13,073	50.0	13,433	56.0	49.3	50.7	46.2

Source: Basic data used for estimates from *Statistics of Income*, Parts 1 and 2.

[a] Rate on adjusted gross income (or estimated equivalent for 1940 and 1941). This column serves only as a rough index of the height of rate schedules because effective rates are affected also by changes in the income distribution. But these data do bring out all that is necessary for our purpose—i.e., that income tax rates (comparing the years cited and the years directly below them in the table) rose in 1941, rose in 1944 and 1945, fell in 1946 and 1947, in 1948 and 1949, and rose in 1950, 1951, and 1952.   [b] Effective rate of corporate income taxes on net income corporations.

[c] Higher than column 4 because earnings for retention are net of deficits of deficit corporations.

from net corporate earnings determines the degree of over- or under-taxation of stockholders.

The reader is reminded of the amplified treatment of these factors and their interrelations in determining the differential tax burden on stockholders given in the two preceding chapters. This cursory recapitulation will serve as a point of departure for our investigation of the variations found over the period of the study.

COMPARISON OF DIFFERENTIALS OVER THE PERIOD FROM 1940 THROUGH 1952

Over the years 1940 through 1952, what were the trends in differential taxation of stockholders? For tracing the directions and extent of change, four selected income levels are analyzed and shown graphically in Chart 4. For this purpose $3,000 is taken as representative of the bottom of the stockholder income scale, $500,000 to summarize the experience at the top, and $10,000 and $50,000 to cover the range in between.[1] As in Chapter 2, the values are derived in terms of variant 2 (although data for variants 1 and 3 would show essentially similar patterns).

Consider first the trend in the differential against earnings for distribution (panel A). While there are slight variations in its time pattern at the lower and upper income levels; in general there occurs a rise in the first years of our period, then a decline reaching a low in 1946, and finally year-to-year increases up through 1951 with a slight fall in 1952. A detailed analysis, to illustrate the operation of the previously noted factors determining the height of the differential, is given later in this chapter. The chief points relevant to Chart 4 are that a rise in the corporate tax rate increases the differential, and a rise in personal tax rates causes it to decline. The rise in the extra burden on earnings for distribution during the early years of our period is explained, therefore, by the sharper increase in corporate rates compared with personal tax rates. In 1945 the effective rate of corporate income tax was lower than in 1944 (primarily because of a pronounced fall in excess profits tax liability), and with the end of the war corporate rates were cut more sharply than the personal income tax schedule; thus the fall in the differential. Note what happened between 1947 and 1948. The introduction of income splitting in 1948 led to a decline in personal income tax rates—slight at the lower income levels but substantial for higher income stockholders.

---

[1] For tabulations of the differentials for every year of this period at all nineteen selected income levels see Appendix A.

CHART 4—Differentials at Selected Stockholder Income
Levels, 1940-1941 and 1944-1952

Income level (dollars)
------- 3,000   ············· 50,000
-·-·-·- 10,000   ———— 500,000

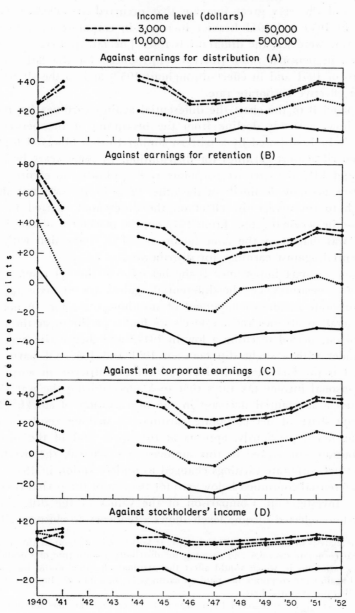

This explains the slight rise between these two years in the differential against earnings for distribution at the $3,000 stockholder income level, and the very great increase that occurred at $500,000. Once again in 1950 and 1951 heavier increases in corporate than in personal rate were set; the differentials rose. The fall in 1952 is due to the rise in personal rates (increases introduced for the last several months of 1951 and in effect throughout 1952) and to the slight fall in the effective corporate rate.[2]

In panel B of the chart the differential against earnings for retention shows a steady decline from the beginning of the period up through 1947, followed by a pattern similar to that observed for the differential against earnings for distribution. In some years between 1940 and 1947 the effective corporate rate applicable to earnings for retention actually declined; in the other years its rise was not sharp enough to counteract the effect on the differential exerted by the increase in personal rates.[3] From 1947 on, the movement of the differential was shaped by the same factors noted in connection with the differential against earnings for distribution.

Of more direct importance is the behavior of the net resultant of these two measures, i.e. the differential against (or in favor of) the net corporate earnings component of stockholder income (panel C). In general, at all four income levels we find a decline over the early part of our period reaching a low in 1947,[4] and then a rise over the remainder with a slight dip between 1951 and 1952. Of particular interest is the fact that coincident with the sharp rise in corporate and personal income tax rates that took place during the war there occurred a substantial decrease in the overtaxation of stockholders' pro rata share of net corporate earnings. A striking result of this decline, noted previously, appears at the upper end of the income distribution, epitomized in this summary by $500,000; the overtaxation of net corporate earnings changed to undertaxation in 1944, and the differential continued below zero for the rest of the period covered by the investigation. Comparison of the values of the differentials at the four selected income levels shows a tendency to cluster in 1940

[2] The analysis in this paragraph is sketchy. It fails to take account of the proportion that corporate earnings and earnings for distribution constitute of stockholder income, variations in which would affect the personal rate that would have been applied against the corporate tax paid on earnings for distribution. But this degree of detail is not required here.

[3] Losses which are subtracted from income to determine earnings for retention were proportionately greater in 1940 than in 1941. That is why the effective rate of corporate tax on earnings for retention was higher in 1940 than in 1941, even though the rates fixed by law were lower.

[4] The exception—a rise at the $3,000 and the $10,000 levels between 1940 and 1941.

and a pronounced widening of the gap between those at the lower income and those at the upper income levels by 1952. Little change in the differential values occurred at the bottom of the income scale, the widening gap being caused by the falling differentials at the top.

Imputed gross income level ($000's)	Differential against net corporate earnings		Change in differential
	1940	1952	
3	35.6%	37.4%	1.8
10	33.5	34.7	1.2
50	21.6	12.3	−9.3
500	8.9	−12.0	−20.9

In the differential against stockholders these same variations among income levels occur (panel D). Note how similar were the values of the differential against stockholders at the extremes of the income range in 1940 and how great the spread between them was in 1952. The differential at the lowest income level rose slightly from the beginning of our period to its end. Over the middle and at the top of the income scale, on the other hand, a fall occurred, particularly

Imputed gross income level ($000's)	Differential against stockholders		Change in differential
	1940	1952	
3	7.4%	8.4%	1.0
10	12.7	9.9	−2.8
50	12.2	7.4	−4.8
500	8.0	−10.8	−18.8

for stockholders with very high incomes. In fact the fall was so great, that we find, in every year but 1940 and 1941, that stockholders at the $500,000 imputed gross income level were "undertaxed." (In several years this was true also of the average $50,000 stockholder.) One further point. The first three differentials reached their maximum at the lowest income level and moved down regularly as income levels rose. The differential against stockholders, however, reached its peak (for the four income levels plotted) at $10,000. At this income level the proportion of stockholder income represented by net corporate earnings was sufficiently higher than the ratio characterizing the average $3,000 imputed gross income to more than compensate for the effect of the higher differential against net corporate earnings found at the lower of these two income levels.

In brief summary: Concentrating on the difference between the years that begin and terminate our period—1940 and 1952—as corporate and personal income tax rates rose, and retentions comprised a higher percentage of corporate earnings, the differentials tended to fall, most notably at the higher income levels. The severity of the overtaxation of corporate earnings and stockholders tended to decline, and, at the higher income levels, undertaxation developed. With the general decline in value of the differentials came a widening of the spread between them because the decline was more pronounced in the upper portion of the stockholder income range than at the lower income levels.

A slightly different way of reviewing the same evidence is furnished by examination of the net corporate tax and the net income tax saving (Chart 5). The net corporate tax (explained in Chapter 1), taken as

CHART 5—Net Corporate Tax and Net Personal Income Tax Saving as Percentages of Stockholder Income at Selected Income Levels, 1940-1941 and 1944-1952

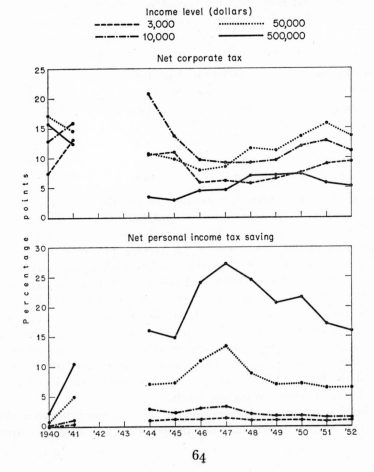

a percentage of stockholder income, can be considered an incremental rate of income tax on stockholders. The net income tax saving, likewise explained in Chapter 1, may be viewed as a rate of income tax "benefit" for stockholders. The excess of the extra burden over the benefit is the differential against stockholders.

Taking as our points for comparison the years 1940 and 1952, the reader will note a slight rise in the net corporate tax percentage at the lowest income level plotted on the upper section of Chart 5, and a fall for the other incomes. The higher the income level, the greater the decline, both absolutely and relatively. In the lower panel where the tax saving is plotted, the pattern is similar but, in this case, more pronounced. The net income tax saving percentages at the two lower income levels rose moderately, and at the two upper levels the rate of tax saving increased substantially. While over virtually the whole income range the differential against stockholders fell, it can be seen why it declined relatively little over the lower portion of this range, and very much in the upper reaches of the income scale.

AVERAGES FOR THE PERIOD AS A WHOLE

Another way of summarizing the findings is to strike averages of the differentials for all eleven years covered by the study. This procedure is also useful in view of the effects on the values of the differentials of variations from year to year in a number of factors. Averaging tends to wash out peculiarities associated with any given year and to provide a more "representative" picture.

Simple averages for each of the four measures, with the values for each year given equal weight, are plotted on Chart 6. Over that portion of the income range in which the majority of stockholders are found (up to about $25,000 of imputed gross income) the part of the corporation income tax levied on earnings for distribution constituted a considerable extra burden on this segment of net corporate earnings— 30 per cent and over. Stockholders with incomes of $500,000 and over were likewise subject to an extra burden on the earnings for distribution portion of their pro rata share of net corporate earnings, but the incremental tax load was much less severe. For the small minority of stockholders with imputed gross incomes from $100,000 to $500,000 the extra tax averaged from 15 to 7.5 per cent. The findings over the period 1940-1952 (1942 and 1943 excluded) on the double taxation of dividends (defined as earnings for payment of dividends or for distribution) may be summarized more starkly: stockholders at the $3,000 imputed gross income level were overtaxed by 34.2 per cent of cor-

CHART 6—Average Differentials for the Period 1940-1952,
Excluding 1942 and 1943

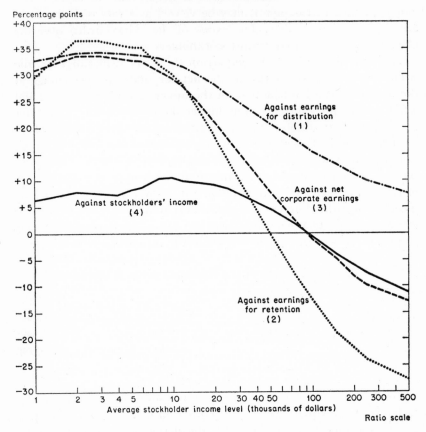

Percentage points

Against earnings
for distribution
(1)

Against net
corporate earnings
(3)

Against stockholders' income
(4)

Against earnings
for retention
(2)

Average stockholder income level (thousands of dollars)

Ratio scale

porate earnings on their behalf for distribution as dividends; stockholders with $500,000 of income were overtaxed by 7.5 per cent.

What about the undistributed segment of net corporate earnings? Averages for the eleven years (see line 2 of Chart 6) reveal that most stockholders were overtaxed on the earnings for retention component of their incomes, while the high income minority were undertaxed.[5] For stockholders with incomes up to about $12,000, the net incremental burden ran between 28 and 37 per cent of their share of earnings for retention; for stockholders with incomes ranging from $100,000 through $500,000, the net tax *benefit* ranged from over 12

[5] The atypical results in 1940 (and to a lesser extent in 1941) when, because of relatively heavy deficits, the differential against earnings for retention, particularly at the lower income levels, exceeded that on earnings for distribution, explains why line 2 lies above line 1 over this portion of the income range.

per cent to about 28 per cent. The differences in the tax liability between the lowest income level ($3,000) and the highest ($500,000) stand out more strongly when the actual tax is compared with the obligation that would have been incurred if earnings for retention had been reached by the personal income tax alone. Stockholders at the lowest income paid as tax 37 per cent more of their share of retained earnings than they would have paid in personal income tax; those at the top of the income range experienced a tax saving equal to 28 per cent of their share of retained earnings.

The extra burdens on earnings for distribution and earnings for retention together constitute the net additional tax liability on the corporate earnings component of stockholder incomes. This incremental tax load expressed in percentage form (i.e. as a per cent of net corporate earnings) is the differential against net corporate earnings, which is a weighted sum of the differential against earnings for distribution and the differential against (or in favor of) earnings for retention. An average of the annual findings plotted on line 3 of the chart shows the following picture of differentials against the net corporate earnings component of stockholder income: a significant degree of overtaxation for stockholders with incomes below $15,000—ranging from an additional tax load of over 30 per cent at the lowest income level to nearly 25 percentage points of additional tax at the $15,000 income point; a more moderate degree of overtaxation for stockholders with incomes over $15,000 and up to $75,000—ranging from an extra tax load of 21 per cent at the $20,000 income level down to an additional burden of less than 3 per cent at the $75,000 level; and a noticeable degree of undertaxation over the $75,000 income level, reaching a maximum tax saving of almost 13 percentage points for stockholders whose imputed gross income averaged $500,000.

One further differential was investigated. How much heavier or (lighter) was the effective tax rate on stockholders than it would have been had there been no corporation income tax and stockholders were called to account fully and promptly on their pro rata share of net corporate earnings under the personal income tax? In other words, the additional net burden was converted to an effective rate on all of stockholder income. The absolute amount of the net extra burden (or tax saving) is, of course, the same used in computing the differential against (or in favor of) net corporate earnings. Since, however, this amount is now related to a larger base, the differentials against or in favor of stockholders will be lower than those against corporate earnings. The ratio of net corporate earnings to imputed gross income, discussed in Chapter 2, tends to rise with income—increasing from about 20 per cent at the lowest income levels, to over 90 per cent at the top of the income scale. Therefore, the differential against stockholders with low imputed gross incomes runs at only one-fifth of the differential against net corporate earnings, but the differential in favor of stockholders at the top of the income range runs at about 90 per cent of the value of the differential in favor of net corporate earnings. Again by way of simple summary, the annual values were computed and plotted as line 4 of Chart 6. Stockholders whose income averaged $25,000 or under, were subject to a sizeable incremental tax levy. In effect they paid an additional tax that averaged between 6 and over 10 per cent of their total income. Over the income interval between $20,000 and $75,000, there existed a smaller and declining additional income tax on stockholders. At the top of the income scale, stockholders were undertaxed. Their combined corporate-personal income tax was lower than what they would have had to pay if all their income had been subject promptly and in full to the personal income tax alone. This tax saving ranged from 0.7 per cent of total income (income from all sources) in the case of the average stockholders at the $100,000 imputed gross income level, to a sizeable 11 per cent for the stockholder with $500,000 of income.

How much difference the corporation income tax alone made can be seen from the data of Chart 7. (The top portion shows the net corporate tax as a rate against net corporate earnings, and the lower section shows it as a rate against all of the average stockholder's income.)

On average, over the years 1940-1952 (excluding 1942 and 1943), the corporate tax represented a heavy net extra burden on stockholders' pro rata share of net corporate earnings. A declining function of the level of stockholder income, this extra income tax liability ranged from 35 per cent of net corporate earnings at the bottom of the stockholder income scale to 7 per cent at the top.

When related to all of stockholder income and not merely to one component of it, the net corporate tax constituted a smaller but not inconsiderable proportion. Stockholders with $1,000 of imputed gross income, on average, were subject to 7 additional percentage points of income tax, and those at the top of the income scale to a similar increment. Over the middle span of incomes the net corporate tax ran higher, reaching a maximum of about 13 per cent. Reading from low to high incomes we find first a rise then a fall in the incremental burden represented by the corporate tax.

But this is only part of the story. The failure of reinvested earnings to be subject to the personal income tax meant a tax saving which

CHART 7—Average Net Corporate Tax and Net Personal Income Tax Saving for the Period 1940-1952, Excluding 1942 and 1943

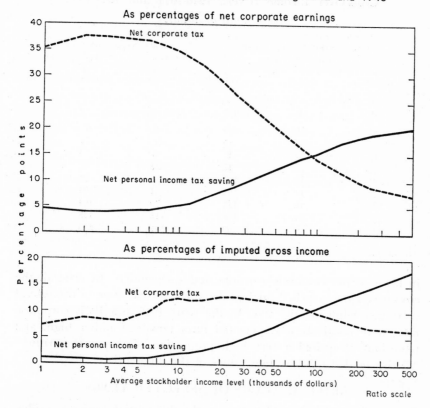

rose with stockholder income (see solid lines on Chart 7). Over the lower portion of the income range, it was quite unimportant, being only 2 per cent of stockholder income at the $12,000 level. After this point, the saving reached sizeable proportions—almost 18 per cent at the top of the income range. The difference between the net corporate tax and the net income tax saving is the differential against stockholders. That story has already been told. It is not necessary to repeat it here.

Differences among the years covered by the study can be pointed up vividly by concentrating on the "cross-over" points, i.e. those income levels at which the differential changes from positive to negative—from a burden to a benefit. Table 7 summarizes the relevant data. In all years except 1940, at some high level of income the differential turned in favor of earnings for retention; similarly in every year except 1940 and 1941, as incomes rose, the differentials turned

69

TABLE 7

Cross-Over Income Levels, 1940-1941 and 1944-1952
(thousands of dollars)

YEAR	DIFFERENTIAL AGAINST EARNINGS FOR RETENTION			DIFFERENTIALS AGAINST NET CORPORATE EARNINGS AND STOCKHOLDER INCOME		
	variant 1	variant 2	variant 3	variant 1	variant 2	variant 3
1940	a	a	a	a	a	a
1941	59	80	397	a	a	a
1944	35	41	63	68	77	117
1945	27	33	56	62	71	102
1946	17	20	45	27	36	69
1947	17	19	41	24	30	63
1948	35	43	101	56	73	159
1949	38	47	108	71	94	192
1950	43	51	115	79	104	195
1951	52	64	116	113	138	214
1952	45	50	99	105	130	206

a No cross-over.

in favor of net corporate earnings and stockholders. In general, the cross-over points reached furthest down the income scale in the several years just following the war. In the years 1946 and 1947, corporate rates were relatively low, personal rates remained rather high, and retentions comprised a very high proportion of corporate earnings. All this tended to cause low values of the differentials.

BRIEF ANALYSIS OF SELECTED YEARS

Factors that determine the values of the differentials varied considerably over the period of the study. Some complexities of the interrelationships which constitute the crux of the problem under investigation can be illuminated by examining these variations and their effect on the height and pattern of the differentials.

The magnitude of the differentials is directly determined by the four variables, described at the beginning of this chapter—the corporate tax rate, the personal tax rate, the relative size and importance of distributions and retentions by corporations, and the weight of corporate earnings in stockholder incomes.[6] On the basis of these magnitudes and also of their income level patterns the years of the whole period fall roughly into four groups. One year from each group has been chosen as representative with 1952 added as the most recent, and four income levels have been selected as focal points for

[6] Each of these, of course, is itself the net result of a number of interacting factors.

this analysis. Summary information on the determining variables for the years 1940, 1944, 1947, 1950, and 1952 appears in Table 8. In the discussion of the findings, the following symbols are used.[7]

C_e = Effective rate of corporate tax on earnings for distribution
C_r = Effective rate of corporate tax on earnings for retention
P = Applicable marginal rate of personal income tax
D_e = Differential against earnings for distribution
D_r = Differential against earnings for retention
D_t = Differential against net corporate earnings
D_s = Differential against stockholders

The discussion is carried out in terms of variant 1 (see the description of the three variants in Chapter 1) because the relevant determinants stand out most clearly, and no essential difference in principle is involved.

1940

In this year, which marks the beginning of our period, legislated corporate and personal income tax rates were lower than in any other covered by the study. This is confirmed by the values for C_e and the personal income tax rate listed in Table 8, but seems contradicted by the C_r of 78.6 per cent. This high C_r, however, is the rate on earnings for retention computed net of deficits, and in 1940 deficits loomed large in relation to retentions. (In the other years deficits were relatively small; C_r was only between 3 and 6 percentage points higher than C_e).

Variations in the corporate and personal income tax rates exercise an opposite effect on the differentials. The higher the corporate rate, the higher the differentials; the higher the personal rate, the lower the differentials. On net balance, these effects at the two lower income levels brought the values of D_e to the lowest for the period, whereas for the two upper income levels in the table the values were smaller in 1947. In that year, at the two upper incomes, the applicable marginal rates of personal income tax, designated by P, had risen relatively more than C_e; therefore D_e, which is equal to $C_e - C_e P$ failed to reach its 1940 values. The very large values for D_r in 1940 are the result of a high ratio of deficits to earnings. The retained earnings of net income corporations were subject to the legal rate, but when this tax liability is applied to net retentions (i.e. earnings for retention of profit corporations minus losses of deficit corporations) the result is a much higher effective rate on net earnings for retention.

---

[7] For simplicity the differentials are designated by single symbols rather than by the fractions used in Chapter 1.

TABLE 8

Factors Determining the Differentials Illustrated for Selected Income Levels, 1940, 1944, 1947, 1950, and 1952 (*per cent*)

AVERAGE STOCK-HOLDER IMPUTED GROSS INCOME ($000's) (1)	Corporate rate on earnings for distribution (2)	Personal rate on corporate tax on earnings for distribution (3)	Complement of personal rate 100 − (3) (4)	Differential against earnings for distribution (2) × (4) (5)	Corporate rate on earnings for retention (6)	Personal rate on earnings for retention (7)	Differential against earnings for retention (6) − (7) (8)	Earnings for distribution as % of net corporate earnings (9)	Earning for retention as % of net corporate earnings (10)	Differential against net corporate earnings (5) × (9) + (8) × (10) (11)	Net corporate earnings as % of IGI[b] (12)	Differential against stockholder income[a] (11) × (12) (13)
1940												
3	27.1	4.0	96.0	26.0	78.6	4.2	74.4	80.9	19.1	35.2	20.9	7.4
10	27.1	8.4	91.6	24.8	78.6	10.9	67.7	80.9	19.1	33.0	37.8	12.5
50	27.1	37.6	62.4	16.9	78.6	39.1	39.5	80.9	19.1	21.2	56.5	12.0
500	27.1	68.1	31.9	8.6	78.6	70.8	7.8	80.9	19.1	8.5	89.3	7.6
1944												
3	57.5	23.0	77.0	44.3	61.6	23.0	38.6	43.8	56.2	41.1	22.8	9.4
10	57.5	28.5	71.5	41.1	61.6	31.7	29.9	43.8	56.2	34.8	50.2	17.5
50	57.5	63.9	36.1	20.8	61.6	70.2	−8.6	43.8	56.2	4.3	56.3	2.4
500	57.5	92.9	7.1	4.1	61.6	94.0	−32.4	43.8	56.2	−16.4	88.9	−14.6
1947												
3	34.5	19.0	81.0	27.9	38.5	19.0	19.5	33.5	66.5	22.3	20.3	4.5
10	34.5	24.8	75.2	25.9	38.5	27.8	10.7	33.5	66.5	15.8	33.9	5.4
50	34.5	55.7	44.3	15.3	38.5	62.5	−24.0	33.5	66.5	−10.9	62.9	−6.8
500	34.5	84.8	15.2	5.2	38.5	86.3	−47.8	33.5	66.5	−30.1	88.0	−26.5
1950												
3	41.3	17.4c	82.6	34.1	44.3	17.4c	26.9	38.6	61.4	29.7	20.9	6.2
10	41.3	20.6c	79.4	32.8	44.3	21.1c	23.2	38.6	61.4	26.9	34.8	9.4
50	41.3	39.6c	60.4	24.9	44.3	48.7c	−4.4	38.6	61.4	6.9	59.7	4.1
500	41.3	75.7c	24.3	10.0	44.3	83.0c	−38.7	38.6	61.4	−19.9	88.1	−17.5
1952												
3	50.0	22.2c	77.8	38.9	56.0	22.2c	33.8	49.3	50.7	36.3	22.4	8.1
10	50.0	25.5c	74.5	37.2	56.0	25.8c	30.2	49.3	50.7	33.6	28.3	9.5
50	50.0	49.9c	50.1	25.0	56.0	59.7c	−3.7	49.3	50.7	10.4	59.4	6.2
500	50.0	86.3c	13.7	6.8	56.0	91.1c	−35.1	49.3	50.7	−14.4	89.3	−12.9

Because rounded values were used in the computations, the figures in this table, in some cases, differ slightly from those in the tabular summary in Appendix A, and the rates in column 7 may differ slightly from those of the Internal Revenue Code.

This result is a logical corollary of our imputation procedure, for deficits should be taken into account equally with earnings in determining the income of stockholders.

D_t is a weighted average of D_e and D_r. The relevant weights appear in columns 9 and 10 of Table 8. Compared with the rest of the years covered, the 1940 weight of earnings for retention was extremely low. D_t generally lies very close to D_e, but note the 1940 behavior of values for D_t compared with those for D_e. At all income levels D_t took a higher value in 1940 than in either 1947 or 1950; at the two upper income levels, it was higher in 1940 than in 1944 and 1952. Note also that the heavy corporate rate on earnings for retention led to the absence of a negative D_t at all income levels. (It is only for 1940 and 1941 that we fail to find, somewhere up the income scale, a negative differential developing on net corporate earnings.)

D_s is equal to that fraction of D_t that corporate earnings constituted of stockholders' imputed gross income. These percentages, listed in column 12, varied but slightly from year to year at any given stockholder income level. Thus, this proportion is not an important determinant of year-to-year changes in the value of D_s. The above explanation of the variations in D_t, therefore, applies also to variations in D_s.

1944

The full weight of wartime tax increases is reflected in the data for 1944. Both corporate and personal tax rates reached levels never since equaled. (The excess profits tax is included here in the corporate tax liability.) The net result was the highest D_e of the period for stockholders at the lower income levels, and the smallest D_e at the top of the income range.

Remember that $D_e = C_e - C_eP$. Between 1940 and 1944, at the $3,000 income level, C_e rose some 30.4 points. The subtracted term, C_eP, rose by 12.1 percentage points, hence an 18.3 increase in D_e. At the top of the income range ($500,000), we have, again, a 30.4 point increase in C_e, but the term to be subtracted in arriving at D_e increased by more than this, i.e. by 34.9. D_e, therefore, *fell* by 4.5.

Since D_r is equal to $C_r - P$, it can be seen that a similar interrelation of the corporate and personal tax sets the value of D_r. Compare once more the change between 1940 and 1944, at the $3,000 level: while C_r declined 17 points, D_r fell by 35.8 points because P, the term to be subtracted, had increased by 18.8.

Reflecting the fact that retentions came to a little more than dividends in 1944, D_t lies somewhat closer to D_r than to D_e. Compared

73

with 1940, the most obvious difference is the negative value at $500,000 of stockholder income. This results from the much lower D_r and its greater weight in the later year. The remaining observations relevant to D_t and D_s have already been made in connection with D_r and D_e.

1947

This year contrasts strongly with 1944, with both relevant tax rates—corporate and personal—being lower. The decline in the corporate rate between these two years was considerably more pronounced than the decline in the personal income tax rate schedule; the differentials in 1947, therefore, were smaller than in 1944. Actually, with only the exception of D_e at the top incomes, the combination of a low corporate rate and high personal rate led to smaller differentials in 1947 than in any other year of the period covered by our study.[8]

C_e was 23 points lower in 1947 compared with 1944. The decline in D_e was less marked. At the $3,000 level C_eP was 13.2 in 1944 and 6.6 in 1947, hence the 16.4 fall in D_e. At the $500,000 stockholder income level, however, we find a slight rise in D_e, for while C_e fell 23 points, C_eP declined 24.1 points, hence a rise in D_e from 4.1 to 5.2. The only noteworthy point about D_r is the extremely large negative differentials at the higher income levels. With retentions comprising approximately two-thirds of corporate earnings, D_t lies closer to D_r than D_e. More precisely D_t is equal to D_r plus about one-third of the difference between D_e and D_r.

1950

Compared with 1947, the 1950 corporate rate shows a rise and the personal rate a decline. Both these factors work in the same direction, exercising an upward push on the differentials which at every income level were higher than in 1947.

At the $500,000 level why were D_r, D_t, and D_s for 1950 higher than in 1944, but lower at the average $50,000 imputed gross income? Because of the much sharper decline between these two years in P at $50,000, which is traceable primarily to income-splitting first introduced for joint returns in 1948. The major portion of returns at $50,000 were joint returns. The weighted average marginal rate (for joint and separate returns combined) was below 50 per cent. The income-splitting effect is gradually lost as income rises to where most of the income lies in the maximum marginal rate bracket; P for both

---

[8] The corporate and personal income tax rates are designated low and high, respectively, only in a relative sense, i.e., compared to what they were in the other years of the period 1940-1952.

types of return is therefore not so disparate. Specifically, comparing 1944 and 1950, the marginal rate of personal income tax applicable to earnings for retention declined by 31 per cent at the $50,000 level, but by only 12 per cent for the average $500,000 stockholder income. Again, the heavier weight of D_r in the determination of D_t is demonstrated by the fact that the D_t values lie closer to D_r than to D_e.

1952

Between 1950 and 1952 the corporate rate (embodying normal and surtax rate increases and excess profits tax in effect throughout 1952 and for only the latter half of 1950) and personal rates both rose. In general the rise in the corporate rate overshadowed that in the personal income tax rate schedule; the values of the differentials were higher in 1952 than in 1950. The only exception occurred for D_e at the $500,000 stockholder income level. Here the C_e increase of 8.7 points was smaller than the C_eP rise of 11.9 points. D_e with C_eP subtracted from C_e in its derivation, fell by 3.2 points, i.e. from 10 to 6.8.

CHAPTER 4

Alternative Measures of the Differentials Against Net Corporate Earnings and Stockholders' Income

THE findings presented so far have been based on a number of assumptions considered to be reasonable and relevant to the problem under investigation. But they are assumptions—made necessary to this investigation either because directly germane data were lacking, or because there appeared to be no firm body of opinion supporting one particular view among scholars of the subject. At each step a choice was made from a number of possible assumptions, definitions, or procedures, as for example: the assumption that the corporate income tax constitutes a levy on stockholders; the definition of income embodied in the tax law; and the imputation of net corporate earnings to stockholders in proportion to their dividend receipts. At some of these points the reader may have found himself a reluctant follower down the selected path; at others he may have decided that he would have chosen to go in another direction.

The most likely stumbling blocks in this connection are the incidence of the corporation income tax and the definition of income generated by the productive activity of corporations. Both these matters lie in the realm of opinion and conjecture rather than of established fact. The conjectures are manifold and diverse. The diversity of opinion about the incidence of the corporation income tax and the appropriate definition of income for tax purposes has made desirable development of several alternative measures to provide some idea of how much our results would be affected by a change in one or another of our basic assumptions.

The presentation in this chapter, then, affords the reader freedom of choice in connection with quantitative measures of the differential taxation of stockholders. Natural limitations—of time for the author, of attention and patience for the reader—preclude an attempt to exhaust the whole range of possible permutations and combinations that could be developed as alternative measures. Fortunately, however, the most important alternatives are easily distinguished, and those discussed below offer enough variety to enable the reader to choose his "favorite" (or at least get some idea of what it would look like), according to his particular views of the shifting and incidence of the corporation income tax and the "right" way to define income for purposes of this tax.

76

This does not mean, however, that all the alternative measures to be analyzed in this chapter are considered to be of the same degree of importance or reasonableness. Compared with our standard measure, developed and discussed in the preceding chapters, some at least of these alternatives are presented with diffidence, although they are based on opinions that seem to be widely held or positively asserted by their supporters. Reservations will be stated below as the particular alternatives are examined. All things considered, variant 2 of our standard measure—the variant used in the earlier chapters—emerges as the best single concept for answering the questions investigated in this study. But the results provided in this chapter will enable the dissenting reader to make the requisite qualifications of some of the earlier conclusions.

The data used in the alternative tests are for 1947, the most recent year for which computations are not complicated by income-splitting. In alternative B—the test that allows, in the definition of income, for the current cost of replacing inventory and depreciable assets—the 1947 data are an additional advantage because the inventory valuation correction was higher in that year than in any other included in the study.

BASIS OF THE ALTERNATIVE MEASURES

Under our so-called standard measure (variant 2) the differential tax load on net corporate earnings and stockholders was determined,

1. assuming no shifting of the corporation income tax, and
2. accepting the Internal Revenue Code definition of corporate net income.

Under these conditions stockholders are credited, on the income side, with the full amount of their pro rata share of net corporate earnings (on the basis of their dividend receipts) and, on the tax side, with their proportionate share of corporation income taxes and an estimated amount of future capital gains tax liability on reinvested earnings. Each of the alternative tests, designated alternatives A through G, involves a change in one of the assumptions or procedures underlying the standard measure.

ALTERNATIVE A—ADJUSTMENT FOR SHIFTING

Here the attempt is made to isolate the effect of using a different assumption about the incidence of the corporation income tax by measuring the differential burden on net corporate earnings and stockholders,

1. assuming that half of the corporation income tax is shifted forward, and
2. accepting the tax law definition of corporate net income.

In this test, stockholders are credited with only half of their pro rata share of corporate earnings, and are assigned only half of their proportionate share of corporation income tax. The other half of the tax is assumed to fall on all individuals in the form of higher prices for the output of corporations.

ALTERNATIVE B—TAKING ACCOUNT OF CURRENT PRICE LEVELS

Here the attempt is to take into account the current cost of replacing inventory and depreciable assets, by measuring the differential burden on net corporate earnings and stockholders,
1. assuming that the incidence of the corporation income tax is on stockholders, and
2. revising the Internal Revenue Code definition of net income, which is based primarily on standard accounting procedures, to allow for the maintenance of inventory at current price levels, and for the replacement of depreciable assets at current cost.

Under these assumptions, the full amount of their proportionate share of corporation income taxes is imputed to stockholders, while corporate income generated on their behalf and credited to them is "corrected" as indicated under 2.

ALTERNATIVE C—COMBINING THE SHIFTING AND CURRENT COST ADJUSTMENTS

This alternative represents the combined effect of A and B. The differentials are derived by
1. assuming that only half the corporation income tax falls on stockholders, the remainder being shifted forward, and
2. adjusting income as defined for the corporate tax to allow for maintenance of inventory and replacement of depreciable assets at current price levels.

ALTERNATIVE D—ADJUSTMENT FOR SAVING THROUGH CORPORATIONS

By the standard method, net corporate earnings are imputed to stockholders on the basis of their dividend receipts. For this purpose the ratio of net corporate earnings to dividends is used no matter what the stockholder's adjusted gross income level. It has been frequently asserted, however, that stockholders with sizeable incomes seek to avoid high marginal rates of personal income tax by investing in corporations that save a high proportion of earnings, for then a part of the income generated on behalf of stockholders will either be subject to the lower rates applicable to capital gains, or it can be passed income-tax free at death. If this argument is accepted, use of the same dividend multiplier for imputation of corporate earnings at all stockholder income levels would be invalid.

This alternative attempts to measure how the results would be affected by the use of dividend to net corporate earnings ratios that vary with stockholder income levels. Thus the differential tax load on net corporate earnings and stockholders is measured,

1. assuming that the incidence of the corporation income tax is on stockholders,
2. accepting the tax law definition of corporate income, and
3. assuming that the higher the stockholder's income, the greater the tendency to hold shares in corporations which distribute a lower than average proportion of their earnings.

ALTERNATIVE E—IMPUTING ONLY EARNINGS FOR DISTRIBUTION

This test is designed, for those who, holding that "a bird in the hand is worth two in the bush," feel that there is something more "real" about what stockholders receive, i.e. dividends, than what they could have received, i.e. retained earnings.

Thus the extra tax load on stockholders is measured in a fashion differing from our standard method in two respects:

1. The income of stockholders includes only earnings for distribution which is the amount that had to be earned before corporate tax to support the dividend outpayments actually made;
2. The tax liability of stockholders includes only that portion of total corporate income tax liability that is allocable to dividends.

Setting up this calculation does not constitute an endorsement of the assumptions on which it is based. My own opinion, set forth in the Introduction and stated again below, is that the appropriate conceptual approach to the questions posed for this study calls for allocation to stockholders of all of corporate net income, and, similarly, allocation to them of the whole of the corporate income tax liability.

ALTERNATIVE F—IMPUTING ONLY A FRACTION OF RETAINED EARNINGS

This alternative is suggested by the adjustment incorporated in variant 2 of our standard method, which assumed, among other things, that only 72 cents of every dollar of reinvested earnings showed up in increased stock prices. Would it not be appropriate, then, to consider only 72 per cent of retained earnings imputable to stockholders, since this is all the market credits them with?[1] For reasons set out in Chapter 1, 100 per cent imputation of retained earnings appears to be more relevant to the problem under investigation, but for those who may judge differently Alternative F is offered.

ALTERNATIVE G—CORRECTION FOR UNDERREPORTING OF DIVIDENDS

Imputation of all of corporate earnings to stockholders on the basis of dividend receipts as reported for personal income taxation (standard method) may be criticized because there is evidence that dividends are not fully reported for this purpose.[2] Moreover, this evidence suggests that the extent of underreporting varies among income classes. Alternative G has been developed to determine whether our findings would be substantially affected by an adjustment for underreporting.

While many other alternatives are possible, the seven outlined above cover the major sources of variation. The conceptual nature of each of these alternatives and the assumptions used in its computation will be developed more fully as each is discussed in the sections that follow. Here, too, the results yielded by the alternative procedures will be compared with the findings derived from our usual method. To aid the reader in interpreting the results of the tests reported below, it should be noted that each test involved a different basis for computing imputed gross income and, consequently, a different array of stockholder income than that furnished by the standard method. Therefore, the comparisons in Tables 9 through 11 and 19 through 22 involve average stockholders with incomes of the same size but differently defined. In other words, the level of income is standardized, but what constitutes stockholders' income varies in each case. The tests do *not* compare the differential against, say, the $3,000 standard method definition stockholder with what it would be on this same person under each of the alternatives. Rather, in every case they compare the results for two average $3,000 stockholders, one obtained from the income definition and array of the standard method, the other from the array based on the income definition appropriate to each of the alternatives.

---

[1] The reader is reminded that the 72 per cent, the average experience for a period ending in 1937, is used for this purpose, although it is not regarded as a precise figure.

[2] *Audit Control Program: A Summary of Preliminary Results*, Bureau of Internal Revenue, May 1951. See also: Selma F. Goldsmith, "Appraisal of Basic Data for Constructing Income Size Distributions," in *Studies in Income and Wealth*, Volume Thirteen, National Bureau of Economic Research, 1951; and Daniel M. Holland and C. Harry Kahn, "Comparison of Personal and Taxable Income," in *Federal Tax Policy for Economic Growth and Stability*, Papers Submitted by Panelists Appearing before the Subcommittee on Tax Policy, Joint Committee on the Economic Report, 1955.

RESULTS OF ALTERNATIVE MEASURES

Alternative A—Adjustment for Shifting

WHAT IF CORPORATION INCOME TAXES ARE SHIFTED?

As already noted several times, our standard method assumes that the corporation income tax constitutes a levy on stockholders in the sense that the earnings made on their behalf are lower than they would have been by the full amount of the tax. This view of corporate income tax incidence is old and venerable; it has "seniority" rights, wide acceptance, and a rationale to recommend it. The theoretical basis of the argument is simple and direct. A tax on net profit like the corporation income tax does not impinge on costs at the margin of production. Therefore, in both competitive and monopolistic markets, the quantity offered for sale will be unaffected by the tax. So too will the quantity of factor inputs. It follows, then, that the price of output and the quantity sold at that price will be unchanged; the same is true of the prices of productive factors, and the quantities employed. The corporation income tax, therefore, is not shifted forward or backward. If this is the case, it must rest on stockholders.

This is the conclusion reached, for example, in two of the most thorough examinations of this problem.[3] It is also, of course, the incidence assumption implicit in the charge of "double taxation" of corporate earnings and its several variants. This view of incidence has been cited to justify exemption from the normal tax of dividends under our personal income tax from its inception until 1936, and also the relief provisions of the Internal Revenue Code of 1954.[4] Similarly, proposals to integrate the personal and the corporate income taxes would make little sense if the incidence of the latter were not on stockholders. If the corporate tax is shifted, it is in effect a sales or payroll tax, or some combination of the two, and the justification for integrating such a tax with the personal tax is not clear-cut. Many of those who have investigated analytical or policy problems whose solution required some conclusion about corporation income tax

---

[3] Report of the Committee on National Debt and Taxation, London, H. M. Stationery Office, Cmd. 2800, 1927, p. 119; The Shifting and Effects of the Federal Corporation Income Tax, National Industrial Conference Board, Vol. 1, Manufacturing and Mercantile Corporations, 1928, p. 157. In the second volume of the latter study, however, a qualification is made for public service corporations where it is concluded that there is probably substantial shifting of the corporation income taxes levied on them.

[4] Internal Revenue Code, 1954, Public Law 591, H.R. 8300, 83d Cong., 2d sess., August 16, 1954, Chap. 736, Secs. 34 and 116 (see Chapter 7 of this study for a discussion of these provisions).

incidence frequently have adopted the view (with or without mis-givings) that it constitutes a burden on stockholders. Examples of this reasoning are found in a number of studies dealing with the allocation of the tax burden among income classes.[5] When faced directly with a decision on incidence, Carl S. Shoup, in his program for reformulation of the Japanese tax system, proposed a measure based on the assumption that the corporation income tax rests on stockholders.[6] But, as an indication that there is considerable dissatisfaction with this conclusion, it was Shoup also, who pointed out in a 1948 article the possibility, at least, that the corporation income tax is shifted or, more accurately, shiftable.[7] This same assumption—that the corporation income tax is not shifted—was adopted by W. L. Crum, who investigated the tax burden on stockholders for 1941.[8] His reasoning is interesting.

"The above-stated point of view of the analysis obviously rests upon a fundamental assumption that the tax paid by a corporation falls proportionately on the stockholder's share of corporate net income and may be regarded as a tax on him. This assumption is in accord not only with the apparent premise of much current discussion of the double taxation of dividends and other aspects of the taxation of corporate income, but also with the doctrine which was formerly accepted that a tax levied on net income could not be shifted. That doctrine rested upon an argument which could be convincing only if the rate of tax were moderate and if the net income were realized

[5] Representative of such studies are the following: Mabel Newcomer, "Estimate of the Tax Burden on Different Income Classes," in *Studies in Current Tax Problems*, Twentieth Century Fund, 1937: *Who Pays the Taxes?* 76th Cong., 3d sess., TNEC monograph 3, 1940; Helen Tarasov, "Who Does Pay the Taxes?" *Social Research*, Supplement IV, 1942.

Some more recent studies of this problem have utilized this assumption, but have also made calculations based on alternative assumptions, for example: R. A. Musgrave, J. J. Carroll, L. D. Cook, and L. Frane, "Distribution of Tax Payments by Income Groups: A Case Study for 1948," *National Tax Journal*, March, 1951; Donald G. Miller, *Taxes, The Public Debt and Transfers of Income*, University of Illinois Press, 1950; John H. Adler and Eugene R. Schlesinger, "The Fiscal System, The Distribution of Income, and Public Welfare," in *Fiscal Policies and the American Economy*, Kenyon E. Poole, editor, Prentice-Hall, 1951.

[6] Carl S. Shoup, "Tax Reform in Japan," *Proceedings of the Forty-Third Annual Conference on Taxation Held Under the Auspices of the National Tax Association*, Ronald S. Welch, editor, 1950, p. 410. "Under this program the 35 per cent tax on corporations is regarded as in essence only a form of withholding tax on dividend income, though not legally so. The tax is assumed not to be shifted forward to consumers. . . ."

[7] Carl S. Shoup, "Incidence of the Corporate Income Tax: Capital Structure and Turnover Rates," *National Tax Journal*, March 1948.

[8] William Leonard Crum, "The Taxation of Stockholders," *Quarterly Journal of Economics*, February 1950, p. 18.

under conditions of competition in which monopolistic elements were absent or negligible. Neither of these requirements is realized in connection with the taxation of corporate income in current and recent years; and the older doctrine has therefore been challenged, although, so far as I am aware, no attempt at revision has won general acceptance.

"I do not herein attempt a revision of the doctrine, or examine in detail the major considerations which must have a bearing upon any valid revision. Instead, I first state without supporting argument my tentative opinion that a substantial, and perhaps large, fraction of the tax levied on corporate net income is probably not borne by corporations or their stockholder-owners, but is shifted to customers or non-executive employees or suppliers. In spite of this opinion, I make herein the stated assumption for the following reason.

"If any portion of the corporation income tax is shifted to one or more of the three groups mentioned above, that portion is less progressive than the prevailing standard of equity, and may even be regressive. I take as the prevailing standard of equity, for this purpose, the scale of effective rates—dependent both upon the steeply graduated surtaxes and upon certain other provisions of the law—of the individual income tax. To the extent that the above fundamental assumption is *not* realistic, we can at once assert that the present corporation tax is inequitable according to the prevailing standards of equity. Question, as to whether the tax is equitable, therefore, remains only if the said assumption *is* realistic."[9]

Many other expressions of dissatisfaction with the assumption that the incidence of the corporation income tax is on stockholders could be cited. More specifically, where does this dissatisfaction arise? It comes from several sources. The most inclusive is a point of view contained in a frequently quoted assertion by D. H. Robertson: "If you throw enough taxation mud at the businessman a good deal of it will stick."[10] A tax that is sufficiently heavy and extensive will have some effect on output and investment. How these effects will be exerted and work themselves out has been analyzed in a number of ways.

Some students, emphasizing the divergence between profits as defined by economists and profits as defined by accountants and tax authorities, have pointed out that the corporation income tax base

[9] *Ibid.*, pp. 18 and 19. Two footnotes that accompany these paragraphs in Crum's article are omitted; the italics are his.

[10] D. H. Robertson, "The Colwyn Committee, The Income Tax and the Price Level," *Economic Journal*, December 1927, p. 581.

really includes elements of cost in an economic sense, i.e. factor rewards such as return to owned capital and recompense for entrepreneurship. It is, therefore, not a tax on net income. Emphasizing this fact, J. Fred Weston takes issue with the traditional view of corporate tax incidence in a paper arguing that "accounting net income on which the corporate net income tax is levied includes elements of economic cost." The element which he considers probably to be of major significance is "the noncontractual interest return on invested capital." He distinguishes between incidence and effects of the tax: "Since this is a fixed cost, the corporate net income tax is levied on a fixed cost and itself represents an element of fixed cost. In the short period, the tax is not shifted under assumptions of competitive conditions, but may be shifted in an oligopolistic market. In the long period, the presumption indicated is that the tax is shifted. If tax incidence is defined as the effect of the tax in the short run and tax effects are defined as the consequences of the tax in the long run, it may be said that the incidence of the tax is on the common stockholder, but its effects may also be on workers in the form of lower wages and on the consumer of the product in the form of higher prices."[11] The conclusion, then, is that there is good reason to question the assumption that the corporation income tax rests in full on stockholders, particularly in the long run. But there is no definite information on how much of the tax is shifted and whether the shifting is forward via higher prices of output, or backward via lower rewards for the factors of production, or both. Weston, for example, considers determination of these unknowns to be an impossible task, and in this attitude he is joined by other students of the problem.[12]

Several types of behavioral response to the corporate tax have been emphasized by those who hold that it tends to be shifted. Representative of one line of reasoning is the set of adjustments described by C. Lowell Harriss, which begins with the premise that ". . . present taxes on business income . . . reduce the net return to investors or risk-takers." The process, in his view, is this: "The funds offered for such investment will be reduced, because of the lowered net attraction and also because business earnings are an exceptionally important source of such capital. The reduction in supply will tend to force up the gross return, until the prospective *net* rate is enough to equal the return available elsewhere. Reduction in the amount of capital will reduce output below what it would otherwise be; the product

11 J. Fred Weston, "Incidence and Effects of the Corporate Income Tax, *National Tax Journal,* December 1949, p. 315.
12 *Ibid.,* p. 313.

84

price will be higher than it would otherwise. In this way, some of the tax is shifted to consumers, and by a method which the business-man may not fully appreciate. Therefore, the tax is increasingly recognized as a mass consumption tax, like sales and pay-roll taxes. However, as some investment is thus shifted to nontax lines—bonds and durable consumer goods—their net yields will tend to fall, reducing also the net rate expected on taxed investment; some of the tax on business income is shifted to investors generally."[13]

In all likelihood, the process of adjustment would not be as clear-cut and direct as Harriss' summary might suggest. The corporate tax affects a good part of business enterprise; the postulated adjustments to it, therefore, will reverberate through all segments of the economy. What happens to the funds that would otherwise have been invested? If alternative forms of assets—bonds for example—are sought, will not the consequent fall in interest rates lead to more investment than would otherwise have occurred? If output is lower than it would have been, would not payments to productive factors likewise be lower than they would have been? If so, demand would be lower than otherwise, and therefore we cannot say positively that the price of output will be higher than it would have been. It could be higher, lower, or unchanged.

Richard B. Goode, apropos of the type of argument presented by Harriss, comments:

"The conclusion that if the corporate tax restricts total investment it will be shifted by a general increase in commodity prices is not admissible. The quantity of investment is so significant that the effects of variations in it are incompatible with the assumptions behind the conventional incidence theory. The long-run effects of the corporate income tax cannot be described by a neat chain of reasoning running from a restriction of total investment to a reduction of output and thence to a higher price level. To determine the effects of the corporate tax on output account must be taken of its impact on aggregate demand, including consumption as well as investment. These effects are meaningful only when viewed in the setting of alternative government budgets. Moreover, changes in aggregate demand and output are likely to result in price movements the opposite of those assumed by extension of the traditional incidence theory."[14]

Goode, then, points out that when aggregate or "macro-economic"

[13] C. Lowell Harriss, "Public Finance," in *A Survey of Contemporary Economics*, Bernard F. Haley, editor, Irwin, 1952, Vol. II, p. 265.

[14] Richard B. Goode, *The Corporation Income Tax*, Wiley, 1951, pp. 57-58. The reader will find a thorough and subtle analysis of corporate tax incidence in Goode's book. This section of our study draws heavily on his incidence chapter.

effects are taken into account doubt is cast on the argument that the corporate tax is shifted because, by restricting investment, it leads to a higher price of output. The very existence of a decline in investment will make unlikely the rise in aggregate demand required for an increase in prices. Rather a fall in investment will probably lead to a decline in demand and a consequent fall in prices.[15]

Another explanation of the process by which the corporate tax might be shifted focuses attention on market structure and price policy under other than purely competitive conditions. Suppose that, for some reason, in a market in which prices can to some extent at least be set by producers, the existing price is lower than that which would have maximized profits. Then the imposition of a tax on corporate income or an increase in the rate of an existing tax might be followed by an increase in prices, because the tax might encourage the producers to take greater advantage of their market power. An example is given by Musgrave, Goode, and Colm: "In the immediate postwar period, the existence of large unsatisfied demands for products such as automobiles is evidence that producers did not raise their prices to the maximum possible, and an increase in tax rates might have induced them to revise their price policy. (This, incidentally, might have meant lower dealer's profits rather than higher customer prices.)" Therefore: "Where monopoly positions are exploited with restraint, imposition of the tax might thus lead to higher prices. Shifting might occur." But the authors doubt the importance of this possibility, for, they argue, ". . . this is not likely to be the typical case. The fact remains that any such price increase would also have been profitable in the absence of the tax, and chances are that the adjustment would be forthcoming in the course of time with or without tax. Shifting, accordingly, is more likely for a new tax (or recent increase in rates) than for an old one. Moreover, shifting in the case of rate increase is more likely than 'unshifting' in the case of rate reduction. Since the public is more likely to react unfavorably to a price increase than to a failure to reduce prices (even though profits will go up equally in both cases), the shifting argument based upon restraint in monopoly pricing is not readily reversible."[16]

It is frequently asserted that in inflationary periods the corporate

---

[15] For some qualification of Goode's criticism, see Richard D. Slitor, "The Corporate Income Tax: A Re-evaluation," *National Tax Journal*, December 1952, p. 306.

[16] Richard A. Musgrave, Richard Goode, and Gerhard Colm, "Economic Effects of the Corporation Income Tax" (Appendix of Preliminary Report of the Committee on the Federal Corporate Net Income Tax of the National Tax Association, 1949), *Proceedings of the Forty-Second National Conference of the National Tax Association*, 1949, p. 462.

tax is passed on to consumers, for the cost of corporate output rises.[17] This is primarily a matter of terminology. Can the rise in prices be attributed to the corporation income tax? Is it not due, rather, to rising money incomes which lead to inflation? In other words, prices would have risen anyway. The real question here (and it is very difficult to assess) is whether, given the expenditure-revenue-borrowing complex of the particular period, a greater price rise can be attributed to the corporate tax than to some other tax that might have been substituted for it.[18]

Somewhat similar considerations cast doubt on the argument that businessmen, reckoning the corporate income tax among their costs, mark up prices as a consequence of the tax, and thereby pass the tax on to the consuming public. For, as Goode points out, "A widespread attempt to raise prices to recoup the tax can succeed only to the extent that total money demand increases relative to real output. The price rise can be maintained only if consumers, business, or government will finance it by saving less and spending more. Some increases in the price level might be effected in this way, provided that the initial markup of prices was not too great, but an offsetting influence would be the probable curtailment of output and cumulative contraction of incomes."[19]

One other possibility remains to be considered—the matter of tax capitalization. Very simply, when, as a result of the imposition of a tax, the net income stream from an asset is cut—as would be the case for the corporate earnings of holders of common stock if the incidence of the tax were on profits—the capital value of the asset should fall as a reflection of this reduction in the net income flow. With stock selling at ten times earnings, i.e., with the capitalization rate at 10 per cent, for example, a reduction in per share earnings of one dollar due to the tax should cause a ten dollar fall in the selling price per share. In other words, the selling price of shares should fall by the present value of all future expected corporate income tax payments. This capital loss is experienced by those holding the shares at the time the tax is imposed. Those acquiring shares after that date buy them "free of tax."

In common with other investigations of the tax burden, the present study leaves out of account the capital losses (if any) suffered by stockholders due to tax capitalization. Throughout the analysis the corporation income tax is taken to be an annual burden in the sense that,

---

[17] This is not a scholarly argument and it cannot be specifically documented, but it is a commonly held opinion.

[18] Goode, *op. cit.*, pp. 61-62.   [19] *Ibid.*, p. 62.

assuming its incidence to be on profits, its imposition lowers the potentially disposable income of stockholders.[20] It is difficult to determine how serious, for the present study, is the failure to allow for tax capitalization. For to the question whether, in fact, the corporate income tax is capitalized and to what degree, it is impossible to find a quantitative answer or even some general consensus on broad ranges of magnitudes. Thus, while Dan T. Smith has pointed out that an "increase in the corporation income tax, assuming a constant price-earnings ratio for the stock, will depress the price of the stock commensurately,"[21] we cannot (and he does not) stop here. Crucial to the argument in this precise form is the assumption of a constant price-earnings ratio, i.e. a constant capitalization rate. But it is unlikely that this will actually be the case. For the corporate tax cuts such a wide swath that repercussions due to it will affect the rate by which the capital value of assets is reckoned; in other words, it partakes of the nature of a general tax whereas the capitalization argument strictly applies to a partial tax—a tax that affects one industry or type of asset.

Further complexities in assessing the degree to which the corporate income tax is capitalized have been pointed out by Goode:

First, "General market conditions are reflected in the level of money income. To the extent that imposition of the corporate tax is deflationary and causes a contraction of money income, it will reduce corporate profits before taxes and hence will depress stock prices more than the capitalization theory alone suggests . . . But, if the corporate tax replaces a more deflationary tax or is itself replaced by such a tax, the change in stock prices will be smaller than the capitalization theory would indicate. These influences may be reinforced by changes in optimism or pessimism of investors that usually accompany significant changes in general business conditions."

Secondly, "The corporate tax may influence the rate at which future earnings are capitalized by the securities market in a way that will partly offset the effects of tax capitalization with respect to stocks but will extend the effect of the tax to prices of other assets. Since stock prices will not be adjusted instantaneously to an increase in the tax rate, stocks will become a less attractive investment as compared with bonds and other assets. Old investors and new investors who would otherwise

[20] The reader is reminded that the amount of this reduction is less than the actual corporate tax liability because from this liability is deducted personal income tax that would have been levied on that portion of corporate income used to meet corporate tax payments.

[21] Dan Throop Smith, *Effects of Taxation: Corporate Financial Policy*, Division of Research, Graduate School of Business Administration, Harvard University, 1952, p. 87.

have bought stock will try to shift from stocks to bonds and other assets and in the process will bid up the price of bonds and other assets. This will reduce the yield of other assets and will check the drop in comparative yield of stocks. Moreover, as the price of stocks falls, funds that would otherwise have been used to buy stocks will be left free to compete for bonds and other assets. The result will be equivalent to a general decrease in the rate of capitalization. The prices of assets whose returns are not directly affected by the corporate tax—high-grade bonds, for example—will rise, while the price of stocks will fall less than in proportion to the decrease in their expected earnings net of tax."[22]

Smith, too, has noted a number of qualifications to the capitalization argument:

"The exact relationship between changes in corporate income tax rates and stock prices is vastly involved. Though prospective earnings per share are probably the most important single factor influencing the market value of most securities, they are certainly not the only, or even at all times the dominant, one. Present dividends, book value, estimated liquidating value, and prospective changes in all of these are among the other interrelated factors which make impossible any assurance about the precise effects of changes in tax rates on market values.

"Also, any general readjustment of stock prices arising from a change in corporate income tax rates would lead to significant but quantitatively indeterminate changes in the yields of other forms of investments, with inevitable readjustment in investors' portfolios and a new pattern of yield differentials. Even more fundamentally, a full analysis of the effects of corporate taxation is complicated by such important but very elusive problems as the effects of the government expenditures financed by the tax on the general level and direction of economic activity and the comparative effects of alternative revenue sources. These more involved analytical problems can only be noted here as important qualifications to any simple conclusions on the extent of influence of corporate income taxation on stock prices."[23]

These comments on capitalization appear to be in agreement at two points: first, for any degree of capitalization to occur the initial incidence of the corporation income tax must be on stockholders; secondly, whether the corporation income tax is capitalized and, if so, to what extent remains a problem fraught with uncertainty, and about which there is no consensus.

Finally, mention should be made of one area where the assumption

[22] Goode, *op. cit.*, p. 70. [23] Smith, *op. cit.*, pp. 86-87.

that the corporate income tax is not shifted is clearly unreasonable. Public utility regulatory bodies are required to take into account income as well as other taxes in determining rates that will yield a fair return. Income taxes are considered an operating expense. Therefore, the corporation income tax on regulated utilities tends to be shifted.[24] The lag in regulation and rate adjustment constitutes a qualifying factor, however.[25] (Relevant in this connection also is the partial abatement of corporate income taxes on dividends of preferred stock issued before 1942 by public utility companies.)[26]

No allowance has been made for the special treatment accorded public utilities. The figures on public utility income and taxes from *Statistics of Income* cover a wide range of such enterprises, some of which are probably not under formal regulation and, therefore, do not as a matter of course treat the corporation income tax as a cost, and others because of the lag in regulation may not have been able to shift taxes promptly or completely. So it cannot be assumed that all of the tax total listed for public utilities was shifted. But some of the tax undoubtedly was shifted. In 1950, about $1.8 billion in corporation income tax was reported for public utilities in *Statistics of Income*. The total of income taxes for all corporations was $17.3 billion. The potentially shiftable taxes on public utilities were a not inconsiderable part of the total—about 10 per cent. An adjustment for the corporation income taxes levied on public utilities would have changed our aggregate totals, but these were not of prime interest. The differentials by income levels, which were the main subject of inquiry, would not have been so greatly affected, for any allowance made for public utility income taxes would apply proportionately to stockholders in each income class.

CONCLUSION ON INCIDENCE

A brief summary of a number of points of view on the problem of the incidence of the corporation income tax cannot do justice to the richness, refinement, and complexity of recent discussions. It is apparent from such cursory treatment that it is impossible to arrive at a general consensus. The conclusions and assumptions on incidence in two previously cited studies merit further examination at this point.

Goode's study—in the author's opinion the most thorough study of the corporation income tax to date—includes the following conclu-

---

[24] This argument implicitly assumes that prices set by regulation are lower than prices that would maximize revenue.

[25] Jesse V. Burkhead, "The Changing Incidence of Public Utility Taxation," *The Journal of Land and Utility Economics*, November 1939, pp. 383-385.

[26] *Internal Revenue Code*, 1954, Chap. 1, Sec. 247.

sions on incidence: "These conclusions do not permit a simple statement that the corporation income tax is 'shifted' or is not. Whether the tax may be said to be shifted is partly a matter of terminology. Certainly it adversely affects groups other than stockholders, and in the long run it probably causes some changes in relative commodity prices. On the other hand, there seems to be little foundation for the belief that a large part of the corporate tax comes out of wages or is passed on to consumers in the same way that a selective excise tends to be shifted to buyers. For both analytical and policy purposes, the most important conclusion is that the initial or short-run incidence is largely on corporate profits."[27]

Or again, and perhaps even more strongly, in explaining the use in some of his computations of the assumption that the corporation income tax is a levy on stockholders, Goode writes: "It is assumed that the whole corporation income tax rests on distributed and undistributed profits. The critical reader will recognize that this assumption is not definitely supported by the findings of the preceding chapter and that indeed it is to some extent inconsistent with them. The argument of Chapter Four, however, holds that in the short run the tax does rest mainly on profits. If this is so, the approach adopted in the present chapter shows what would happen to the distribution of income and wealth immediately after increase or decrease of the corporate tax. This itself is a matter of great importance for tax policy. Even for the long run it is not clear what other assumption would be more realistic or useful. In particular, there is no basis for assuming that any specific fraction of the tax is passed on to consumers. The assumption that the corporate tax rests on corporate profits seems only slightly less justifiable than the usual working hypotheses that assign excises entirely to consumers and the individual income tax wholly to its original payers."[28]

In 1947 the National Tax Association (with a membership of accountants, lawyers, tax administrators, and academic students of public finance) appointed a committee headed by Harold M. Groves "to make a thorough study of the federal income tax with attention to fiscal, economic and legal aspects. . . ." In its final report (1950) the committee summed up its views as follows:

"Our preliminary report analyzed the problem of short-run incidence and, as previously stated, concluded that the corporate tax is passed on in the short period to a minor extent only." The report then asks, "Is a different answer required when the long run is brought

[27] Richard B. Goode, The Corporation Income Tax, Wiley, 1951, p. 72.
[28] Ibid., p. 75.

into the picture?" No definite conclusions emerge from an extended discussion which admits its inability to go beyond deductive reasoning in an "area not amenable to much empirical evidence." The section on incidence closes with this sentence: "Whereas short-run shifting of the corporate tax figures heavily in equity considerations, long-run effects are seen to be relevant principally as they bear on a desired level of investment."[29] This conclusion is particularly germane to our study, for ours is primarily a study in equity, i.e., a study of the equality or inequality of tax burdens on individuals with incomes of similar sizes but derived in part from different sources.

While no general agreement exists on where the burden of the corporation income tax rests, enough evidence has now been marshalled to show that the assumption that it rests on profits is neither unreasonable nor unsupported. This choice—a part of the framework of this study—is open to criticism but is probably less vulnerable than any other choice. In view of the uncertainties, however, an alternative computation was undertaken to explore the effects of the assumption that the corporation income tax is shifted in part.[30]

RESULTS ASSUMING SHIFTING

For this test computation the most reasonable alternative possibility appears to be that, as under alternative A, half the corporation income tax is assumed to be shifted forward. This arbitrary choice of half the tax is the simplest sort of compromise—between full forward shifting and zero shifting.[31] Since, as will be seen, the results based on this

---

[29] *Final Report of the Committee on the Federal Corporate Net Income Tax*, Proceedings of Forty-Third National Conference, National Tax Association, 1950, pp. 56-58.

[30] While the personal income tax is assumed in this study and widely among scholars not to be shifted, its incidence is also open to some of the arguments that are relevant to the corporate tax. For instance, since some personal taxable income arises from the activity of business units (individually owned and partnerships), the question of shifting arises—in this case shifting of the personal tax. The argument that corporation income taxes limit the spirit of enterprise and the rate of investment and lead to lower output, higher prices, and hence shifting of the tax might with equal force be applied to the personal income tax of businessmen. It might also be claimed that workers would be spurred by higher income taxes to seek higher wages to maintain the same take-home pay, thus tending to force costs and prices up, if suitable finance for this higher level of payments is forthcoming.

[31] Miller (*op. cit.*) used two assumptions: (1) that the corporate tax falls fully on stockholders, and (2) that one-third of the tax is shifted forward, leaving two-thirds resting on stockholders. Musgrave, Carroll, Cook, and Frane (*op. cit.*) used as their standard case the assumption that one-third of the tax is shifted forward to consumers, one-eighth backward to wage-earners, and the rest falls on profits. In addition they considered two limiting cases: (1) full forward shifting, and (2) the incidence solely on profits. Adler and Schlesinger (*op. cit.*) used two assumptions: (1) that the tax is borne solely by stockholders (this was necessary for comparability with a previous study), and (2) that half of the tax is shifted forward to consumers.

assumption differ systematically from the results based on our standard method, the reader may assess, qualitatively at least, the effect of assuming the percentage shifted to be more or less than 50. More specifically, under this alternative corporations are assumed to act as tax collectors for the government—as retailers do in the case of a retail sales tax—to an amount of 50 per cent of the corporate tax. Therefore only half the corporate tax is taken to be a direct liability on stockholders and only half of the corporate tax is included in the earnings imputable to stockholders.

The procedures outlined earlier in connection with the standard method were employed, except that a smaller amount of income was imputed to stockholders and a smaller corporate tax burden was allocated to them. The pattern of these results compared with those of the standard method is therefore predictable, at least in direction. With the same absolute adjustment made on both the income and tax side, a greater proportionate reduction will occur in the tax liability. The effective rate of corporate tax is lower, and therefore the net extra burden against corporate earnings (both distributed and retained) and stockholders will be smaller. The differentials as measured under alternative A are significantly lower than those obtained by the standard method.

A comparison of the differentials against net corporate earnings and stockholders under the 50 per cent shifting assumption with the results by the standard method appears in Table 9.[32] Note how much smaller the alternative A values are. Compared with the results by the standard method, the differential against net corporate earnings is from 9 to over 13 percentage points lower (column 3). The standard method indicates an extra burden equal to 25 per cent of net corporate earnings at the bottom of the income scale; the assumption that 50 per cent of the corporate tax was shifted results in a differential less than half as great. At the $25,000 stockholder income level, the standard method results in an extra burden of 2 per cent; alternative A results in a tax benefit of 10 per cent. For the average stockholder with $500,000, the standard method shows an actual tax rate on the net corporate earnings component of his income some 26 percentage points

[32] This and the following tables compare the differentials against average stockholders having incomes of the same size but defined differently according to the standard method and to that of each of the alternatives. The level of income is standardized, but the constituents of the stockholder's income vary in each case. The comparison is *not* of the burden on the $3,000 income level (standard method definition) stockholder, for example, with the burden on the same stockholder under the alternative A assumption; rather, the comparison is of results for two $3,000 average stockholders under different income definitions.

TABLE 9

Comparison of Differentials under Standard Method and Alternative A, 1947
(*per cent*)

AVERAGE STOCKHOLDER IMPUTED GROSS INCOME ($000's)	DIFFERENTIAL AGAINST NET CORPORATE EARNINGS			DIFFERENTIAL AGAINST STOCKHOLDER INCOME		
	Standard method (1)	*Alternative A* (2)	(2) — (1) (3)	*Standard method* (4)	*Alternative A* (5)	(5) — (4) (6)
1	24.6	11.1	—13.5	5.9	2.3	—3.6
3	23.8	10.7	—13.1	4.8	2.5	—2.3
5	22.5	9.4	—13.1	5.2	2.4	—2.8
10	17.7	5.0	—12.7	6.0	1.6	—4.4
25	2.0	—10.0	—12.0	1.0	—4.5	—5.5
50	—7.6	—18.1	—10.5	—4.8	—10.9	—6.1
100	—16.2	—26.3	—10.1	—11.9	—18.4	—6.5
250	—24.5	—33.9	—9.4	—19.4	—26.6	—7.2
500	—25.7	—34.8	—9.1	—22.7	—31.1	—8.4

lower than would have been the case had this component been reached promptly and in full by the personal income tax; the assumptions of alternative A, however, result in a greater degree of undertaxation—an effective tax rate almost 35 points lower than that of the personal income tax alone. As a corollary of the lower effective rates of alternative A we find its cross-over point (the income level at which undertaxation begins) to be much lower down the income scale than that of the standard method—$15,000 of imputed gross income as compared with $30,000.

The value of this test lies not in the precise amounts of the differentials based upon the assumption that half the corporate tax is shifted. The 50 per cent is an arbitrary choice and the differentials would change with assumptions of a greater or a smaller degree of shifting. The test does enable us to conclude that if the corporate tax is in fact shifted, the measures derived from our standard method overstate the extra burden against net corporate earnings (understate it where it is negative). If shifting occurs to a degree greater than 50 per cent of the tax, the overstatement is greater than Table 9 indicates; if, however, less than 50 per cent of the tax is shifted, the overstatement is smaller. As among different income levels, the overstatement of the differential against corporate earnings by our standard method, if shifting actually is the case, is greatest in absolute terms for the lower incomes. But the income level differences are not large. Finally, the general pattern traced out by the differentials against net corporate earnings in our standard method appears distinctly in the alternative A values—a steady decline in the differential as the level of stockholder income rises.

What shifting of the corporation income tax implies for the extra burden related to the whole of stockholder income is shown in columns 4-6 of Table 9. If as much as half of the corporation income tax was shifted in 1947, it appears that the double taxation of stockholders compared with the single taxation of other personal income taxpayers led to a relatively slight extra burden on the owners of corporate shares. In no case did it result in more than 2.5 percentage points of extra tax liability. The benefit to stockholders with larger incomes was more significant; at the $500,000 level the tax burden was more than 30 percentage points lower than it would have been if there had been no corporate tax and all their corporate earnings had been taxed as personal income (see column 5 for the differential at other levels). How much these results differ from those provided by our standard method can be determined by the comparison in column 6 of Table 9.

CONCLUSION ON SHIFTING

We may conclude from the results of the test that, if there is any validity in the contention that the corporate tax is shifted and if the degree of shifting is significant (as much as 50 per cent of the tax), the main concern on equity grounds is "undertaxation" of stockholders. In 1947, for example, the "overtaxation" that occurred for the stockholders in income classes of $10,000 and below was relatively slight compared with the results based upon imputation of the whole corporate tax to stockholders. For those in the classes above $10,000 (more precisely, $15,000), however, "undertaxation" of sizeable proportions would have existed if half the corporate tax was really shifted forward.[33]

[33] These generalizations apply to our test as far as it was carried. But it might be argued it was not carried far enough for it does not trace out the burden of the shifted part of the corporate tax on stockholders and others. To do this would be difficult, but the type of difference it would have made can be suggested.

Stockholder income always includes an imputed component. Consumption expenditures, however, upon which the shifted corporate tax would fall, are geared more closely to income actually received than to imputable income. If our comparison is taken to be between stockholders and non-stockholders with a similar amount of income, albeit differently defined, the non-stockholders will show a larger amount of consumption and will bear more of the shifted corporate tax than the stockholders. Thus the differentials against corporate earnings and stockholders would be smaller and the negative differentials would be larger than those shown in Table 9, with the difference being more pronounced the higher the income level.

Alternative B—Taking Account of Current Price Levels

So far, throughout this study we have used the Internal Revenue Code definition of corporate net income, which generally follows the accepted usages of accounting practice,[34] and therefore is most valid for periods of unchanging prices. In the last decade and particularly since the end of the war, this definition of corporate income has been criticized because conservative accounting usages provide inadequate allowance for the cost of replacing inventory and plant in the determination of taxable income. Some part of what is called net corporate earnings in this study, it is contended, is not net at all because it is required to maintain capital intact in real terms. However, there is disagreement about what this connotes for the proper definition of taxable income. This section presents briefly some representative points of view on this matter and the results of a test designed to take account of current price levels in the determination of taxable income.

CHANGING PRICE LEVELS

While there is general agreement that there exists no one definition of income that is most appropriate for all the uses to which the concept of income is put, the discussion of what income is, or should be, is very voluminous and complex. This section proposes not to add to this discussion or to explore many of the facets of it, but simply to explain what alternative B is and why it was developed.

With constant price levels, the conventional accounting practices for computing cost of inventory used up (or converted) and value of physical capital destroyed during the productive process provide an accurate measure of net income. This view implies that if dividends equal to the designated net income were paid out, a company would be able to continue a physical level of operations exactly similar to its previous scale, with its capital remaining intact. Stationary price levels would limit a change in value of inventory to a physical change, and estimated depreciation would amount to a total just sufficient to purchase replacement units of capital.[35] Under conditions of changing price levels, however, this strict equivalence is destroyed. With rising prices, part of what is reported as net income, by conventional accounting standards, must be devoted to replenishing inventories and replacing depreciated assets. The steep rise in prices during the period following World War II focused attention on this problem. But even

---

[34] Dan Throop Smith and J. Keith Butters, *Taxable and Business Income*, National Bureau of Economic Research, 1949, p. 9.

[35] This neglects any changes in technology that would make it less costly to obtain replacements for the depreciated assets.

before this, there had been noticeable discontent with acceptance of standard accounting procedures by the Internal Revenue Service, particularly in connection with the valuation of inventories.[36]

There is general agreement that, for some purposes at least, standard accounting usages do not provide the most relevant measure of income generated during a given period. As set forth by Lintner in 1949:

"When the purpose in view . . . is to evaluate the results of ordinary current operations of business firms, it is generally most appropriate to use profits figures which exclude, so far as is practicable, all elements of capital gains and losses which reflect changes in price levels as such, rather than the operating characteristics of the enterprise. To this end it is necessary to express all costs as well as all receipts in terms of current price levels, and this requires that the entire amount of what are generally called 'inventory profits' be eliminated from reported profits data, together with the excess of current replacement costs of book values of the capital equipment 'used up' in the course of producing current outputs."[37] Or, again, as stated by Fabricant in 1950:

"To obtain comparable figures that measure business income from a consistent economic point of view, economists are therefore driven to make adjustments of accounting data, or at least to attach qualifications to them. Economists follow the principle that costs should be related to revenues on the same price level basis, and that the income of one period should be compared with the income of another period on the same price level basis. In accord with this principle, economists believe that inventory revaluations should be excluded from business income, and the income estimates of the National Bureau of Economic Research and of the Department of Commerce do exclude them. Economists believe, also, that revaluations of fixed assets should be excluded from business income, and the income estimates of the National Bureau and Department of Commerce both exclude realized capital gains and losses. The estimates of the National Bureau further exclude revaluations of fixed assets arising from the charging of depreciation at original cost. The Department of Commerce also accepts the prin-

---

[36] Since 1938, taxpayers have been permitted to use the last-in-first-out method of inventory valuation which tends to tone down inventory profits and losses. In 1947, it is estimated, this method, Lifo, was being used by companies with inventories representing about 9 per cent of the total book value of manufacturers' inventories, or, translated to 1947 prices, somewhere between 13 and 17 per cent (see J. Keith Butters, assisted by Powell Niland, *Effects of Taxation: Inventory Accounting and Policies*, Harvard University Press, 1949, pp. 54-55). The inventory valuation adjustment of the National Income Division of the Department of Commerce, used in the test to be described below, makes allowance for the fact that some companies use Lifo.

[37] John Lintner, *Corporate Profits in Perspective*, American Enterprise Association, 1949, p. 13.

ciple, but has so far implemented it only by a textual qualification of its figures."[38]

Acceptance of this concept of income as most appropriate for income tax purposes is not, however, universal. An illustration is Lintner's statement:

"For many purposes, however, it is entirely appropriate that elements of capital gain or loss be included in profit figures. For instance, one of the distinguishing characteristics of the ownership and management of property and business enterprise, as compared with supplying current labor services, is that the former provide opportunities for the realization of capital gains, as well as risks of incurring capital losses. An appraisal of the relative changes which have occurred in the *total* economic position of different groups in the economy over any period of time which failed to allow appropriately for such changes in capital position would obviously be incomplete and misleading."[39]

Goode has made a strong case for historical cost valuations in defining income for tax purposes:

". . . Lifo in practice has proved to be a tax-relief device for a relatively small group of taxpayers. The method cannot be convincingly defended on general grounds as a refinement of the definition of taxable income. To be sure, it has eliminated a speculative element of profit that is largely extraneous to the primary activities of the businesses using it. But general price fluctuations make speculators of everyone who holds tangible wealth or money claims or who engages in long-term contracts. A case in equity can be made for eliminating inventory profits and losses from the tax base, while including other speculative gains and losses, only by showing that the situation of the inventory holders is peculiar to a degree warranting special classification. This case has not been made for that group of taxpayers who have found it feasible to use Lifo. . . .

". . . An objection to the adoption of the current-cost approach for depreciation, however, is that the economic-power concept is not consistently followed in the statutory definition of taxable income. Gains and losses are ordinarily recognized for tax purposes only when 'realized' as the result of a bona fide transaction. Unrealized gains and losses are ignored. As a matter of principle, recognition of an increase in costs not yet objectively realized in a transaction can hardly be

[38] Solomon Fabricant, "Business Costs and Business Income Under Changing Price Levels," in *Five Monographs on Business Income*, Study Group on Business Income, American Institute of Accountants, 1950, p. 154.
[39] Lintner, *op. cit.*, p. 13 (italics are his).

justified unless unrealized gains on capital assets are also recognized for tax purposes, or all capital gains and losses are ignored.

"The problem may be illustrated by considering an asset with a normal life of twenty years bought in year 1 at a cost of $100. At the end of year 5 one-fourth of the original cost will have been written off if the straight-line method is followed, and the depreciated value will be $75. Suppose that in year 6 the price of comparable new assets rises by 20 per cent, to $120. On the current cost basis the true cost of the old asset in year 6 will be one-twentieth of $120, or $6, rather than the $5 of normal depreciation. But the price increase has also raised the value of the remaining useful life of the asset, from $75 to $90. If both this unrealized capital gain of $15 and the unrealized increment in cost are taken into account, the taxpayer has a net gain in year 6 of $14. In each of years 7 through 20, the taxpayer's income will be $1 smaller than under normal depreciation. Over the whole period the unrealized gain and the unrealized cost increment will exactly cancel. Of course, the net tax may be affected by the timing of income in the absence of complete averaging of income for tax purposes.

"The foregoing illustration brings out an elementary fact that, surprisingly enough, has been largely ignored in recent discussion of depreciation policy: Owners of physical assets benefit from an inflation as compared with holders of fixed money claims . . . Along with organized labor and farmers, the owners of business assets enjoy an increase in money income. Since the additional money income is generally subject to taxation, regardless of source and its real purchasing power, there seems to be no case in equity for special tax treatment of the owners of depreciable property."[40]

On the other hand, a substantial body of opinion holds that for income tax purposes the costs of replacing inventory and depreciable assets at current price levels should be taken into account. Representative of this point of view are: a statement by W. A. Paton,

". . . It is to be hoped that, in revising the Internal Revenue Code, Congress will give serious attention to the possibility of authorizing the use of current replacement cost of materials used and the replacement cost of plant facilities expired, as of the end of the taxable year, as deductions in lieu of deductions based on unadjusted book costs. I understand that developments along this line have occurred in the

[40] Goode, *op.cit.*, pp. 171 and 174-175. For a more extended treatment of this question see E. Cary Brown, *Effects of Taxation: Depreciation Adjustment for Price Changes*, Harvard University Press, 1952, especially Chap. IV.

income-tax statutes of some foreign countries."[41] And one by G. O. May,

"If the Group should feel, as the present writer does, that an increase in charges for exhaustion is called for in the public interest as well as by sound accounting, the best prospect of implementing that view would seem to lie in a revision of the tax law which would (as in the case of LIFO inventorying) allow the increased deduction for tax purposes, provided the same method was employed in the regular accounting of the taxpayer."[42]

In summary, both standard accounting techniques and the tax code regulations, with the exception of the Lifo option, include inventory profits in income and make no allowance for increased cost of replacing fixed assets. To some students it is not completely clear on equity grounds that any change in this practice is required in defining taxable income. Others, however, support a change to allowances based on current costs. In deference to this latter point of view adjustments were devised to assess the change in findings that would result from use of a more "real" concept of income.[43]

TAKING ACCOUNT OF INVENTORY PROFITS AND
DEPRECIATION AT CURRENT COST

To compare the 1947 differentials obtained by the standard method with those taking account of current prices for replacement of inventory and depreciable assets, adjustments were made in net corporate earnings to be allocated to stockholders.

The fact that the sharp price rises in the course of 1947 led to inventory profits was first taken into account. As a measure of the change in inventories due to price rather than quantity changes the inventory valuation adjustment figure estimated by the National Income Division of the Department of Commerce was used.[44] The adjustment figure for 1947 of $5.8 billion was subtracted from corporate earnings imputable to stockholders. The adjustment for inventory valuation is difficult to estimate and is not among the more firmly

41 William A. Paton in *Profits, Report of a Subcommittee of the Joint Committee on the Economic Report on Profits Hearings*, 80th Cong. 2d sess., 1949, p. 143.

42 George O. May, *Business Income and Price Levels, An Accounting Study*, Study Group on Business Income of the American Institute of Accountants, 1949, p. 65.

43 This does not imply support (or condemnation) of a "real" definition for tax purposes. It was not employed for our standard method because the approach in this study has been to compare stockholders with other personal income taxpayers, and the latter including business enterprises subject to the personal tax have received no special tax abatements because of inflation.

44 *Survey of Current Business*, Dept. of Commerce, July 1953, p. 13.

based items in the national income accounts,[45] but it is the best figure available. Choice of 1947 for the year of test was, as previously noted, fortunate, for in this year the inventory valuation adjustment was higher than in any other of the period and points up the change most dramatically. Parenthetically, had the test been made for 1949 or 1952, an addition to stockholder income would have been necessary on this score.[46]

The second adjustment deals with depreciation. Data bearing on this are scant, but fortunately, there is E. Cary Brown's estimate of the extent to which current costs of replacement exceeded historical costs[47]; for 1948-1951 he estimated that current costs exceeded historical costs by about 50 per cent.[48] Assuming the same ratio to have been applicable in 1947, an adjustment was made in the total of corporate earnings imputable to stockholders by subtracting $2.6 billion, half of the total depreciation reported by all corporations in that year.[49] Table 10 gives figures for comparison of the differentials by the standard method and by alternative B.

For 1947, after defining income net of costs computed in relation to current price levels, we find the differentials against net corporate

[45] *National Income Supplement, 1954, Survey of Current Business,* Dept. of Commerce, pp. 122-125.

[46]

Inventory Valuation Adjustment
(*billions of dollars*)

Year	Amount
1940	−0.1
1941	−2.6
1942	−1.2
1943	−0.8
1944	−0.3
1945	−0.6
1946	−5.2
1947	−5.8
1948	−2.1
1949	2.1
1950	−5.0
1951	−1.3
1952	1.0

Source: *Survey of Current Business,* Dept. of Commerce, July 1953, pp. 12-13.

[47] Brown, *op. cit.,* p. 28. Details of his estimate will be found on pp. 151-154.

[48] Actually, it is his judgment that 30 per cent is more correct, but he rounded to 50 to "prevent any understatement." This, then, constitutes an upper limit of possibilities.

[49] Another source provides a figure on the same order of magnitude. In a study published by the National Association of Manufacturers ("Major Tendencies in Business Finance," Economic Policy Division series No. 57, p. 69) depreciation at current price levels was estimated as $2.2 billion higher than corporations actually took for 1947.

TABLE 10

Comparison of Differentials under Standard Method and Alternative B, 19
(per cent)

AVERAGE STOCKHOLDER IMPUTED GROSS INCOME ($000's)	DIFFERENTIAL AGAINST NET CORPORATE EARNINGS			DIFFERENTIAL AGAINST STOCKHOLDER INCOME		
	Standard method (1)	Alternative B (2)	(2) — (1) (3)	Standard method (4)	Alternative B (5)	(5) — (4) (6)
1	24.6	39.5	14.9	5.9	7.9	2.0
3	23.8	39.5	15.7	4.8	8.2	3.4
5	22.5	38.1	15.6	5.2	9.4	4.2
10	17.7	33.4	15.7	6.0	11.1	5.1
25	2.0	18.3	16.3	1.0	7.4	6.4
50	—7.6	10.1	17.7	—4.8	5.7	10.5
100	—16.2	1.7	17.9	—11.9	1.2	13.1
250	—24.5	—5.3	19.2	—19.4	—4.1	15.3
500	—25.7	—6.1	19.6	—22.7	—5.6	17.1

earnings to run anywhere from 15 to 20 points higher than the values provided by our usual method. Whereas the latter procedure, at the $1,000 income level, for example, indicates that 25 per cent more of stockholders' pro rata share of net corporate earnings went into taxes than would have been the case under the personal income tax alone, alternative B places the extra tax liability at almost 40 per cent. At the $25,000 average stockholder income level, the usual method shows a slight degree of overtaxation of net corporate earnings—some 2 per cent; under alternative B, however, it is much greater—over 18 per cent. At the top of the income range a similar discrepancy exists. By the standard method stockholders, on average, were undertaxed on the net corporate earnings component of their income to a much larger degree—nearly 26 per cent—than by alternative B just about 6 per cent.

However, it should be noted that, while the alternative B differentials are higher, they follow the same general pattern disclosed by our standard method; the higher the average stockholder's income, the lower the differential against the net corporate earnings component of his income. Also, both methods show, after a point, a tax benefit for stockholders who enjoyed a lower tax under the combined corporate-personal income tax structure than would have been due if there had been no corporate tax but instead the whole of the corporate earnings component of their income had been subject currently to the personal income tax. In the case of alternative B, however, the tax saving was much lower and started higher up the income scale, the "cross over" point being about $135,000 while for the usual method it was $30,000. The same type of difference shows up in the differential against stockholders when the results of the standard method and alternative B are compared. The differences between results by the alternative adjustments and by the usual method become increasingly pronounced as the proportion of corporate earnings increases with rising imputed gross income level of stockholders (column 6).

CONCLUSION ON COST ADJUSTMENTS

We may conclude that the reader who thinks that alternative B embodies a more meaningful definition of income than our standard method should view the results of the latter as understating the differentially heavier effective rates of tax to which most stockholders are subject, and overstating the degree of tax benefit that the stockholders at the top of the income scale received.[50]

Alternative C—Combining the Shifting and Current Cost Adjustments

Alternatives A and B are not mutually exclusive. Some readers may hold it most realistic to assume that the corporation income tax is shifted and also that it is appropriate to define income for purposes of the corporation income tax exclusive of the cost of inventory maintenance and depreciable asset replacement at current price levels. To illustrate how much, under these conditions, the results would differ from those obtained through our standard procedure, alternative C has been developed.

This alternative is a simple combination of alternative A (in which the adjustments tend to lower the differentials) with alternative B (in which the adjustments tend to raise them). What is the net result when both sets of adjustments are incorporated in our calculations? The data of Table 11 provide the answer.

Over the lower portion of the average stockholder income range up to about $10,000, the alternative C differentials are about the same as those obtained by the standard procedure; but above this level, the

[50] This interpretation of results holds for most years of the study which, however, show variations in the degree of over- and understatement, probably most pronounced in 1947, and least in 1952 when the inventory valuation adjustment was opposite in sign to (but smaller than) the adjustment for current cost depreciation. For 1949, however, the two definitions would probably give closely similar results, for the inventory revaluation allowance was positive, necessitating an addition to stockholder income, and was just large enough to cancel out the excess of current over historical cost of depreciable assets.

TABLE 11

Comparison of Differentials under Standard Method and Alternative C, 1947

(per cent)

AVERAGE STOCKHOLDER IMPUTED GROSS INCOME ($000's)	DIFFERENTIAL AGAINST NET CORPORATE EARNINGS			DIFFERENTIAL AGAINST STOCKHOLDER INCOME		
	Standard method (1)	Alternative C (2)	(2) — (1) (3)	Standard method (4)	Alternative C (5)	(5) — (4) (6)
1	24.6	24.0	0.6	5.9	5.4	—0.5
3	23.8	24.8	1.0	4.8	4.4	—0.4
5	22.5	23.7	1.2	5.2	5.0	—0.2
10	17.7	19.4	1.7	6.0	5.1	—0.9
25	2.0	7.1	5.1	1.0	3.0	2.0
50	—7.6	0.2	7.8	—4.8	0.1	4.9
100	—16.2	—7.1	9.1	—11.9	—4.1	7.8
250	—24.5	—12.5	12.0	—19.4	—8.9	10.5
500	—25.7	—13.2	12.5	—22.7	—10.9	11.8

differentials are larger. Also, from this point on, the higher the stockholder income, the greater the difference between results of the two procedures. The cross-over from over- to undertaxation, which in the usual procedure occurred at $30,000, takes place under alternative C at about $51,000.

The reader who regards alternative C as the most accurate and reasonable framework in which to analyze our problem probably will have few reservations about the standard method's findings over the lower portion of the income range, but he will consider those findings over the rest of the income array an understatement of the extra burden on net corporate earnings and stockholders. He is reminded that columns 3 and 6, providing some idea of the quantitative nature of the amendments he will want to make, apply strictly only to 1947. For most other years, except 1949, the changes would be in the same direction as for 1947. Moreover, the 1947 adjustments are derived from a 50 per cent shifting assumption. Should the reader prefer to assume a greater degree of shifting than this, the alternative C values of the differential would lie closer to those of the standard method at the top of the income scale, and below them at lower stockholder incomes. On the other hand, if a smaller than 50 per cent assumption were employed, the comparative understatement of differentials by the standard method would be greater.

Alternative D—Adjustment for Saving through Corporations

WHAT IF CORPORATE SAVINGS ARE USED TO AVOID
PERSONAL INCOME TAXES?

In this investigation, the standard method imputes all of net corporate earnings to stockholders on the basis of their dividend receipts, the ratio for imputation being the same for every income-dividend size stockholder cell.

However, it has been frequently pointed out that, because corporate distributions are subject upon receipt as dividends to personal income tax, stockholders (particularly in the higher income classes subject to stiff marginal rates) are induced to save via the corporate mechanism and thereby avoid personal income taxes on the retained portion of corporate earnings, until realized in the form of (less heavily taxed) capital gains or passed on income-tax free at death.

Such an attitude has been expressed by one investor as follows: "We, that is, my wife and I, prefer common stocks as an investment, but not for all our funds. We choose corporations which pay out a minimum of earnings in order to have our holdings grow in intrinsic value. We like to save by having corporations plow back a substantial portion of their earnings tax-free to us. If the corporations pay us dividends, we have to pay taxes on the income."[51]

If there is a systematic tendency for upper-income stockholders to blunt the impact of high personal income surtax rates by holding shares in corporations known to pay out a small fraction of their earnings, and if this is quantitatively important enough so that the distribution ratio (i.e. the ratio of dividends to net corporate earnings) for high-income taxpayers is lower than the average distribution ratio for all taxpayers, then the results obtained by our standard method may be in error. The upper-income stockholders will really be claimants to more of the total of net corporate earnings than our method credits them with; those lower down the income scale should really be credited with less. For example, suppose that there are only two classifications of stockholders, one "high-income" and the other classification comprising the rest. Let dividends received total $20,000 for all stockholders, with the high-income group receiving $5,000 and all the rest $15,000. Net corporate earnings are assumed to equal $100,000. Now assume that the high-income group purposely holds stock in high-saving corporations which have only a 10 per cent distribution

[51] J. Keith Butters, Lawrence E. Thompson, and Lynn L. Bollinger, *Effects of Taxation: Investments by Individuals*, Harvard University Press, 1953, p. 200. The investor quoted had a net worth over $1,000,000 and an income of about $100,000.

ratio. The other shareholders, on average, receive their dividends on shares in corporations which average a 30 per cent distribution ratio. Thus, the high-income stockholders should be credited with $50,000 or 50 per cent of the net corporate earnings, and all other shareholders with a similar amount. However if, as in our standard method, the over-all average distribution ratio of 20 per cent for both classes of stockholders were used, the high-income shareholders would have $25,000 (which is less than their actual share) allocated to them, and to the others would be imputed $75,000 (which is more than their actual share). While the average distribution ratio is 20 per cent for all stockholders, for the high-income group it is only 10 per cent (i.e. below average) and for the other, 30 per cent (i.e. above average).

It is desirable, therefore, to assess the quantitative importance of the choice of distribution ratios by a comparative test. Unfortunately little information is available for this purpose. The only data I have been able to find that bear on this problem are not focused directly on it, but they are better than nothing.

ANALYSIS OF AVAILABLE EVIDENCE

There is available for 1936 a cross-tabulation which gives the asset size of dividend paying corporations and the net income class of dividend recipients filing income tax returns for that year.[52] The dividends received by shareholders, tabulated by 27 net income classes, are classified on the basis of asset size (10 in all) of the originating corporations. For instance, stockholders in net income class $70,000 and under $80,000 received 0.37 per cent of their dividends from corporations with assets less than $50,000; they received 0.52 per cent from corporations with assets of $50,000 and under $100,000, etc. These data, more refined than those available for any other year, can be used to estimate differences in average distribution ratios associated with the dividend receipts of taxpayers in the various net income classes, because, on average, corporations in each asset size class had different distribution ratios. These ratios tend to increase with the asset sizes of the dividend distributing corporations.[53] (See Table 12.) Note that these ratios, at best, only approximate the information relevant to the problem posed for alternative D. Directly relevant would be data derived from an array in which the distribution ratio itself constituted the basis for classifying the data. Use of an approximation qualifies the result of

[52] *Bulletin of the Treasury Department*, Dept. of the Treasury, January 1943, pp. 3-6.
[53] Cf. George E. Lent, *The Impact of the Undistributed Profits Tax*, Columbia University Press, 1948, p. 43.

TABLE 12

Ratio of Net Dividends Paid Out to Net Corporate Earnings for Net Income Corporations, by Asset Size Classes, 1936

(dollars in thousands)

ASSET SIZE CLASS	Net dividends paid out	Net corporate earnings	Distribution ratio
Under $50	$ 79,902	$ 148,818	0.5369
$50 and under 100	93,349	154,577	0.6039
100 and under 250	218,687	349,336	0.6260
250 and under 500	238,476	374,159	0.6374
500 and under 1,000	272,306	453,423	0.6006
1,000 and under 5,000	718,404	1,234,418	0.5820
5,000 and under 10,000	343,452	567,963	0.6047
10,000 and under 50,000	902,773	1,334,255	0.6766
50,000 and under 100,000	414,546	548,464	0.7577
100,000 and over	1,280,608	1,531,202	0.8363
All net income corporations	4,562,500	6,696,613	0.6813

Source: *Statistics of Income for 1936*, Part 2, Bureau of Internal Revenue.

the test (summarized in Table 13) and tends to damp the figures finally obtained compared with the results that would have been obtained from data classified directly by dividend distribution ratios. Basically, the test involved computing a distribution ratio for each net income class, by weighting each asset size distribution ratio (Table 12) by the proportion that dividends paid by corporations in this asset size class comprised of the total dividend receipts in each net income class.

These test procedures and their results are merely indicative and are not directly comparable with the standard method developed in this study. In the latter, stockholders in each adjusted gross income class were divided into a number of dividend size groups, corporate earnings were imputed on this basis, and stockholders were rearrayed in imputed gross income classes. In the test a much rougher calculation was undertaken. Corporate earnings were allocated to stockholders in each income class (net for 1936) in accordance with the average amount of dividends for all stockholders in that class, without rearraying. The relevant values for all net income classes appear in Table 13. The pattern of deviations from the overall average distribution ratio is surprisingly regular.[54] Starting with the lowest net income class

[54] The deficit income class is neglected for purposes of this discussion because the calculations covered taxpayers only. Moreover, purposeful conduct cannot be inferred from the deficit class since, presumably, deficits are involuntary.

TABLE 13

Net Income Class Weighted Average Distribution Ratios, 1936

NET INCOME CLASS ($000's)	Weighted average distribution ratio
Under 1	0.730
1 and under 2	0.737
2 and under 3	0.729
3 and under 4	0.720
4 and under 5	0.710
5 and under 10	0.701
10 and under 15	0.691
15 and under 20	0.686
20 and under 25	0.685
25 and under 30	0.682
30 and under 40	0.682
40 and under 50	0.678
50 and under 60	0.679
60 and under 70	0.683
70 and under 80	0.690
80 and under 90	0.689
90 and under 100	0.696
100 and under 150	0.693
150 and under 200	0.695
200 and under 250	0.710
250 and under 300	0.735
300 and under 400	0.726
400 and under 500	0.734
500 and under 750	0.735
750 and under 1,000	0.754
1,000 and over	0.775
Total	0.701

and moving up, we find distribution ratios above the overall average, but the extent of departure from the general average tends to decline. Dividends representing distribution ratios below average were received by all classes from $10,000 up to $200,000. The lowest ratio was reached in the $40,000 and under $50,000 net income class; above this class the extent of departure from the overall average distribution ratio becomes gradually less until at the $200,000 and under $250,000 net income level a distribution ratio above average is once more reached. This above-average ratio is characteristic of the rest of the income distribution, with the extent of departure from the average increasing steadily as the income level increases, and reaching its maximum in the $1,000,000 and over class. If the behavior of these divergences in distribution ratio were plotted with income on the horizontal axis, above-average distribution ratios on the vertical axis above the origin, and below-average distribution ratios below the origin, then a plot of the net income class distribution ratios would be U-shaped.

How important are these differences in the distribution ratios characterizing the investments of the various net income classes? They are really very small. It is only at the extreme levels that the divergence from the average for all classes is over 5 per cent. But, as pointed out above, if the data were classified by distribution ratio of each dividend paying corporation, relatively greater differences would probably have been obtained. An interesting feature of this pattern of distribution ratio is its regularity. With only a few minor exceptions it varies smoothly from one income class to the next falling constantly to a minimum and thereafter rising constantly. This pattern is not exactly what would have been expected solely on personal income tax avoidance grounds. It is true that over a significant range the distribution ratios for the higher net income receivers are below average and this is reasonable. But if it is rational for a $45,000 net income shareholder to seek to hold personal taxes down more than average, via corporate saving, is not the pressure to do this even greater on the $450,000 net income stockholder? But the latter typically received dividends representing a distribution ratio higher than average.

The results of this test do not permit positive generalizations for 1936 for a reason beyond the lack of precise and suitable data: uncertainty arises because the undistributed profits tax, instituted in 1936, stimulated dividend distribution and changed the relative pattern of distribution ratios of different asset size class corporations.[55] There is certainly no basis for concluding that many higher income class taxpayers did not choose investments in companies with very meager distribution policies in order to forestall high personal surtaxes. But, in 1936 at least, this tendency appears to have been almost completely counterbalanced and even swamped (in the case of top income classes) by the opposite choice of stock in corporations with distribution ratios above average.[56] In that year, considerations other than corporate

[55] Cf. Lent, *op. cit.* According to Lent, while all but one asset size class were induced by the undistributed profits tax to distribute more liberally, the greatest relative increase was made by corporations in asset size classes in which a higher proportion of stock was held by taxpayers in the middle range of net income classes. Over this income interval the test disclosed distribution ratios below average—despite the influence of the new tax. Therefore, in the absence of the undistributed profits tax, the overall average distribution ratio of Table 13 would have been higher and, for each income class, the extent of the deviation from this average would have been greater (but in the same direction as the table shows).

[56] There may be, in some cases, a close relationship between capital gains or resale value of a stock and the corporation's distribution policy which would encourage

saving rates evidently affected the relationship between size of personal income, including dividends, and distribution ratios of corporations from which the dividends were received.

While the above test, fragmentary though it is, suggests that there was on net balance no pronounced tendency in 1936 for the rich to seek investment in high-saving corporations, it is possible that in the years after 1936, when opportunities for tax saving on capital gains increased, such a tendency became marked. Table 14 provides the effective tax rate on an added dollar of ordinary income and the effective rate on an added dollar of net long-term capital gains for taxpayers at selected net income levels. In the years after 1936, the effective rate on an incremental dollar of ordinary income increased substantially and the tax saving represented by the preferential rate on capital gains was much greater. These factors should create an impetus for those subject to high marginal rates of personal income tax to hold shares in high-saving corporations, but against this is the deterrent imposed by the fact that the market prices of shares frequently fail to reflect reinvested earnings. However, other things equal, the rate could be an important factor in the pattern of investment choices of taxpayers in the higher income classes and also in the distribution policies of corporations controlled by them. Hence the necessity for an inquiry into the effects of such a possibility upon the relationships under investigation.

---

investors to choose stock in corporations that distribute a high proportion of their earnings. A stockholder explained it in this way:

"One of the main factors that enters into the market value of stock is the dividend it pays.

"To show how dividends affect prices, I have tried to find a parallel example with which to compare Jersey, and I believe that American Can fills the bill. Both are fine companies; their stocks are really 'prime.' They are rated equally by Fitch. In 1947 they closed within a half point of each other, around 81. Their high prices of 1948 were within one-eighth point, around 93. The book value of Can is $10 or so less than that of Jersey, yet Can sold at 91⅜ yesterday, and Jersey sold at 64⅜. Why? Perhaps because Can, while earning only $9.71 a share in 1948 increased its dividends from $3 to $4, while Jersey, earning over $12 in 1948, decreased its dividends from $4 to $2. I venture the theory that if Jersey had paid us $4 last year the stock would now be selling right up where Can is, perhaps even higher" (from a statement by Mr. Wolf, a stockholder, at the 1949 Annual Meeting of Standard Oil Company [New Jersey], pp. 20-21 of a transcript published by the company for its stockholders, July 18, 1949).

Cf. also J. Keith Butters, John Lintner, and William L. Cary assisted by Powell Niland, *Effects of Taxation: Corporate Mergers*, Harvard University Press, 1951, p. 49: "It is entirely conceivable that Ashland's policy of paying out a larger percentage of earnings as dividends would increase the market value of its securities more than a policy of negligible distributions; the market value of listed securities—as contrasted with closely held, untraded securities representing a controlling interest in a company—depends in considerable part on their dividend records."

TABLE 14

Effective Rate on an Added Dollar of Ordinary Income (Odd Numbered Columns) and on an Added Dollar of Net Long-Term Capital Gains (Even Numbered Columns) for Selected Statutory Net Incomes[a] and Years, 1935-1952

(per cent)

YEAR	Net income $5,000		Net income $10,000		Net income $25,000		Net income $50,000		Net income $100,000		Net income $1,000,000	
	(1)	(2)	(3)	(4)	(5)	(6)	(7)	(8)	(9)	(10)	(11)	(12)
1935b	4.0	2.4	9.0	5.4	19.0	11.4	31.0	18.6	54.0	32.4	62.0	37.2
1936-37b	4.0	2.4	9.0	5.4	19.0	11.5	31.0	18.6	59.0	35.4	76.0	45.6
1938-39c	4.0	2.0	9.0	4.5	19.0	9.5	31.0	15.0	59.0	15.0	76.0	15.0
1940d	4.4	2.2	11.0	5.5	34.1	16.5	48.4	16.5	66.0	16.5	78.4	18.5
1941	13.0	6.5	21.0	10.5	48.0	15.0	59.0	15.0	68.0	15.0	78.0	15.0
1942	22.0	11.0	34.0	17.0	58.0	25.0	69.0	25.0	83.0	25.0	88.0	25.0
1943e	24.8	11.0	36.8	17.0	60.8	25.0	71.8	25.0	88.0	25.0	90.0f	25.0
1944-45	25.0	12.5	37.0	18.5	62.0	25.0	75.0	25.0	90.0	25.0	90.0f	25.0
1946-47	20.9	10.5	32.3	16.2	56.1	25.0	68.4	25.0	82.7	25.0	86.5	25.0
1948-49	16.6	8.3	19.4	9.7	33.4	16.7	51.9	25.0	63.4	25.0	82.1	25.0
1950	17.4	8.7	20.0	10.0	34.6	17.3	53.7	25.0	65.5	25.0	84.4	25.0
1951	20.4	10.2	22.4	11.2	39.0	19.5	60.0	25.0	73.0	25.0	91.0	25.0
1952	22.2	11.1	24.6	12.3	42.0	21.0	66.0	26.0	75.0	26.0	92.0	26.0

Source: For 1935-1950, Lawrence H. Seltzer, *The Nature and Tax Treatment of Capital Gains and Losses*, National Bureau of Economic Research, 1951, pp. 523-4; for 1951 and 1952, Internal Revenue Code.
a Married person, two dependents, maximum earned income credit.
b Rates on gain from sale of capital assets held over two, but not over five years.
c Rates on gain from sale of capital assets held more than two years.
d Includes Defense Tax.
e Includes Victory Tax.
f Takes account of maximum effective rate limitation of 90 per cent.

111

Data for 1949 on the patterns of financial asset holdings of individuals in Wisconsin, made available by Thomas R. Atkinson, permit inferences to be drawn as to whether high income taxpayers, as a group, take advantage of the preferential tax rate on capital gains by concentrating their holdings in corporations having low distribution ratios. The Wisconsin law requires reporting on state income tax returns not only dividend receipts but also stock holdings. Having access to the returns, Atkinson was able to estimate the value of the stock from which a sampled group of taxpayers received dividends in 1949.[57] For this purpose he divided common and preferred stocks into two categories—traded and untraded. Stock issues for which dividend and price quotations were available in investment manuals fall in the traded category and the rest are classified as untraded. The value of traded stock holdings was determined by multiplying the average number of shares of the particular issue held by the individual in 1949 "by the unweighted mean between the high and low 1949 market price." For untraded stock Atkinson used book value.[58] His estimates for all Wisconsin taxpayers are presented in Table 15.

The hypothesis that the stock investments of the rich as a group

TABLE 15

Yield on Traded and Untraded Common Stock
Held by Wisconsin Individuals, Arrayed
by Income Classes, 1949
(*per cent*)

| | YIELD ON COMMON STOCK | |
INCOME CLASS	traded[a] (1)	untraded[b] (2)
Negative	5.6	7.4
$0-4,999	7.3	3.2
5,000-5,999	6.8	3.1
10,000-19,999	6.7	4.3
20,000-49,999	6.5	4.9
50,000 and over	7.3	5.1
All income classes	6.9	4.6

Source: Thomas R. Atkinson, *The Pattern of Financial Asset Ownership: Wisconsin Individuals, 1949*, Princeton University Press for National Bureau of Economic Research, 1956, p. 131.
a Based on market value.
b Based on book value.

[57] Thomas R. Atkinson, *The Pattern of Financial Asset Ownership: Wisconsin Individuals, 1949*, Princeton University Press for National Bureau of Economic Research, 1956.
[58] *Ibid.*, p. 49.

are characterized by a lower pay-out percentage than the average percentage for stock holdings of all dividend recipients can be tested most straightforwardly by the data for untraded corporations. For these companies are more typically small and closely held, and the operations of such enterprises can be more easily geared to the owners' personal requirements than is the case for widely owned corporations. Moreover, with traded stock, a low dividend pay-out policy might lead to a fall in the value of the stock (or prevent a rise); therefore the ratio of dividends to stock value, i.e. the yield, would not be useful data for testing the hypothesis. Book valuation would not be affected in this way.

An examination of the data most relevant here (column 2, Table 15) shows that in general the higher the income class, the greater the dividend return in proportion to stockholders' equity. On the face of it, these figures appear to contradict the hypothesis under test, but such a direct conclusion is not warranted. It is not the ratio, D/B ($D =$ dividends and $B =$ book value) which is relevant evidence in this connection, but more properly it is D/Y ($Y =$ earnings) which is the product of D/B and B/Y. Only if B/Y is constant or rises from one stockholder income class to another can the pattern of movement of the values of D/B be taken definitely to indicate the direction of the ratio D/Y. In other words, since D/B increases reading up the stock holder income scale, if B/Y rises or remains constant then D/Y will increase with stockholder income. Without evidence on the behavior of B/Y by stockholder income classes, the argument must be inferential. For income corporations (responsible for almost all corporate net dividend payments in the years covered) W. L. Crum has demonstrated that the rate of return on net worth, Y/B, tends to fall as asset size rises.[59] This means that its inverse, B/Y, rises with asset size. And since the 1936 data suggest a loose correlation between corporate asset size and dividend recipient income class, the D/B ratios in the untraded column of the table can be taken to indicate a D/Y that moves in the same direction, rising with stockholder income class. The same result would follow if it were the case that corporations whose stock is untraded tend to fall within a narrow asset size range, with B/Y roughly constant for all relevant corporation asset size and stockholder income classes.

Thus, the analysis apparently ends with the conclusion that the

[59] William Leonard Crum, *Corporate Size and Earning Power*, Harvard University Press, 1939, pp. 27-30. Crum's findings are for each of the years 1931 through 1936. Similar computations for 1944, 1947, and 1952 confirm the occurrence of this pattern over the period of this investigation.

data do not support the hypothesis that high income stockholders, as a group, tend to invest proportionately more heavily than lower income stockholders do in corporations that save a higher than average proportion of their earnings. But this is not a conclusion to be pressed strongly. The chain of argument is not complete; some links are missing. In particular, the transition from corporation asset size to stockholder income classes is a rather rough and ready procedure. Moreover, data for one state in one year are obviously not a valid basis for generalization.[60] The data are too tangential to the problem at hand and generally too imperfect to sanction a firm conclusion that, in fact, personal income tax relief via the route of retained earnings is not sought to a greater relative extent by stockholders in the higher income classes.

[60] Indicative of the need for caution in interpreting these data is the following information supplied by Atkinson:

"Finally I did some investigating on the reason that the per cent return on closely-held stocks behaves in an opposite manner than your thesis would require. I broke the tabulation down into holdings of stocks in corporations from which the holder also received wages, and stocks in corporations from which they did not. No luck there. The ratios continued to rise for each type of holding. However, the proportion of low yielding bank stock out of the total closely held stocks owned by each income group falls as income rises which may account for some of it. Similarly, the holdings of stock in personal holding companies rise percentage-wise as income increases and these stocks have an extremely large rate of return when computed on book value basis as the underlying assets, real estate and stocks for the most part, are carried on the books, for the most part, at purchase price. For instance, the Able Company is a holding company whose principal assets consist of Baker Company stock. The Baker stock must have been valued at the original cost for Able paid out almost as much in dividends as its total book value in 1949. Thus, even if the operating company retained a high percentage of earnings, the per cent return on the book value of the holding company would be very high.

"These factors may account for some of the reasons that the ratios rise. However, I think the more important reasons have to do with the character of the closely held corporations the stock of which is held by people in different income groups. Low income groups hold closely held stock of banks, retail and wholesale concerns and service concerns, all of which are small businesses which have extremely low earnings after payment of the wages of the manager who is probably also the principal stockholder. Their earnings would be much smaller both absolutely and relative to book value than some larger closely held corporations. Furthermore, undoubtedly the larger closely held corporations are owned somewhat more widely, i.e., outside of management and family circles, and there is a pressure to distribute dividends to the outsiders, perhaps due to mistrust, and also due to the inability in many cases for capital gains to be taken by the outsiders because of lack of market or a market composed only of 'insiders.' Finally, perhaps unions will accept a six per cent return on investment more easily than high salaries to management in their bargaining considerations." Letter from Thomas R. Atkinson, February 25, 1951. Able and Baker are substituted for the names of specific companies in this quotation.

A TEST DESIGNED TO MEASURE THE POSSIBLE EFFECT ON THE FINDINGS OF SAVING THROUGH RETAINED EARNINGS

Because information on the differential rate of individual saving via corporate reinvestment is fragmentary, because pressures toward minimizing personal surtaxes have become increasingly powerful in the last decade, and because of a widespread feeling that this applies particularly to higher income stockholders, it seemed desirable to undertake a test calculation on the assumption of a distribution of net corporate earnings reflecting this practice. This test, like those devised for the preceding alternatives, was made with data for 1947.

The possibility of preferential tax rates on realized capital gains, an important part of the argument, was used in setting up the alternative distribution. It was assumed that the degree to which stockholders at various income levels consciously sought retained earnings varied directly with the degree of tax saving achieved by obtaining an incremental dollar as long-term capital gain rather than as ordinary income. This of course is a rather mechanical view of human nature, particularly when applied to something as complex as the motives that surround stock ownership. Nonetheless it serves to focus directly on the point whose effects, if any, the test is designed to isolate.

Nontaxable dividend recipients, having the same marginal rate on their capital gains and dividend receipts, were assigned a benchmark weight of one. For all taxable persons, on the other hand, there was a difference between the marginal rates, a difference that always ran in favor of long-term capital gains, but varied in relative strength, growing stronger the higher the taxpayer's income level. For example, as in Table 16, for the class with taxable incomes ranging between $0 and under $10,000, the marginal rates on capital gains were on average only half the rates on dividends, a proportion expressed by the multiplier of 2 assigned to this class; for the income class $100,000 and under $500,000, the capital gains marginal rates were on average just over three-tenths of the personal income tax marginal rates, a proportion expressed by the multiplier of 3.311. Such multipliers were developed for a number of broad income classes. (See Table 16.)

These multipliers were applied to the amount of retained earnings after taxes as computed by our standard method. But, of course, the total retained earnings obtained by this method greatly exceeded the actual amount of retained earnings. The new values were reduced proportionately to bring them into line with the actual totals. This set of figures takes into account the postulated tendency for stockholders at the higher income levels to hold stock in corporations that retain a higher than average proportion of their earnings. With the

TABLE 16

Multipliers Used for Alternative D

TAXABLE INCOME CLASS ($000's) (1)	Ratio of marginal capital gain rate to marginal personal rate (2)	Multiplier [reciprocal of (2)] (3)
0 and under 10	0.500	2.000
10 and under 25	0.473a	2.114
25 and under 50	0.406b	2.463
50 and under 100	0.334c	2.994
100 and under 500	0.302d	3.311
500 and under 1,000	0.295e	3.390
1,000 and over	0.289f	3.460

Source: For data, column 2, Lawrence H. Seltzer, *The Nature and Tax Treatment of Capital Gains and Losses*, National Bureau of Economic Research, 1951, p. 525.

a Average of rates applying at $10,000 and $25,000.
b Average of rates applying at $25,000 and $50,000.
c Average of rates applying at $50,000 and $100,000.
d Rate applicable to $100,000 (little variation between $100,000 and $1,000,000).
e Average of rates applicable at $100,000 and $1,000,000.
f Rate applicable to $1,000,000.

total of corporate earnings given, these figures mirror also the assumption that stockholders in the lower income classes receive dividends from corporations that retain a lower than average proportion of their earnings.

For 1947, the standard method implied for every income class a ratio of retained earnings after taxes to dividends of 1.86. For alternative D, after adjustment, the ratio varies with income class, as shown in Table 17. With these ratios, the next step was to impute new

TABLE 17

Ratio of Retained Income after Taxes to Dividends under Alternative D, by Taxable Income Classes, 1947

TAXABLE INCOME CLASS ($000's)	Ratio of retained income after taxes to dividends
0 and under 10	1.52
10 and under 25	1.61
25 and under 50	1.87
50 and under 100	2.27
100 and under 500	2.52
500 and under 1,000	2.58
1,000 and over	2.63
Average	1.86

Note: There is nothing peculiar about the fact that all but two classes in the table show a ratio above average, because the nontaxable and the taxable under $25,000 classes together account for a high proportion of total dividends.

amounts of corporate earnings and corporate income tax liability to each stockholder dividend-income size cell used in the standard method. What did all this computational maneuvering achieve? In our standard method, at all levels of imputed gross income, the ratio of dividends to corporate earnings net of corporation income tax stood at 0.349. Under alternative D the distribution ratio varies all along the line, tending to fall as stockholder income rises. (See Table 18.)

TABLE 18

Distribution Ratios under Alternative D, 1947

AVERAGE STOCKHOLDER IMPUTED GROSS INCOME ($000's)	Distribution ratios
1	0.399
2	0.396
3	0.397
4	0.396
5	0.397
6	0.396
8	0.396
10	0.395
12	0.393
15	0.393
20	0.389
25	0.386
50	0.373
75	0.363
100	0.350
150	0.332
200	0.318
250	0.312
500	0.293

CONCLUSION

With the rearrayed data, by procedures previously described in connection with the standard method, values of the differentials against earnings for distribution, earnings for retention, net corporate earnings and stockholders' income were calculated. The results (variant 2 only) are presented in Table 19.

These data suggest that, in all likelihood, the findings of our standard method are substantially correct, even if it should turn out that there is a consistent tendency (its strength correlated with the degree of tax saving involved in converting a dollar of income into a dollar of long-term capital gain) for the higher income taxpayers so to arrange their stockholdings that a higher than overall average

TABLE 19

Comparison of Differentials under Standard Method and Alternative D, 19
(per cent)

AVERAGE STOCKHOLDER IMPUTED GROSS INCOME ($000's)	DIFFERENTIAL AGAINST NET CORPORATE EARNINGS			DIFFERENTIAL AGAINST STOCKHOLDER INCOME		
	Standard method (1)	Alternative D (2)	(2) — (1) (3)	Standard method (4)	Alternative D (5)	(5) — (4 (6)
1	24.6	24.5	—0.1	5.9	5.4	—0.5
3	23.8	24.1	0.3	4.8	4.5	—0.3
5	22.5	23.0	0.5	5.2	5.5	0.3
10	17.7	18.4	0.7	6.0	6.5	0.5
25	2.0	2.4	0.4	1.0	1.2	0.2
50	—7.6	—7.0	0.6	—4.8	—4.3	0.5
100	—16.2	—16.1	0.1	—11.9	—11.8	0.1
250	—24.5	—26.1	—1.6	—19.4	—20.8	—1.4
500	—25.7	—28.5	—2.8	—22.7	—25.1	—2.4

proportion of the earnings made on their behalf is retained in the corporate till.

Alternative E—Imputing Only Earnings for Distribution

Up to this point, the imputed gross income of stockholders used in the study has included all of net corporate earnings—distributed as dividends, paid out as taxes, and retained by corporations—on the premise that this is what they could have had as part of their personal income if there had been no corporate tax, and if corporations had distributed all of their earnings. This appears to be the most reasonable concept as a basis for analysis of the differential taxation of stockholders. However, some recent policy proposals have been primarily concerned with the distributed segment, and some students have suggested that the problem be analyzed on this basis.

President Eisenhower proposed, in his Budget Message to Congress for the fiscal year 1955, that relief from the "double taxation of dividends" be granted stockholders. The relief provisions finally incorporated in the Internal Revenue Code of 1954 called for an exclusion from taxable income of the first $50 ($100 for joint returns) of dividends from domestic corporations, and a personal income tax credit of 4 per cent of all dividend receipts in excess of the excluded amount.[61] This tax relief applies solely to the distributed portion of

[61] *Internal Revenue Code of 1954*, Public Law 591, H.R. 8300, 83d Cong., 2d sess., August 16, 1954, Chap. 736, secs. 34 and 116. These relief provisions are analyzed in Chapter 7 of this study.

corporate earnings. Similarly, in criticizing a study of the 1948 tax burden by Richard Musgrave and three associates, Rufus S. Tucker stated that "there is no justification for allocating undistributed profits to the income of stockholders. They are not available to the stockholders, except to the extent that they may result in raising the market price of the stock. They usually have only a slight influence on the market price, and even if that were not the case the stockholder could only realize them by selling, and his profit from such sales is generally not regarded as income, either by accountants or economists or statisticians, but as capital gains. Even tax authorities do not regard unrealized capital gains as income."[62]

For reasons given earlier, the view appears justified that the full answer to the question of the differential heaviness of the tax load on stockholders should run in relative terms, i.e., relative to how heavy their tax load would have been under the personal income tax. This can be assessed only if stockholders' potential personal income levels are ascertained, and for this, imputation of undistributed earnings is necessary.

But, at this point in our examination of the effects of alternatives of the standard method on the results, it appeared desirable to provide the reader with some information on what the picture would look like if the comparison were to deal only with distributed earnings (and the corporate taxes allocable to them). For this purpose, alternative E has been developed. For it earnings for distribution serve as the measure of personal income from corporate activity. Therefore to stockholders' income is imputed the excess of what corporations had to earn before corporation income tax over dividends received by stockholders, i.e. the corporate tax liability on earnings for distribution.[63] This same figure is, of course, included in their tax liability also. The rearrayed stockholder incomes are then processed as under the standard method. Alternative E gives two differentials, one against net corporate earnings (equal to earnings for distribution) and the other against stockholders. The assumptions and methods embodied in alternative E lead to results substantially different from those produced by the assumptions

[62] Rufus S. Tucker, "Distribution of Tax Burdens in 1948," *National Tax Journal*, September 1951, p. 277.

[63] As before, let E equal the earnings made for distribution, D the dividends paid out, and C_e the effective rate of corporate tax (as a fraction), then

$$E - C_e E = D \quad \text{or}$$
$$E = \frac{D}{1 - C_e}$$

and the difference between E and D is equal to $C_e E$.

of the standard method. A comparison of the results under the two methods is found in Table 20.

TABLE 20

Comparison of Differentials under Standard Method and Alternative E, 1947

(*per cent*)

AVERAGE STOCKHOLDER IMPUTED GROSS INCOME ($000's)	DIFFERENTIAL AGAINST NET CORPORATE EARNINGS			DIFFERENTIAL AGAINST STOCKHOLDER INCOME		
	Standard method (1)	*Alternative* E (2)	(2) — (1) (3)	*Standard method* (4)	*Alternative* E (5)	(5) — (4) (6)
1	24.6	27.9	3.3	5.9	7.3	1.4
3	23.8	27.9	4.1	4.8	4.9	0.1
5	22.5	27.3	4.8	5.2	4.2	—1.0
10	17.7	24.7	7.0	6.0	5.2	—0.8
25	2.0	16.4	14.4	1.0	4.2	3.2
50	—7.6	11.9	19.5	—4.8	3.6	8.4
100	—16.2	7.9	24.1	—11.9	3.5	15.4
250	—24.5	5.0	29.5	—19.4	2.7	22.1
500	—25.7	4.7	30.4	—22.7	2.2	24.9

Differentials against the net corporate earnings component are higher under alternative E at all levels of stockholder income. (Remember, this comparison is undertaken for stockholders with incomes of similar size but different definition.) As a corollary, for alternative E there is no cross-over, even at the peak incomes, from extra burden to benefit. For the differential against stockholders a somewhat different result makes the extra burden, compared with that of the standard method, about the same at the lower income levels, and considerably more severe at the upper income levels. The result over the lower portion of the income range occurs because, while the differential against net corporate earnings is higher under alternative E, net corporate earnings comprise a much smaller proportion of stockholders' total income under the definition used in this alternative than in our standard method. We can conclude that if it is deemed more "sensible," in analyzing the differential tax burden on stockholders, to consider only that portion of net corporate earnings distributed to stockholders then our standard method involves an understatement of the differentials against net corporate earnings over the whole income range, and of the differentials against stockholders at the higher income levels.

Alternative F—Imputing Only a Fraction of Retained Earnings

In Chapter 2, in estimating the future increase in capital gains tax liability due to retained earnings imputed to each average stockholder income, it was assumed (according to variant 2 which is the standard method) that stock prices mirror only 72 per cent of the earnings retained by corporations. In imputing to stockholders their proportionate share of retained earnings, however, the full value—100 per cent—was considered appropriate for the problem at hand. Because some readers may feel that the proportionate share of retained earnings credited to stockholders should be no more than the change in the value set on their assets by the market, alternative F has been developed. The adjustment incorporated in this alternative is simple and direct: only 72 per cent of stockholders' pro rata share of total retained earnings is imputed to them.[64] Stockholders' corporate earnings and total income are lower than under the usual procedure, but their tax liability is unchanged.[65] It follows, therefore, that the alternative F differentials would be larger than those derived by our usual procedure. That these differences are not very important, however, can be seen from an examination of the data of Table 21.

TABLE 21

Comparison of Differentials under Standard Method and Alternative F, 1947
(per cent)

AVERAGE STOCKHOLDER IMPUTED GROSS INCOME ($000's)	DIFFERENTIAL AGAINST NET CORPORATE EARNINGS			DIFFERENTIAL AGAINST STOCKHOLDER INCOME		
	Standard method (1)	Alternative F (2)	(2) — (1) (3)	Standard method (4)	Alternative F (5)	(5) — (4) (6)
1	24.6	27.7	3.1	5.9	6.0	0.1
3	23.8	27.7	3.9	4.8	5.3	0.5
5	22.5	26.3	2.8	5.2	6.3	1.1
10	17.7	21.5	3.8	6.0	7.7	1.7
25	2.0	5.1	3.1	1.0	2.4	1.4
50	—7.6	—4.5	3.1	—4.8	—2.8	2.0
100	—16.2	—13.8	2.4	—11.9	—9.8	2.1
250	—24.5	—21.8	2.7	—19.4	—17.1	2.3
500	—25.7	—22.8	2.9	—22.7	—20.3	2.4

The alternative F differentials against net corporate earnings exceed those of our standard method by between 2.5 and 4 points, lying close to the upper value at the lower income levels, and nearer 2.5 at the

[64] In a sense, alternative F is another way of allowing for the same considerations that suggested variant 3 of our standard method, in which the 28 per cent attrition is treated as an additional tax and stockholder income is unchanged.

[65] The adjustment here is not precise. In view of the time required for retained earnings to be reflected in stock prices, the present value of this component is somewhat less than 72 per cent of reinvested earnings.

top of the income range. The familiar pattern of decline in severity as stockholder income rises and, after a point, a turn in favor of net corporate earnings persists under alternative F. The cross-over point is higher, however—$38,000 compared with $30,000 for the standard method. The differential against stockholders is also slightly higher as measured under alternative F than by our usual method. The difference between them is almost imperceptible at the lower incomes, but it rises with stockholder income, reaching a peak of 2.4 percentage points at the top of the income range. The growing divergence between the differentials of alternative F and the standard method is explained by the increase in the proportion of corporate earnings as stockholder income rises.

Those who prefer as more appropriate inclusion of a fraction rather than the whole of retained corporate earnings in the income of stockholders will conclude that the standard procedure overstates the differentials against net corporate earnings and stockholders. But if imputing 72 per cent is judged to be reasonable, the overstatement is quite small. While the specific findings of this test rest, of course, on the data for 1947, the general conclusions they suggest hold for the other years in our period. Moreover, in these other years, the overstatement would be even smaller because in 1947 retentions represented a higher proportion of corporate earnings than in any other year covered by the study.

Alternative G—Correction for Underreporting of Dividends

One step in the standard method is imputation to stockholders of their full pro rata share of corporate earnings (before tax) on the basis of their dividend receipts as reported on their personal income tax returns. But there is evidence suggesting that dividends have not been fully reported for this purpose.[66] (While this is true of other types of income also our concern here is with dividends.) For example, for 1952 there was an estimated gap of about $1.1 billion between the dividends paid out to individuals and total dividends reported on personal income tax returns.[67] The data do not permit a precise statement, but, undoubtedly some of this gap, perhaps a very high fraction, can be attributed to purposeful underreporting. Thus, the Treasury has estimated for 1950 that if dividends "not accounted for" on personal income tax returns (about $1 billion) were reached by a

---

[66] *Audit Control Program: A Summary of Preliminary Results*; Goldsmith, *op. cit.*; Holland and Kahn, *op. cit.*; Revenue Revisions of 1950, Hearings on H.R. 8920 before the Senate Committee on Finance, 81st Cong., 2d sess., pp. 15-19.

[67] Holland and Kahn, *op. cit.*, pp. 320 and 336.

withholding tax an increase in revenue of $150 million would have resulted.[68] That stockholders have failed to report all their dividends under the personal income tax is clear. The Audit Control Program obtained data suggesting that the degree of underreporting varies among income classes, generally tending to decline in relative importance as stockholder incomes rise. Unfortunately the full statistical substantiation for this statement, based upon unpublished material examined by the author, cannot be set forth here.

In brief summary this was the procedure: The data consisted of the amount of tax change disclosed by audit on returns with major errors in dividends and minor errors in dividends so classified that they could be arranged in four broad adjusted gross income classes—under $7,000,[69] $7,000 and under $25,000, $25,000 and under $100,000, and $100,000 and over. By assuming all of the tax change disclosed by audit on returns with major dividend errors and half of the tax change on returns with minor errors to be due to dividend underreporting, and applying the average marginal rates prevailing in each of these four broad income classes (different rates for separate and joint returns), an estimate was obtained of the amount of unreported dividends.[70] Underreporting showed a general tendency to decline in relative importance as stockholder income increased.

Estimated Underreporting, 1948

Adjusted gross income class ($000's)	Unreported dividends as a per cent of all dividends
Under 7	6.0
7 and under 25	7.9
25 and under 100	2.2
100 and over	0.6
Total	4.4

[68] Revenue Revisions of 1950, op. cit., p. 19.

[69] This class includes returns with up to $25,000 of gross receipts from business or profession.

[70] The criteria for placing a return in the major error in dividends category were: the error was responsible for the largest portion of the change in adjusted gross income; the change in adjusted gross income, in turn, was responsible for a larger part of the tax change than that due either to exemptions, personal deductions, or arithmetical error. The estimate of the amount of unreported dividends in our test is too high because it is likely that less than the assumed 100 per cent (for major dividend errors) and 50 per cent (for minor errors in dividends) of the tax change were due to the dividend errors. It seemed appropriate, in view of the illustrative nature of the figures, to make these extreme assumptions which provided the maximum possible value for the factor the effect of which the test incorporated in alternative G was designed to isolate.

Finally, on the assumption that these same ratios applied in 1947, they were used to "correct" the imputation ratios employed in the various dividend-size income class cells. Whereas our standard method used a single imputation ratio of net corporate earnings to dividends, 4.56, for all income classes, the alternative G ratio varied as follows:

Adjusted gross income class ($000's)	Imputation ratio— net corporate earnings to dividends
Under 7	4.85
7 and under 25	4.94
25 and under 100	4.66
100 and over	4.58

Application of these ratios furnished the corporate earnings and imputed gross income that would have been obtained if stockholders had been more "truthful" or more accurate in remembering or recording their dividends reported.

The previously noted lack of precision in this test stems also from the unknown degree of success attained by the Audit Control Survey in digging up unreported dividends,[71] and from the whole string of assumptions made. But the adjustment under alternative G has illustrative value. What does it show?

RESULTS OF TEST OF ALTERNATIVE G

Had the data used incorporated "fuller" reporting of dividends, the findings would have been virtually the same as those drawn from the standard method (see Table 22). In general under alternative G the differentials are slightly higher at the lower income levels; the degree of tax saving slightly greater at the top of the range.

[71] Very rough calculations indicate quite a gap between the total underreporting estimated from the Audit Control data and that suggested by the other studies cited in footnote 66.

TABLE 22

Comparison of Differentials under Standard Method and Alternative G, 1947
(per cent)

AVERAGE STOCKHOLDER IMPUTED GROSS INCOME ($000's)	DIFFERENTIAL AGAINST NET CORPORATE EARNINGS			DIFFERENTIAL AGAINST STOCKHOLDER INCOME		
	Standard method (1)	Alternative G (2)	(2) — (1) (3)	Standard method (4)	Alternative G (5)	(5) — (4) (6)
1	24.6	23.6	—1.0	5.9	6.0	0.1
3	23.8	24.0	0.2	4.8	4.8	0.0
5	22.5	22.4	—0.1	5.2	5.9	0.7
10	17.7	17.9	0.2	6.0	6.7	0.7
25	2.0	2.1	0.1	1.0	1.1	0.1
50	—7.6	—7.4	0.2	—4.8	—4.8	0.0
100	—16.2	—16.3	—0.1	—11.9	—12.1	—0.2
250	—24.5	—25.4	—0.9	—19.4	—20.1	—0.7
500	—25.7	—26.6	—0.9	—22.7	—23.6	—0.9

CHAPTER 5

The Taxation of Corporate Earnings and Progressivity

IT is sometimes argued that, whatever its merits or demerits on other grounds, the corporation income tax does add to the progressivity of our tax system. Starting "from the two propositions: (1) the tax is proportional to corporation income, and (2) a larger proportion of the income of individuals in the higher-income classes is corporation income paid to or accruing to them as shareholders than is the case in the income of poorer individuals," the National Industrial Conference Board reached the conclusion that to "the extent that it is not shifted, the burden of the federal corporation income tax, considered by itself, is what is technically known as 'progressive'—the tax constitutes a heavier burden in proportion to total income upon individuals in the higher-income classes than upon individuals in the lower income classes."[1] Among similar views expressed more recently is: "Another consideration with respect to a tax on corporate income, even if it is deemed as a tax on the shareholders, is that such a tax serves to burden the unearned income, as compared with earned income, and to increase the progressiveness of the individual income tax."[2]

These contentions, even if valid (and cause for disagreement will be set forth below), are subject to the obvious qualification that this effect, i.e. increased progressivity, applies only to stockholders. Therefore an inequality is injected into our tax system; since all taxpayers at any given income level are not stockholders, individuals with incomes of the same size (but different composition) are subject to different rates of tax. Much the same consideration is relevant when we limit the analysis to stockholders, for not all stockholders at a given income level receive the same proportion of their income from corporation earnings.

Two approaches used in the preceding chapters in the examination of the differential taxation of stockholders are particularly pertinent to the alleged progressivity effect of the corporation income tax: the findings in connection with the net corporate tax; and evidence assembled under the heading of the differential against stockholders. The first approach will be employed to determine the progressivity effect of the corporation income tax per se. The latter approach con-

[1] *The Shifting and Effects of the Federal Corporation Income Tax*, National Industrial Conference Board, Vol. II, 1928, p. 102.

[2] From Congress of Industrial Organization memorandum, *A Federal Tax Program to Promote Full Employment*, reprinted in *Revenue Revision of 1950*, Hearings before the House Committee on Ways and Means, 81st Cong., 2d sess., Vol. I, *Excise Taxes*, 1950, p. 762.

siders the effect on progressivity of the existing method of taxing stockholders during the period of our study, by analyzing the effect of both the net corporate tax and the personal income tax saving due to the failure of corporations to distribute all of their earnings.

More specifically, this chapter will examine the question of progressivity effect on two bases.

(1) First, the effect of the corporation income tax alone will be discussed, using the net corporate tax, which is the excess of the corporation income tax on earnings for distribution and earnings for retention over the personal income tax that would have been due had these corporation income tax payments been part of the taxable income of stockholders. It is a measure of the net effect of the corporation income tax alone. This may be considered the narrow definition of the problem, for it fails to take account of corporate distribution policy—more specifically, it fails to take account of the fact that retained earnings (after corporation income tax) escape personal income taxes currently, and, at best, this is made up only partially via future capital gains taxation.

(2) Secondly, the progressivity effects are also considered from a broader perspective that takes account of both the net corporate tax and the personal income tax saving. The excess of the former over the latter is the differential against stockholders.

THE NET CORPORATE TAX AND PROGRESSIVITY

The community's consensus as to the desirable degree of progressivity in our income tax structure is presumably mirrored by the personal income tax schedule. This is taken as the standard or benchmark against which the progressivity effect of the net corporate tax is measured. The comparisons are confined to "average" stockholders, overlooking the complications, noted above, actually introduced by the varying proportions of corporate earnings included in individual incomes. Limiting the examination of progressivity effects to stockholders is consistent with the previously described incidence assumption by which they alone are considered to be affected by the corporation income tax.[3]

The term "progression" is here employed in its usual sense to denote an increase or decrease in the rate of tax relatively greater than the increase or decrease in the size of the base on which the tax is assessed. Various measures of the degree of progressivity, each of which has

[3] Goode makes a similar computation, but for distributed earnings only, and expresses the results in terms of the income of all taxpayers not merely stockholders (Richard B. Goode, *The Corporate Income Tax*, Wiley, 1951, pp. 93-94).

its own peculiarities, are consistent with this general concept, and different indications as to changes in progressivity may be obtained according to the formula adopted. For this reason two measures have been used.[4]

1) *Average rate progression,* which is based on the rate of change of the effective rate of tax and is defined as

$$\frac{(T_1/Y_1) - (T_0/Y_0)}{Y_1 - Y_0}$$

where T stands for tax liability and Y for income, and the subscripts *1* and *0* denote adjacent income levels. Average rate progression remains unchanged if a rate schedule is raised or lowered the same number of percentage points at all levels of taxable income.[5]

2) *Liability progression* which is "the ratio of the percentage change in tax liability to the concurrent change in income."[6] It is defined as

$$\frac{T_1 - T_0}{T_0} \cdot \frac{Y_0}{Y_1 - Y_0}$$

The coefficient of liability progression remains unchanged if the rates of a given schedule are raised or lowered proportionately.[7]

[4] The measures and the methods used in their computation are taken from R. A. Musgrave and Tun Thin, "Income Tax Progression, 1929-48," *Journal of Political Economy,* December 1948, pp. 498-514.

[5] Write T_0/Y_0 as E_0 (E standing for effective rate) and T_1/Y_1 as E_1. Then the formula for average rate progression becomes $(E_1 - E_0)/(Y_1 - Y_0)$. Let there be an increase of a given number of percentage points in effective rate, say K. Then average rate progression will equal $[E_1 + K - (E_0 + K)]/(Y_1 - Y_0)$. But this, of course, is the same as $(E_1 - E_0)/(Y_1 - Y_0)$. Therefore, if one effective rate schedule exceeds another by the same number of percentage points they are, in terms of this measure, equally progressive. Thus a comparison of progressivity based on average rate progression is relatively simple. A constant ratio of net corporate tax to imputed gross income signifies that the personal and the combined corporate-personal income taxes were equally progressive; a falling ratio differential, moving up the income scale, is an indication that the corporate-personal tax system was less progressive, while the converse conclusion follows from a rising net corporate tax ratio (*ibid.,* p. 501).

[6] *Ibid.,* p. 504.

[7] In any comparison of two schedules at a given income level or over a given range $Y_0/(Y_1 - Y_0)$ will be unchanged, so it is necessary only to watch what happens to $(T_1 - T_0)/T_0$. Let the tax due at each income level be raised by a fixed percentage K. Then $(T_1 - T_0)/T_0$ is replaced by $(KT_1 - KT_0)/KT_0$. But this is the same as $(T_1 - T_0)/T_0$. Thus a proportionate change in tax liability (and hence tax rate) associated with a given income level leaves the degree of liability progression unchanged (see *ibid.,* p. 505). This facilitates comparison of the progressivity of two rate schedules under this definition. When the net corporate tax rate, reading up the income scale, represents a continually growing percentage increase in the effective rate of tax, liability progression has increased. The opposite result connotes a decrease in progressivity, while a constant proportionate increase in effective tax rates signifies an equal degree of progressivity.

The findings on average rate progression are summarized in Table 23, those on liability progression in Table 24. The $+$ sign means that, because of the net corporate tax, stockholders were taxed more progressively than they would have been under the personal income tax; the $-$ sign indicates the reverse result, and the $=$ sign denotes equal progressivity for the two systems.[8]

TABLE 23

Summary of the Progressivity Effect of the Net Corporate Tax, 1940-1941; 1944-1952

AVERAGE RATE PROGRESSION

IMPUTED GROSS INCOME RANGE ($00's)	1940	1941	1944	1945	1946	1947	1948	1949	1950	1951	1952
-2				+	+	−		+	+		+
-3	−	+	+	+	−	−	−	−	+	+	+
-4	−	+	+	−	+	+	+	−	−	−	−
-5	+	+	+	+	+	+	+	+	+	−	−
-6	−	+	+	+	+	+	+	+	−	−	−
-8	+	=	+	+	+	+	+	+	+	+	+
-10	+	−	−	+	+	−	+	+	+	+	+
-12	−	−	−	−	=	+	−	+	+	+	−
-15	+	−	−	−	−	−	+	+	+	+	−
-20	+	+	−	−	−	−	+	+	+	+	+
-25	−	=	−	−	−	−	+	+	+	+	−
-50	−	−	−	−	−	−	=	+	+	−	−
-75	+	+	−	−	−	−	=	−	−	−	−
-100	−	−	−	−	−	−	−	−	−	−	−
-150	−	−	−	−	−	−	−	−	−	−	−
-200	−	−	−	−	−	−	−	−	−	−	−
-250	−	=	−	−	−	−	−	−	−	−	−
-500	+	−	−	−	+	=	−	−	−	−	−

$+$) means that, because of the net corporate tax, stockholders were taxed more progressively than they would have been under the personal income tax.

$-$) means the reverse finding.

$=$) means equal progressivity for the two systems.

[8] These two measures of progressivity did not correspond at all points, and the results, therefore, are not precisely comparable. But they serve for the rough purpose at hand. Much laborious computation was saved by using a slightly different base for each of the measures. The change in average rate progressivity was measured by computing the excess of the actually effective rate for stockholders over the potential rate if their full pro rata share of corporate income tax payments had been paid to them as personal income. With liability progression, the net corporate tax was computed as a proportion of the effective rate of personal income tax on adjusted gross incomes of the same size as the selected imputed gross income levels. This comparison is not strictly confined to stockholders, the adjusted gross income

TABLE 24

Summary of the Progressivity Effect of the Net Corporate Tax, 1940-1941; 1944-1952

LIABILITY PROGRESSION

IMPUTED GROSS INCOME RANGE ($000's)	1940	1941	1944	1945	1946	1947	1948	1949	1950	1951	1952
1-2						−	−	−		+	−
2-3	−	−	−	−	−	−	−	−	+	−	−
3-4	−	−	−	−	+	−	−	−	−	−	−
4-5	+	−	+	−	−	−	−	−	−	−	−
5-6	−	−	−	−	+	+	−	−	−	−	−
6-8	−	−	+	−	−	−	+	+	+	+	+
8-10	−	−	−	−	−	−	−	−	−	−	−
10-12	−	−	−	−	−	−	−	−	−	−	−
12-15	+	−	−	−	−	−	+	−	−	−	−
15-20	−	−	−	−	−	−	−	−	−	−	−
20-25	−	−	−	−	−	−	−	−	−	−	−
25-50	−	−	−	−	−	−	−	−	−	−	−
50-75	+	−	−	−	−	−	−	−	−	−	−
75-100	−	−	−	−	−	−	−	−	−	−	−
100-150	−	−	−	−	−	−	−	−	−	−	−
150-200	−	−	−	−	−	−	−	−	−	−	−
200-250	−	−	−	−	−	−	−	−	−	−	−
250-500	+	−	−	−	−	−	−	−	−	−	−

(+) means that, because of the net corporate tax, stockholders were taxed more progressive than they would have been under the personal income tax.
(−) means the reverse finding.
(=) means equal progressivity for the two systems.

The effect of the corporate income tax on the degree of progressivity applying to the taxation of stockholders is clearly uneven. If one particular definition—average rate progression—is adopted, the general conclusion is that stockholders were taxed more progressively than other income taxpayers similarly circumstanced in terms of the size of their income, up to about the $12,000 income level, in the earlier years of the decade, and to the $50,000 level from 1948 through 1952; taxation was less progressive over the rest of the income range. Under

---

levels being derived from averages for all taxpayers. The adjusted gross incomes are of different compositions, and, because they include different proportions of capital gains, are subject to somewhat different rates from those implied in the average rate progressivity computation. But this difference in base is a relatively minor factor that tends to be submerged by the much more pronounced force exercised by the net corporate tax in the final results. The findings on progressivity are, therefore, both comparable and, for the purpose at hand, informative.

the second definition—liability progression—we find a less equivocal picture. Here, almost without exception, it appears that stockholders were taxed less progressively than other taxpayers with a similar amount of income subject only to the personal income tax.

PROGRESSIVITY EFFECT TAKING ACCOUNT OF THE INCOME TAX SAVING

These conclusions hold when the income tax saving is also taken into account. For this test, the three variants of the differential against stockholders (see Chapter 1) are utilized. To recapitulate: this differential is equal to the difference between (i.e. the algebraic sum of) the net corporate tax and the net income tax saving. The results tabulated in Tables 25 and 26 indicate the effects on progressivity in the taxation of stockholders caused by the two income taxes on stockholders compared with the hypothetical effects of the personal income tax on their full pro rata share of corporate earnings.

As in the case of the net corporate tax, we find under the average rate progression definition an uneven effect; an irregular increase in progressivity over the lower portion of the income range and, above a certain point, lower progressivity than under the personal income tax. Under the liability progression definition, the indications are that over almost the whole of the income range stockholders were taxed less progressively by the combined corporate-personal income tax system than they would have been by the personal income tax alone.

Average rate and liability progression can be measured only as between specified ranges of income, and these values vary over the income scale. It has been suggested that progressivity could be measured also (and perhaps more meaningfully) in terms of a single value for the entire income distribution. In this connection, Musgrave and Thin have developed a definition—effective progression—based on the degree to which the area between the line of "complete equality" and the Lorenz curve derived from a particular distribution is reduced by taxation.[9] This measure has been investigated specifically for four years—1947, 1949, 1950, and 1952 (see Chapter 6). In brief summary, the findings for all years were that, if stockholders had been taxed in full on their pro rata share of corporate earnings, the after-tax distribution of stockholder income would have bent away less from the line of "complete equality" than it did for the distribution which took account of the corporate tax on all earnings and the personal tax on the distributed portion. In other words, in terms of effective pro-

[9] *Ibid.*, p. 510.

TABLE 25

Progressivity of the Corporate-Personal Income Tax on Stockholders Compared with the Progressivity of the Personal Income Tax, 1940-1941; 1944-1952

AVERAGE RATE PROGRESSION

IMPUTED GROSS INCOME RANGE ($000's)	1940	1941	1944	1945	1946	1947	1948	1949	1950	1951	1952
					Variant 1						
1-2				+	+	−		+	+	=	+
2-3	−	+	+	+	−	−	−	−	+	=	+
3-4	−	=	+	−	+	+	+	−	−	−	−
4-5	+	+	+	+	−	−	+	+	=	−	=
5-6	−	+	+	+	+	+	−	+	+	+	+
6-8	+	−	+	+	−	−	+	+	+	+	+
8-10	+	−	−	−	−	−	+	+	+	=	−
10-12	−	−	−	−	−	−	+	=	+	=	−
12-15	+	−	−	−	−	−	=	−	−	−	−
15-20	+	−	−	−	−	−	−	−	−	+	+
20-25	−	−	−	−	−	−	−	−	−	+	+
25-500a	−b	−	−	−	−	−	−	−	−	−	−
					Variant 2						
1-2				+	=	−		+	+	+	+
2-3	−	+	+	+	−	−	−	−	+	+	+
3-4	−	=	+	−	+	+	+	−	−	−	−
4-5	+	+	+	+	−	−	+	+	+	−	−
5-6	−	+	+	+	+	+	+	+	=	−	=
6-8	+	−	+	+	−	−	+	+	+	+	+
8-10	+	=	−	−	−	−	+	+	+	=	−
10-12	−	−	−	−	−	−	+	−	+	=	−
12-15	+	−	−	−	−	−	+	−	−	−	−
15-20	+	−	−	−	−	−	−	=	+	+	+
20-25	−	−	−	−	−	−	−	−	−	+	+
25-500a	−b	−	−	−	−	−	−	−	−	−	−
					Variant 3						
1-2				+	=	−		+	+	+	+
2-3	−	+	+	+	−	−	−	−	+	+	−
3-4	−	+	+	−	+	+	+	−	−	−	−
4-5	+	+	+	+	=	−	+	+	=	−	−
5-6	−	+	+	+	+	+	+	+	=	+	+
6-8	+	−	+	+	+	=	+	+	+	+	−
8-10	+	=	−	−	−	−	+	+	+	+	−
10-12	−	−	−	−	−	+	+	+	+	+	−
12-15	+	−	−	−	−	−	+	=	−	−	−
15-20	+	−	−	−	−	−	+	+	+	+	−
20-25	−	−	−	−	−	−	=	=	=	+	−
25-500a	−b	−	−	−	−	−c	−	−	−	−	−

(+) means that stockholders were taxed more progressively than they would have been under the personal income tax.

(−) means the reverse finding; (=) means equal progressivity for the two systems.

a (−) applies to each of the following income classes (thousands of dollars), for which separate calculations were made: 25 to 50; 50 to 75; 75 to 100; 100 to 150; 150 to 200; 200 to 250; 250 to 500.

b For 1940, the progressivity was + in the $50,000 and under $75,000 class.

c Under variant 3, in 1947, the progressivity was equal for the $150,000 to $200,000 class.

TABLE 26

Progressivity of the Corporate-Personal Income Tax on Stockholders Compared with the Progressivity of the Personal Income Tax, 1940-1941; 1944-1952

LIABILITY PROGRESSION

IMPUTED GROSS INCOME RANGE ($000's)	1940	1941	1944	1945	1946	1947	1948	1949	1950	1951	1952
Variant 1											
1-2					—	—	—		—	—	—
2-3	—	—	—	—	—	—	—	—	+	—	+
3-4	—	—	—	—	+	+	—	—	—	—	—
4-5	+	—	+	—	—	—	—	—	—	—	—
5-6	—	—	=	—	+	+	—	—	—	—	—
6-8	—	—	+	—	—	—	—	=	+	+	+
8-10	—	—	—	—	—	—	—	—	—	—	—
10-12	—	—	—	—	—	—	—	—	—	—	—
12-15	+	—	—	—	—	—	—	—	—	—	—
15-500a	—	—	—	—	—	—	—	—	—	—	—
Variant 2											
1-2					—	—	—		—	—	—
2-3	—	—	—	—	—	—	—	—	+	=	+
3-4	—	—	—	—	+	+	—	—	—	—	—
4-5	+	—	+	—	—	—	—	—	—	—	—
5-6	—	—	+	—	+	+	—	—	—	—	—
6-8	—	—	+	—	—	—	+	+	+	+	+
8-10	—	—	—	—	—	—	—	—	—	—	—
10-12	—	—	—	—	—	—	—	—	—	—	—
12-15	+	—	—	—	—	—	—	—	—	—	—
15-500a	—	—	—	—	—	—	—	—	—	—	—
Variant 3											
1-2					—	—	—		—	—	—
2-3	—	—	—	—	—	—	—	—	+	—	+
3-4	—	—	—	—	+	+	—	—	—	—	—
4-5	+	—	+	—	—	—	—	—	—	—	—
5-6	—	—	=	—	+	+	—	—	—	—	—
6-8	—	—	+	—	—	—	+	+	+	+	+
8-10	—	—	—	—	—	—	—	—	—	—	—
10-12	—	—	—	—	—	—	—	—	—	—	—
12-15	+	—	—	—	—	—	—	—	—	—	—
15-500a	—	—	—	—	—	—	—	—	—	—	—

(+) means that stockholders were taxed more progressively than they would have been under the personal income tax.

(—) means the reverse finding.

(=) means equal progressivity for the two systems.

a (—) applies to each of the following income classes (thousands of dollars), for which separate calculations were made: 15 to 20; 20 to 25; 25 to 50; 50 to 75; 75 to 100; 100 to 150; 150 to 200; 200 to 250; 250 to 500.

gression, the actual combination of corporate and personal tax led to less progressive taxation of stockholders than would have followed from the personal income tax alone.

ERRATIC IMPACT OF THE PROGRESSIVITY EFFECT

Finally, it will be instructive to return to a problem noted as a complication and temporarily set aside—the unevenness of the alleged progressivity effect of the corporation income tax due to the fact that stockholders with about the same total income have varying amounts of net corporate earnings.

From stockholder cells for 1947, the chosen sample year, entries were picked for individuals having almost identical levels of taxable income after full imputation of corporate earnings. But the corporate earnings component comprises different proportions of total taxable income; thus the combination of corporate tax on all earnings and of personal tax on dividends constitutes a varying incremental burden. How uneven and indiscriminate the progressivity effects actually are is demonstrated by the evidence in Table 27.

Among three stockholder cells, for example, for which the taxable income was about $1,850, the extra burden due to the corporate tax amounted in one cell to 3 per cent of income, in another to 9 per cent, and in a third to 28 per cent.[10] Reasons for the highly uneven effect on progressivity are suggested by the data in column 8: the extra burden of a 3 percentage point increase in effective rate of tax occurred in a stockholder cell in which corporate earnings represented only 12 per cent of taxable income; the extra burden of 9 percentage points characterized a cell in which 38 per cent of taxable income came from corporate earnings; while the 28 percentage point extra burden arose in a cell in which income was very heavily weighted with corporate earnings, about 115 per cent of taxable income. (This happens when income from sources other than corporate earnings is so small that it is outweighed by deductions.) The type of results found at this particular taxable income level was also observed at others (see Table 27).

This evidence warrants the conclusion that even if it were true at least over much of the income scale that, because of the corporation income tax, stockholders are taxed more progressively than other tax-

[10] These calculations are based on a comparison of the actual combined corporate-personal tax and an estimate of what would have been due under the personal tax both currently and in the future (from capital gains taxes on realized increments in stock prices due to reinvestment). They correspond, therefore, to our variant 2 measure described in Chapter 1 and discussed in Chapter 2.

payers, the progression is of a rude, uneven, and indiscriminate type. Of the 711,683 stockholders in the sample potentially subject to an effective rate of personal income tax between 19 and 20 per cent (see column 4), over three-fifths were actually taxed at between 20 and 25 per cent; one-quarter at between 25 and 30 per cent; one-tenth at between 30 and 35 per cent; 1.6 per cent at between 35 and 40 per cent; and almost 2 per cent at more than 45 per cent.

TABLE 27

Examples of Varying Effective Rates of Corporate-Personal Tax on Stockholders with Taxable Incomes of Substantially the Same Size, 1947

AVERAGE TAXABLE INCOME LEVEL OF STOCK-HOLDERS[a] (1)	Number of stockholders (2)	Potential personal income tax (3)	Effective rate of potential personal income tax (3) ÷ (1) (4)	Total estimated corporate-personal tax[b] (5)	Effective rate of corporate-personal tax (5) ÷ (1) (6)	Difference in effective rates (6) — (4) (7)	Corporate earnings as a per cent of taxable income (8)
$1,491	7,513	$283	19.0%	$ 685	45.9%	27.0	112
1,470	136,238	279	19.0	335	22.8	3.8	16
1,855	243,694	352	19.0	408	22.0	3.0	12
1,833	44,662	348	19.0	520	28.4	9.4	38
1,861	5,997	354	19.0	869	46.7	27.7	115
2,192	23,673	420	19.2	695	31.7	12.5	53
2,215	98,720	425	19.2	587	26.5	7.3	31
2,925	61,953	573	19.6	729	24.9	5.3	24
2,933	26,840	575	19.6	945	32.2	12.6	55
2,915	11,457	571	19.6	1,055	36.2	16.6	71
3,281	33,614	648	19.7	907	27.6	7.9	35
3,292	17,322	650	19.8	1,125	34.2	14.4	63
5,292	17,155	1,117	21.1	1,544	29.2	8.1	40
5,294	15,657	1,118	21.1	2,395	45.2	24.1	109

(continued on next page)

Table 27, concluded

AVERAGE TAXABLE INCOME LEVEL OF STOCK-HOLDERSᵃ (1)	Number of stockholders (2)	Potential personal income tax (3)	Effective rate of potential personal income tax (3) ÷ (1) (4)	Total estimated corporate-personal taxᵇ (5)	Effective rate of corporate-personal tax (5) ÷ (1) (6)	Difference in effective rates (6) — (4) (7)	Corporate earnings as a per cent of taxable income (8)
$ 8,894	1,580	$ 2,151	24.2%	$ 4,189	47.1%	22.9	117
8,862	36,957	2,140	24.2	2,728	30.8	6.6	40
13,623	21,047	3,893	28.6	4,033	29.6	1.0	12
13,658	5,290	3,907	28.6	5,759	42.2	13.6	94
18,560	21,770	6,172	33.2	6,610	35.6	2.4	43
18,476	8,035	6,130	33.2	8,515	46.1	12.9	112
33,864	20,578	14,888	43.9	15,488	45.7	1.8	105
33,378ᶜ	4,948	14,588	43.8	14,337	43.0	—0.8	17
74,160	25,953	43,215	58.3	35,954	48.5	—9.8	107
74,513ᶜ	589	43,487	58.4	40,364	54.2	—4.2	28
194,284ᶜ	3,218	144,092	74.1	107,320	55.2	—18.9	90
190,906ᶜ	548	141,204	74.0	124,771	65.4	—8.6	89

ᵃ Includes imputed pro rata share of net corporate earnings.
ᵇ Equals sum of personal income tax on taxable income from sources other than corporate earnings, plus personal income tax on dividends, plus corporate tax on pro rata share of net corporate earnings.
ᶜ Estimated returns with normal and surtax only.

CHAPTER 6

Differential Taxation of Stockholders in the Aggregate

TURNING from the average measures of the differentials that have occupied our attention up to this point, in this chapter we consider the aggregate amount of the "extra" burden on stockholders. For this purpose the relevant material is organized around three questions: What would be the effect on the revenue of the federal government were the "unequal" taxation of stockholders to be abolished by extension to them of the tax treatment accorded members of a partnership? What is the total extra burden (or benefit) of stockholders, and how is it distributed among income classes? Which method would have a more equalizing effect on the distribution of income—that method of taxing corporate earnings on the corporate level when earned and the personal level when distributed, or that involving the abolition of the corporate tax and the full taxation to stockholders of their pro rata share of corporate earnings as personal income?

THE PARTNERSHIP METHOD

Were shareholders to be taxed as partners, the corporate entity, as such, would drop out of the tax picture. Since stockholders would be held accountable under the personal income tax for their pro rata share of corporate earnings, all such earnings would be fully and promptly called to account. Taxwise, corporate earnings would be treated like property income from other sources, and stockholders would be treated as all other taxpayers are. "Under-", "over-", or "differential taxation" of corporate earnings would no longer exist. It is not surprising, therefore, that a number of students have proposed abolishing the corporation income tax and substituting for it current taxation as personal income of stockholders' pro rata share of corporate earnings.[1] (The corporate tax need not be abolished. If the personal

---

[1] See, for example: T. S. Adams, *The American Economic Review*, Supplement, March 1918, pp. 25-26. Note, however, an apparent change of heart on Adams' part, in 1923, in a speech before the National Tax Association (see page 310 of the *Proceedings* of their 16th Annual Conference, edited by Alfred E. Holcomb); Robert M. Haig, "Final Report of the Committee of the National Tax Association on Federal Taxation of Corporations, 1939," in *Proceedings of the National Tax Association for 1939*, pp. 539-540 and 544; Paul Ellis, *Corporate Tax Structure for Post-War Progress*, an address before Temple Institute on Tax Policies, Temple University, April 6, 1944, p. 10; Edward S. Shaw and Lorie Tarshis, "A Program for Economic Mobilization," *American Economic Review*, March 1951, pp. 44-45. In this article Shaw and Tarshis suggest the partnership method for a period of economic mobilization and make no reference to its desirability one way or another for "normal" periods.

income tax base were defined to include all of corporate earnings, the corporation income tax could be retained but converted to a withholding appendage of the "partnership" method by permitting stockholders to subtract their proportionate share of the corporate levy from their personal income tax liability.)

In what follows, this procedure, i.e., taxing stockholders on their pro rata share of corporate earnings fully and promptly under the personal income tax, will be referred to as the "partnership" method, for this is the way in which members of a partnership are called to account under the personal income tax.[2] Extension of the partnership method to stockholders has been criticized on a number of grounds.[3] In particular, serious doubts have been cast on its administrative feasibility.[4] Also, along with other possible methods of taxing undistributed corporate earnings, it has been opposed, especially for widely-owned corporations, as having undesirable economic effects.[5] Some critics have dismissed it as an impractical ideal. Despite adverse opinions, however, the method invites our interest not solely because, either in its stark form or with modifications toward practicability, it has been suggested by serious students of the subject. More particularly, in the framework of our study it serves as a benchmark, for, accepting the assumption that the incidence of the corporation income tax is on profits only, the partnership method would prevent differential taxation of stockholders. Obviously, a quantitative examination of the partnership method of taxation for stockholders is warranted. And this our data permit rather conveniently.

It cannot be emphasized too strongly that this study neither supports nor opposes this particular proposal.[6] The objective here is two-fold:

[2] There is a minor exception. A provision of the Internal Revenue Code of 1954 (Public Law 591, Chap. 736, Subchap. R, sec. 1361) permits unincorporated business, both individual proprietorships and partnerships, to elect to be taxed as domestic corporations. (A number of qualifications, enumeration of which is not necessary here, attach to this right of election.) But very few partnerships are so taxed.

[3] Full partnership treatment for stockholders would require also raising the basis of valuation (for the determination of capital gains) of their shareholdings by the excess of imputed over distributed earnings.

[4] For example, Richard B. Goode, *The Corporation Income Tax*, Wiley, 1951, pp. 184-190; William Vickrey, *Agenda for Progressive Taxation*, Ronald, 1947, pp. 161-162; Harold M. Groves, *Postwar Taxation and Economic Progress*, McGraw-Hill, 1946, pp. 55-59.

[5] "Both as technicians and as businessmen they [accountants] should oppose any attempt to tax to stockholders, in any way, the undistributed income of the widely owned business corporation, which is the main source of the capital needed for the constant extension of the scope of business activities upon which in turn reasonably full employment depends." (George O. May, "Stock Dividends and Concepts of Income," *The Journal of Accountancy*, October 1953, p. 431.)

[6] At this point it is convenient to note also that the study's sole preoccupation

first, to explore by an additional approach evidence relevant to an evaluation of the differential taxation of stockholders; and secondly, to develop a measure of the aggregate extent of the unequal taxation of stockholders. Such a measure emerges, within the context of the whole investigation, from estimates of the change in federal revenue to be expected from a hypothetical change in the tax structure—substituting, for the corporation income tax, the current taxation to stockholders under the personal income tax of their full share of corporate earnings (both distributed and retained).

Aggregate estimates of this type will complement the findings of Chapters 2, 3, and 4. The four measures used there—the differentials against earning for distribution, earnings for retention, net corporate earnings, and stockholders—summarize the experience at selected "average" or "representative" stockholder income levels; they do not provide, therefore, evidence on the total amount of over- or undertaxation.

EFFECT OF THE PARTNERSHIP METHOD
ON TAX REVENUE

Many considerations, of course, are involved in evaluating a possible change in the tax structure. Not the least important of these considerations is the effect on the public revenue, especially if the existing level of government expenditures is to be maintained. The effect on government receipts is not the only basis for evaluation of a proposed change, but it must always be taken into account. Some changes, however desirable on other grounds, might cause such a decline in tax revenue that they would be inadmissible without an alternative proposal that would recoup a substantial part of the revenue loss, and would, on net balance, leave the tax structure improved in terms of equity and economic effects. Such a substitute may be hard to find.

Can we afford to institute the partnership method? What would be its effect on public revenue?[7] This question cannot be answered in the abstract. The answer depends on a number of factors which vary from year to year—the rates of corporate and personal income taxes,

---

with the differential taxation of stockholders should not be interpreted to imply a stand either in support of or against the contention that a corporate tax is justifiable and desirable, per se, and should not stand or fall as a substitute for or appendage to the personal income tax. (See Gerhard Colm, "The Corporation and the Corporation Income Tax in the American Economy," *American Economic Review*, May 1954, pp. 486-503.)

[7] The discussion which follows waives the question of the administrative feasibility of the partnership method.

the amount of corporate earnings and its distribution between dividends and retained earnings, and, because the personal income tax is progressive, the degree of concentration of dividend receipts and stockholder incomes. To anchor the discussion, rather careful estimates were made for four of the more recent years for which detailed data were available—1952, 1950, 1949, and 1947—and less refined and accurate estimates for the other years between 1944 and 1955.

What follows is predicated on the assumption that the total of corporate earnings would not have changed had the corporation income tax been rescinded. This assumption, that the corporation income tax is not shifted either forward via higher prices of corporate output or backward through a lower level of returns to the factors of production, qualifies our findings. More particularly, to the extent that removal of the corporation income tax would result in a lower level of corporate earnings due either to a fall in the price of the output of corporations or a bidding up of the cost of their inputs (or some combination of the two), the estimates of the revenue loss presented below are too low. More tax revenue would be lost to the National Treasury than our estimates show because a smaller amount of earnings would be imputable to stockholders. While lower prices of consumer goods are usually followed by increased sales and excise tax collections, and higher incomes for workers and other suppliers of productive factors mean increased personal income tax liability, neither of these expansions would be likely to offset the loss completely. The reasons are not far to seek: not all goods and services are subject to excise taxes, rates of which are probably lower than the prevailing marginal rates for stockholders; the marginal tax rate for the average taxpayer is substantially lower than for the average dividend-receiving taxpayer.

Only a brief description of the procedures used in estimating the effect on public revenue of the partnership method of taxing stockholders appears in this chapter, a more detailed explanation will be found in Appendix B.

Many changes in financial asset prices and the relative attractiveness of stock to various investor groups that would have an effect on federal revenue collections might follow the introduction of the partnership method. For example if, because of this change, the stockholdings of nonprofit institutions were to increase, other things unchanged, tax collections would be lower. No account is taken of this or similar possible effects in the revenue estimates presented in this chapter.

1950

If the corporation income tax had been abolished, the federal government's revenue in 1950,[8] other things unchanged, would have declined by $16.8 billion.[9] This represents a significant proportion—one third—of total federal tax receipts, $50.2 billion.[10] But, of course, everything else would not remain unchanged. Imputation to stockholders of their full pro rata share of net corporate earnings would raise their personal income tax liability. To what extent would this have served to offset the loss of corporation income tax revenue?

Briefly, the offset, while not large enough to prevent a net decline in tax revenue, would have been large enough to keep the decline somewhere in the neighborhood of $3 to $4.5 billion.[11]

How was this conclusion reached? Very simply, by computing the difference between stockholders' personal income tax liability before and after imputation of their full pro rata share of net corporate earnings. For this purpose, the stockholder income-dividend class array was broken down on two bases—joint and separate returns, and returns with and without the alternative tax on capital gains. For each of the 585 stockholder cells, the increase in personal income tax liability that would follow the introduction of the partnership method was com-

[8] As explained previously (see Chapter 2) the data for 1950 were the latest available for analysis when this investigation was under way. Later, 1951 and 1952 tabulations were published, and an analysis for 1952 appears below.

[9] *Statistics of Income for 1950*, Bureau of Internal Revenue, Part 2, pp. 40 and 90. This figure equals the corporate tax liability incurred in that year (including $1.4 billion excess profits tax liability) minus the credit claimed for foreign taxes paid ($0.5 billion). Our discussion runs in terms of liabilities rather than of actual collections. *Statistics of Income* liability figures, used throughout, take no account of revisions due to audit, which, in every year without exception, are positive in the aggregate. Failure to take account of them, however, probably entails only slight error in our estimate of revenue loss because, not only is the foregone tax liability somewhat greater after audit revisions, but also the total of corporate earnings to be imputed to stockholders. Use of these revised aggregates would have yielded a higher personal income tax liability under the partnership method, tending to offset the larger corporation income tax loss. For example, for 1950, increased corporation income tax due to audit has been estimated at about $0.2 billion (*National Income Supplement, 1954, Survey of Current Business*, Dept. of Commerce, p. 93). The same source places profit increases disclosed by audit at $0.6 billion. Since, from the estimate to be discussed below, we find an over-all marginal rate of personal income tax on imputed corporate earnings of something over 40 per cent, the revisions due to audit for 1950 would leave our revenue loss estimate unchanged.

[10] *National Income Supplement, 1954, Survey of Current Business*, p. 171.

[11] The findings are presented in broad ranges initially to point up two features of our estimates: (1) it would be misleading to suggest by a single figure greater precision than the data and our estimating techniques make possible; and (2) different conclusions are reached if we consider the current revenue decline or the aggregate revenue loss over time. This latter problem is elaborated below.

puted. Stockholders' actual personal income tax liability was estimated at $7 billion and their potential partnership method tax liability at $19.1 billion—an increase of $12.1 billion in personal income tax liability. In addition, full taxation of proportionate shares of net corporate earnings applied to taxable fiduciaries (estates and trusts that failed to distribute all their income to beneficiaries) would have increased their personal income tax liability by $1.4 billion.[12] In consequence it appears that the increase in personal income tax liability would have been on the order of $13.5 billion, which leaves $3.3 billion of the foregone corporation income tax not recouped. This revenue loss—about 9 per cent of the total corporate and personal income tax liabilities incurred in 1950[13]—is not unimportant but it is significantly less than the corporate tax liability figure that is frequently cited to support the argument that, good or bad on other grounds, the corporate tax is a mighty revenue raiser, and its abolition cannot be countenanced. One way of placing the revenue loss in perspective is this: In 1950, if the partnership method of taxing corporate earnings had been introduced by Congress, a current fall in federal revenue could have been prevented by raising personal income tax rates (on stockholders and all other taxpayers) by about 3.0 percentage points all along the line.[14]

This is not the end of the story. A further loss in revenue is to be expected from a change not apparent in 1950. No allowance has been made thus far for the change in basis of valuation used to determine the amount of capital gain that would be the logical corollary of full imputation of corporate earnings. For personal income tax purposes, the amount of capital gain attendant upon the sale of a partnership share is equal to the proceeds from the sale, minus the sum of the initial purchase price plus the partner's pro rata share of all undistributed earnings from the date of purchase to the date of sale. To accord, then, with the procedure now used in the taxation of partner-

[12] This estimate is made assuming that fiduciaries would distribute no more to beneficiaries after imputation than they actually did in 1950 and that, therefore, the full amount of the income imputed was taxed to the fiduciary. This assumption probably provides a minimum figure for the increment in tax liability, for it is reasonable to conjecture that if tax considerations led to less than full distribution of the fiduciary's income the marginal rate for beneficiaries was higher than for fiduciaries. Therefore, if part of the imputed income had been distributed to the beneficiaries the increase in tax liability would have been greater.

[13] As tabulated in *Statistics of Income for 1950*, personal income tax liability (including fiduciaries) came to $18.4 billion; corporate tax liability net of foreign tax credits equalled $16.8 billion.

[14] This figure is merely illustrative. It is not intended to imply that this would have been either the only or the most appropriate way of recouping the revenue loss.

ship shares, the basis of stock valuation for capital gains tax purposes should be raised by the excess of net corporate earnings over dividends received, i.e., by the amount of retained earnings. If this is done, future capital gains and capital gains tax liability would be smaller than they otherwise would have been.

How much smaller? Several imponderables are involved in estimating the quantitative importance of this part of the complex and it is possible to provide only a very rough idea of what its magnitude might be. Our assumptions seem reasonable, but they could be rather far from actuality. However, much the same results would have followed from different assumptions.

Two sets of factors are involved in this estimate. It is not likely that under the partnership method of taxing corporate earnings the entire sum formerly paid as corporation income tax would be distributed to stockholders. The amount of retained earnings probably would be higher than before, and consequently, sometime in the future, stockholders' tax liability for capital gains would be larger. This increase in tax revenue would be outweighed by the revenue effect of the change in basis of valuation of corporate stock described above; because of this adjustment future capital gains and the tax liability on them would be lower. Since the increase in capital gains tax liability would be related to an increment in retained earnings, while the decrease due to the change in basis would be associated with total retained earnings, on net balance these factors would lead to a decline in revenue. It would not show up currently but over time in the form of a lower capital gains tax liability than would have been the case in the absence of the partnership method. Precisely how this revenue loss was estimated is too detailed a matter to go into here.[15]

15 A full explanation of our method is found in Appendix B. Lest the reader, however, feel that he is being asked to accept too much on faith, a very brief outline of the procedure follows: It was assumed that the rescinded corporation income tax would go into dividends and retentions in the same proportion as corporate earnings (net of the corporation income tax) were actually divided in 1950. Following the reasoning behind variant 2 (see Chapters 1 and 2) it was assumed that only 72 per cent of the increase in retained earnings would show up as capital gains. This sum was subtracted from the new total of retained earnings to get the net future decline in capital gains caused by the change in basis due to the current taxation to stockholders of income not distributed to them. To get from this figure to a revenue loss estimate required two assumptions: only two-thirds of capital gains are realized in taxable form (the remaining one-third being realized by persons who are not taxable, who are negligent about reporting capital gains for tax purposes, or who pass them income-tax free at death); the gains would be long-term, and, therefore, only half would be included in taxable income; on average, an effective rate of 30 per cent would apply to them. (This is reasonable since the alternative tax sets a ceiling of 50 per cent on them.) So far this suggests a revenue

Our principal concern is the result: an estimated loss of $1.4 billion in capital gains tax liability would occur over time due to the retention of earnings in 1950. This figure, it should be noted, is characterized by a much lower order of accuracy than the above current revenue loss estimate.

In summary, under the conditions prevailing in 1950, changing to the partnership method of taxing corporate earnings would have meant an immediate loss in revenues of $3.3 billion, and an additional decline aggregating about $1.4 billion over the years that followed. Interpreting the current revenue loss as the net revenue contribution of the corporate income tax on net corporate earnings, we may conclude that this net contribution came to only a small fraction—less than one-fifth—of the total actual corporate income tax liability.

These findings are particularly dependent on the specific values of the relevant variables in 1950, the relative heights of the corporate and personal income taxes, and the aggregate of corporate earnings and their divisions between dividends and retentions. How will variations in these determinants change our estimate of the revenue effect of the partnership method? One means of tracing the effects of such variations is the previously mentioned analysis of data for other years, to be discussed later. Another means is examination of the effects of hypothetical changes in one or another of the determining variables for the year now under consideration, 1950. For this purpose, tax rates prevailing in 1947 were substituted for 1950 rates.

With other things equal, the higher the effective rate of corporation income tax, the greater the revenue loss connected with a switch to the partnership method. If instead of the actual 1950 effective corporate tax rate (42.5 per cent) the 1947 rate of 36.7 per cent had been in effect in 1950, the current revenue loss would have been considerably less—$1.1 billion as against our estimated $3.3 billion.[16] Again other things unchanged, the higher the personal income tax rate schedule, the smaller the revenue loss if stockholders were taxed as partners. In 1947, personal income tax rates were higher than in 1950; in 1947, the increase in personal income tax liability came to 48.0 per cent of the additional amount imputable to stockholders under the

loss of 10 per cent of the decline in capital gains due to the change in basis. But since it is a loss to be experienced in the future, its present value would be somewhat lower. By assuming the decline to take place evenly in the five years following the year of imputation, and taking 5 per cent as an appropriate rate of discount, a figure for the present value of the future capital gains tax liability revenue loss was obtained equal to 8.6 per cent of the total amount of the decline in capital gains due to imputed retained earnings.

[16] Both rate computations take into account the credit for foreign income taxes paid.

partnership method; in 1950, the percentage was only 44.2. If the 1947 personal income tax rate schedule had been in effect in 1950 with the marginal rate of tax on the amount imputable at 48.0 per cent, the current revenue loss in 1950 would have come to only $2.1 billion.[17] (See Table 28 for evidence on the level of personal income tax rates.)

TABLE 28

Comparison of Effective Rates of Personal Income Tax, 1947, 1949, 1950 and 195? (per cent)

NET INCOME LEVEL ($000's)	Single person—no dependents				Married person—two dependents			
	1947	1949	1950	1952	1947	1949	1950	1952
3	16.2	13.6	14.3	18.1	6.3	3.3	3.5	4.4
5	18.4	16.2	16.9	21.0	11.8	8.6	9.0	11.5
10	23.5	21.2	22.0	27.2	18.6	13.6	14.2	17.7
25	37.5	34.4	35.6	43.8	34.1	21.9	22.7	28.0
50	50.3	46.4	48.0	56.9	48.2	33.2	34.3	42.2
100	63.5	58.8	60.8	69.7	62.3	45.6	47.2	56.0
500	81.6	77.0	79.2	87.2	81.3	71.7	73.9	82.2
1,000	84.0	77.0	80.0	88.0	83.9	76.9	79.1	87.1

Source: *Annual Report of the Secretary of the Treasury on the State of the Finances for the Fiscal Year Ended June 30, 1950*, pp. 248 and 250; and *for 1951*, p. 502.

Finally, if effective rates equal to the 1947 corporate rate and personal rate had prevailed in 1950 there would have been no current revenue loss accompanying the institution of the partnership method. On the contrary, a slight current increase in revenue, something on the order of $100 million, would have resulted.

Since the partnership method would involve no differential taxation of stockholders, the net revenue contribution of the corporate tax may be taken to be the excess of corporate tax liability over the tax liability stockholders would have if they were taxed as partners. More specifically, the net revenue contribution of the corporate tax is here defined as equal to the current revenue loss under the partnership method. From this point of view it is interesting to note that the net revenue contribution of the corporation tax can be traced in large part to a specific segment of stockholders—viz., those stockholders not reached by the personal income tax either because they were not subject to it as nonprofit institutions or because their income fell short of their exemptions, and those stockholders who failed to report their total dividend receipts.

[17] Reduction in personal income tax rates after 1947 reflects primarily the income-splitting introduced in 1948, and the resulting lower rates applicable to joint returns.

If we restrict our examination to those stockholders who paid the personal income tax (both individuals and taxable fiduciaries) we find that their actual corporate-personal income tax liability for 1950 exceeded their potential current partnership method liability by a very slight margin—about $0.8 billion.[18] But such stockholders accounted for only 83 per cent of all net dividends paid out by corporations. The remaining 17 per cent were not reported for reasons enumerated above. It is from the corporate earnings imputable to this segment of dividends that most of the net revenue contribution of the corporate income tax came. These findings for 1950 also apply for 1947, 1949, and 1952. In other words, the major part of the net revenue contribution of the corporation income tax can be explained by two facts: it is the less discriminating of the two taxes and thus reaches the corporate earnings of those exempt from the personal tax; and it is probably more difficult to underreport corporate earnings for corporate tax purposes than it would be under the personal income tax.

The fact that some dividends were either inadvertently or deliberately not reported on personal income tax returns suggests another qualification to our revenue loss estimates. For if, with enactment of a change in the method of taxing corporate earnings, safeguards were incorporated in the revenue code to insure fuller reporting of dividends, the current revenue loss would be lower than our estimates indicate. In support of a withholding provision for dividend payments, the Treasury has "estimated that the withholding tax system would increase net income tax receipts by $150,000,000."[19] Corporate earnings in 1950 were almost four and one-half times as large as dividends. Therefore, with full taxation of each stockholder's share of corporate earnings, one would expect at least a $0.6 billion increase in personal income tax receipts if unreported dividends (and, presumably, corporate earnings) were ferreted out.[20]

1949

Corporate earnings (and, of course, corporate tax liability) were considerably lower in 1949 than in 1950 ($26 billion of earnings as against $40 billion) but were divided between dividends and retentions in about the same proportion in both years. The corporate rate and the

[18] $0.6 billion for individuals, $0.2 billion for fiduciaries.

[19] *Hearings before the Committee on Finance,* United States Senate, on H.R. 8920, 81st Cong., 2nd Sess., 1950, p. 19.

[20] "At least" because for all of corporate earnings personal income tax marginal rates higher than for dividends alone would be applicable.

personal rate for 1949 were lower than for 1950. In general, then, the factors involved in the revenue change associated with the partnership method were noticeably different from those operating in 1950.

A shift to the partnership method in 1949 would have meant giving up $9.5 billion of corporation income tax liability. But, in that year, all but $2.3 billion of this foregone revenue would have been recouped via increased personal income tax collections. To put this revenue loss in perspective: an estimated over-all percentage point increase of 2.6 in the personal income tax rate schedule would have been required to prevent any revenue loss; or $2.3 billion represents 9.5 per cent of the total corporate and personal income tax liability in 1949. The future revenue loss would be an estimated $0.9 billion. All in all, a decline in tax liabilities of $3.2 billion would have accompanied a shift to prompt and full taxation of stockholders' pro rata share of net corporate earnings under the personal income tax in 1949.

1947

The 1947 results are perhaps the most surprising. For indications are that a revenue gain (albeit of modest proportions) rather than a loss would have been the immediate consequence of a shift to the partnership method. A conjunction of circumstances—relatively high personal rates, a comparatively low corporate rate, and a high proportion of undistributed earnings—led to this result. Corporate income tax liability (after allowance for foreign tax credits) of $10.8 billion would have been lost to the Treasury. But the additional personal income tax liability of stockholders would have come to $9.8 billion, and fiduciaries would have been liable for an additional $1.1 billion. The immediate revenue gain, some $0.2 billion, would have been overbalanced, however, by a revenue loss in later years due to lower future capital gains tax liability of about $1.2 billion.

An apparent oversight in our procedure should be explained. Our revenue calculations have been limited to individuals, estates, and trusts that were liable for personal income tax in a given year. Upon full taxation of corporate earnings under the personal income tax, would not some previously nontaxable stockholders be pushed into the taxable category and should this not be taken into account in our estimate? Such an adjustment made for 1947 was found to be very unimportant—on the order of $20 million. Given the inherent ranges of error in the revenue estimates (making reasonable their rounding to the nearest tenth of a billion for present purposes), it seems unnecessary to take account of this refinement.

1952

Corporate earnings were $4 billion lower in 1952 than in 1950, yet because of rate increases between these two years corporate tax liability was $1.6 billion greater in 1952. This presages a larger revenue loss under the partnership method for 1952, a loss made more substantial by the fact that less would have been recouped under the 1952 personal income tax. The added loss, despite increased personal income tax rates, would result from the smaller total to be imputed in 1952, causing the increment in personal income tax liability to fall short of the comparable 1950 figure by $800 million.[21]

More particularly, the revenue loss that would have occurred in 1952 had the partnership method been instituted would have been around $5.7 billion, the amount by which the estimated increase (partnership method) in personal income tax liability of $12.7 billion would have fallen short of the corporate tax liability of $18.4 billion.[22] A loss in revenue of this amount could have been recouped by raising the 1952 personal income tax rate schedule by 4.4 percentage points. That the current revenue loss would have come to $5.7 billion indicates that the corporate tax, when evaluated against the alternative procedure of taxing corporate earnings as part of personal income, was responsible for a net addition to federal revenue of less than one-third of the total sum ostensibly raised by it. As in the preceding years, the future capital gains tax liability would be lower than it might have been; for 1952 this future revenue loss is estimated at $900 million.

1955

Especial interest always attaches to the most recent experience. Therefore, the net revenue contribution of the existing method of taxing corporate earnings was estimated with the data for 1955. This estimate, it must be pointed out, is considerably rougher than those we have just discussed; the data used were less reliable; the method of estimation much more summary.

If the partnership technique had been adopted in 1955, the Treasury would have suffered a considerable loss in revenue. Increased personal income tax liability would have fallen short of the foregone corporate tax liability by some $4.9 billion.[23] A 3.3 point increase in

---

[21] The amount imputed was $30.6 billion in 1950, $26.5 billion in 1952. The difference is due to the lower level of corporate earnings and the greater relative importance of distributed earnings in 1952.

[22] The corporate tax liability is taken net of the credit for foreign corporation income taxes paid.

[23] This figure takes no account of the individual tax relief provisions introduced

the personal income tax rate schedule would have been required to recoup the current revenue loss. In addition, the future capital gains tax revenue loss would have been on the order of $1.3 billion.

Summary

By way of summary Table 29 presents the revenue effects (both current and future) of a shift to the partnership method. Also, to place the current revenue loss in perspective, the estimated percentage point rise in the personal income tax rate schedule necessary in each year to recoup the loss appears in column 3. (Table B-13 incorporating greater detail appears in Appendix B.) Of the data in Table 29, the entries for 1947, 1949, 1950, and 1952 are the most firmly based.

Quite varied are the results for these twelve years. In every one of them, of course, the net contribution of the corporate income tax to the public fisc was substantially less than its face amount.

1. In 1946 and 1947, no loss in revenue would have occurred currently by a shift to the partnership method.

2. Nor was the corporate tax a very powerful revenue raiser on a net basis in a number of other years—1948, 1949, and 1950. Most of its net contribution in these years can be explained by the fact that it reached the corporate earnings of stockholders who were either exempt from or failed to report their dividends for the personal income tax.

3. In the other years of this period, however, sizeable amounts of revenue resulted from the fact that two income taxes—corporate and personal—were levied on corporate earnings.

4. One way of giving the current loss figure some meaning, as noted above, is to estimate by how much the schedule of personal income tax rates (personal income now defined to include stockholders' pro rata share of net corporate earnings) would have to be raised to recoup it (see column 3). This figure, of course, varied considerably over our period; between 1950 and 1955 it ranged from 3 to 5 points. In 1955, by a rough estimate it would have required a 3.3 percentage point rise in personal income tax rates to leave the federal revenue intact after switching to the partnership method.

5. The net revenue obtained currently by taxing corporate income separately when earned and again when distributed—i.e., the revenue loss associated with the partnership method—represented only a fraction of the total corporate income tax liability (column 4). This fraction varied considerably from slightly less than zero (1947) to a little over one-third (1944). These findings suggest that, at the present time, were the federal revenue requirements to develop in such a way

TABLE 29

Estimated Partnership Method Revenue Loss, 1944-1955
(dollars in billions)

YEAR (1)	Current revenue loss due to shift to partnership method (2)	Percentage point rise in personal tax rates required to recoup current revenue loss[a] (3)	Net current revenue yield of corporate tax as % of total corporate tax liability (4)	Present value of future revenue loss by shift to partnership method (5)	Total revenue loss due to shift to partnership method (2) + (5) (6)
1944	$5.2	7.3	35.1%	$0.7	$5.9
1945	3.5	5.1	32.7	0.5	4.0
1946	0.3	0.4	3.4	0.9	4.2
1947	—0.2	—0.2	—1.9	1.2	1.0
1948	1.9	2.0	16.4	1.3	3.2
1949	2.3	2.6	24.2	0.9	3.2
1950	3.3	3.0	19.6	1.4	4.7
1951	6.5	5.2	30.2	1.2	7.7
1952	5.7	4.4	31.0	0.9	6.6
1953	6.1	4.3	30.8	1.0	7.1
1954	4.5b	3.3	28.3	0.9	5.4
1955	4.9b	3.3	24.4	1.3	6.2

a 1944-1947 based on taxable income estimates in Joseph A. Pechman, "Yield of the Individual Income Tax During a Recession," *National Tax Journal*, March 1954 (Vol. VII, No. 1) p. 7. For 1944 and 1945, income subject to normal tax was used; for 1946 on, when exemptions applied to both normal and surtax, surtaxable income was used. From 1948 on, Pechman's worksheet estimates were used. The imputations under the partnership method were added to taxable income. The method used in deriving the values in column 3 leads to an overstatement of the rate increase required. A somewhat smaller rise than indicated would probably be sufficient to recoup the current revenue loss (see footnote j to Table B-13).

b These estimates take no account of the dividend credit and exclusion, in effect since 1954. Very roughly, these two relief provisions lowered the personal income tax burden on stockholders, in the aggregate, by about $200 million in 1954 and $300 million in 1955. The entries in column 2 might more accurately be, therefore, $4.3 and $4.6 respectively because, with the partnership method in effect there would be no reason, on equity grounds at least, to keep the exclusion and credit. These changes, of course, carry through the rest of the columns in the table.

that a cut of, say, 25 per cent in corporation normal and sur-tax rates could be seriously contemplated,[24] it would also be feasible, from the revenue point of view, to abolish the corporation income tax entirely if corporate earnings were fully and promptly taxed to stockholders as part of their personal income.

in 1954. (They are discussed in the next chapter.) We estimate the revenue loss due to the dividend exclusion and credit at $350 million in 1955. So the current revenue loss under the partnership method (which implies also the repeal of these relief provisions) might more properly be set at $4.5 to $4.6 billion.

24 This would leave them a little above the rates prevailing in the period 1946-1949.

6. Additional comparisons are represented in Table 30. The corporation income tax, apparently, is a mainstay of our revenue structure. Over the years included in this investigation corporate tax liability was second to the personal income tax as a source of federal revenue. (Compare lines 1 and 2.) On these simple grounds alone it might be called our "second best" tax, accounting for anywhere from one-fifth to over one-third of total revenue.[25] But as a net revenue raiser, i.e., in terms of additional revenue over and above the aggregate liability calculated by the partnership method of taxing corporate earnings, the picture is not so imposing (line 8).[26] In only two years did the net revenue contribution of the corporation income tax exceed 10 per cent of federal revenue. Typically it ran between 5 and 9 per cent of federal tax and non-tax receipts, and in two years came to less than 1 per cent of this total (line 9). Moreover, on a net revenue basis, the corporate tax was less important in the flow of federal receipts than excise taxes or contributions to social security (lines 12 and 13), and, also, of course, than the personal income tax.

It would be interesting to check our figures against those of other investigators. The only somewhat comparable estimate I have discovered was made by Louis Shere who found that, in 1948, the repeal of the corporate tax and the introduction of the partnership method would have involved a probable revenue loss of around $3 billion.[27] This estimate is one billion dollars higher than ours for the 1948 current revenue loss.[28] Allowing for the wide margins of error attaching to all such estimates, our estimate and Shere's can be considered to constitute mutually corroborative rather than conflicting evidence.

[25] Total revenue in Table 30 is defined as the sum of personal and corporate tax liability as tabulated in *Statistics of Income*, plus all other tax and non-tax collections. This definition fits most appropriately the data used in our study, but it means for some taxes we use liability and for other collections. If the collections figures had been used in all cases, the results would not have been very different.

[26] The net revenue contribution is the current revenue loss estimated for the partnership method.

[27] Louis Shere, "Federal Corporation Income Tax—Revenue and Reform," *National Tax Journal*, June 1949, p. 114. Shere does not state explicitly that the estimate is for 1948, but his text implies it. In *Corporate Tax Structure for Post-War Progress*, Paul Ellis provided a figure for 1945. But, in deriving it, he was forced to use estimated data that fell so far off the mark from the actual data for that year that his figure and ours are not comparable. W. L. Crum has estimated the partnership method revenue loss for 1941, not for all returns, but for a major category—individual returns with normal and surtax only (W. L. Crum, "The Taxation of Stockholders," *Quarterly Journal of Economics*, February 1950, p. 53).

[28] It is likely, from the context and the lack of any explicit statement that he was allowing also for future losses in capital gains tax revenue, that Shere's estimate is concerned solely with the revenue loss effective in the given year 1948.

TABLE 30

Net Revenue Contribution of the Corporation Income Tax Compared with
Other Sources of Federal Revenue, 1944-1952

(dollar amounts in billions)

	1944	1945	1946	1947	1948	1949	1950	1951	1952
Sources of federal revenue:									
1. Personal income tax liability	$16.3	$17.3	$16.3	$18.3	$15.6	$14.6	$18.6	$24.4	$28.0
2. Corporation income tax lia-bility a	14.8	10.7	8.7	10.8	11.6	9.5	16.8	21.5	18.4
3. Excise taxes	5.3	6.2	7.3	7.3	7.5	7.6	8.3	8.7	9.6
4. Contributions for social in-surance	4.8	5.8	5.5	5.1	4.5	4.9	5.9	7.1	7.5
5. Other tax and nontax revenue	1.7	1.8	1.5	1.5	1.6	1.5	1.6	1.7	1.9
6. Total revenue	42.9	41.8	39.3	43.0	40.8	38.1	51.2	63.4	65.4
Corporation income tax:									
7. Liability as a per cent of total revenue	34.5%	25.6%	22.1%	25.1%	28.4%	24.9%	32.8%	33.9%	28.1%
8. Its net revenue contribution b	$5.2	$3.5	$0.3	$ —0.2	$1.9	$2.3	$3.3	$6.5	$5.7
Net revenue contribution of corporation income tax as a per cent of:									
9. Total revenue	12.1%	8.4%	0.8%	—0.5%	4.7%	6.0%	6.4%	10.3%	8.7%
10. Personal income tax liability	31.9	20.2	1.8	—1.1	12.2	15.8	17.7	26.6	20.4
11. Gross corporation income tax liability	35.1	32.7	3.4	—1.9	16.4	24.2	19.6	30.2	31.0
12. Excise taxes	98.1	56.5	4.1	—2.7	25.3	30.3	39.8	74.7	59.4
13. Contributions for social in-surance	108.3	60.3	5.5	—3.9	42.2	46.9	55.9	91.5	76.0

Source: For lines 1 and 2, *Statistics of Income;* for line 3, line 12 of Table 8, *National Income* (1954 ed.); for line 4, line 21 of Table 8, *National Income* (1954 ed.); for line 5, lines 16, 17, and 18 of Table 8, *National Income* (1954 ed.).
a Net of credit for foreign taxes paid.
b Current revenue loss under partnership method.

AGGREGATE DIFFERENTIALS

In deriving the differential against earnings for distribution, earnings for retention, net corporate earnings, and stockholders' income at selected levels of imputed gross income, by the standard method developed in this investigation (see Chapters 1 and 2), it was assumed that the incidence of the corporate tax is on profits. On this assumption stockholders are currently subject to what is called here the corporate-personal income tax system, i.e., one income tax on corporate earnings at the corporate level when earned and another at the personal level when earnings are received as dividends. The corporate tax in this complex is a gross tax; on a net basis it would be lower because if the amount taken away by the corporation income tax had been distributed to stockholders it would have been reached by the personal income tax. Likewise, if retained earnings had been distributed personal income taxes would have increased. This section is concerned, not with the average experience at selected levels of imputed gross income, but with a comparison for all stockholders, arrayed by imputed gross income classes, between the aggregate tax liability incurred under the corporate-personal income tax system and the aggregate tax liability calculated by the partnership method. The difference between the two liabilities constitutes a differential measured on an aggregative basis—i.e., the total differential for all the stockholders in each imputed gross income class.[29]

Results of such a comparison made with the data for 1947, 1949, 1950, and 1952 are shown in Table 31. Much the same sort of comments are in order for all four of these years; the discussion concentrates on one of them—1950. In that year, as far as taxable dividend recipients were concerned, both income tax systems—the actual corporate-personal and the personal income tax alone (the partnership method)—involved substantially the same amount of aggregate tax liability.[30] But this virtual equality masks important diversities among

[29] Because our computations deriving the aggregate differential take no account of the future capital gains tax liability due to the retained earnings of a given year, the measure used corresponds conceptually to variant 1 rather than variant 2 which was used as the standard measure in earlier chapters (see Chapter 2), and to the current revenue loss under the partnership method.

[30] That for "double-taxed" stockholders a relatively slight decline in tax liability of $600 million would have been associated in 1950 with the partnership method is not a contradiction of our earlier conclusion that a current revenue loss of about $3.3 billion could have been expected had a switch to the partnership method been made in that year. For not all net dividend outpayments of corporations show up on taxable returns; for this year I was able to trace only 83 per cent of net corporate dividends to the taxable returns of individuals and estates and trusts. (Percentages were similar in the other years.) For a variety of

TABLE 31

Comparison of Tax Liability of Stockholders under the Corporate-Personal Income Tax System and the Partnership Method, 1947, 1949, 1950, and 1952

IMPUTED GROSS INCOME CLASS ($000's) (1)	TAX LIABILITY		(3) as a per cent of (2) (4)	Number of stockholders with liability higher under partnership than under corporate-personal income tax (5)	Per cent of total returns in class undertaxed (6)
	Corporate-personal tax system ($ in millions) (2)	Partnership method ($ in millions) (3)			
		1947			
Under 2	56.7	36.1	64		
2 and under 4	475.6	316.5	67		
4 and under 5	274.0	191.5	70		
5 and under 7	557.2	383.4	69		
7 and under 10	739.2	526.0	71		
10 and under 25	2,575.5	2,211.7	86	16,401	2.9
25 and under 50	2,309.2	2,447.0	106	155,110	92.3
50 and under 100	2,549.2	3,213.6	126	75,691	100.0
100 and under 500	2,894.9	4,136.8	143	28,939	100.0
500 and under 1,000	658.8	1,034.5	157	1,790	100.0
1,000 and over	803.1	1,281.1	160	648	100.0
Total	13,893.4	15,778.2	114	278,579	8.6
		1949			
Under 2	26.7	14.5	54		
2 and under 4	276.7	167.5	61		
4 and under 5	231.8	144.7	62		
5 and under 7	628.4	391.6	62		
7 and under 10	714.8	438.7	61		
10 and under 25	2,393.1	1,652.0	69		
25 and under 50	1,649.4	1,353.9	82	10,220	6.1
50 and under 100	2,093.7	1,983.4	95	28,363	32.2
100 and under 500	2,985.5	3,492.8	117	37,447	99.5
500 and under 1,000	699.2	945.7	135	2,321	100.0
1,000 and over	849.6	1,153.3	136	801	100.0
Total	12,548.9	11,738.1	94	79,152	2.5

(*continued on next page*)

income classes. By the partnership method, a smaller aggregate tax than actually levied would have been set on stockholders in the income classes (imputed gross income definition) below $50,000, while a higher

reasons cited above the remaining 17 per cent escapes or evades the personal income tax mill. Thus the partnership method corporate earnings tax base used in calculating the revenue loss was only 83 per cent of the corporate income tax base.

Table 31, *concluded*

IMPUTED GROSS INCOME CLASS ($000's) (1)	TAX LIABILITY Corporate-personal tax system ($ in millions) (2)	Partnership method (3)	(3) as a per cent of (2) (4)	Number of stockholders with liability higher under partnership than under corporate-personal income tax (5)	Per cent of total returns in class undertaxed (6)
		1950			
Under 2	23.0	13.1	57		
2 and under 4	269.8	160.4	59		
4 and under 5	250.8	153.9	61		
5 and under 7	729.7	473.0	65		
7 and under 10	720.8	406.3	56		
10 and under 25	3,077.0	2,032.7	66		
25 and under 50	2,896.8	2,316.9	80	12,252	5.3
50 and under 100	3,706.6	3,619.8	98	63,182	55.5
100 and under 500	5,104.3	6,022.3	118	50,496	99.3
500 and under 1,000	1,216.7	1,660.1	136	3,149	100.0
1,000 and over	1,692.4	2,225.4	131	1,213	100.0
Total	19,687.9	19,083.9	97	130,292	4.0
		1952			
Under 2	34.9	19.5	56		
2 and under 4	339.6	204.2	60		
4 and under 5	350.7	231.7	66		
5 and under 7	1,046.5	747.0	71		
7 and under 10	1,178.2	729.9	62		
10 and under 25	4,288.5	3,086.6	72		
25 and under 50	3,361.8	2,553.9	76	246	0.1
50 and under 100	4,148.7	3,832.2	92	12,428	11.1
100 and under 500	5,139.6	5,622.3	109	45,920	96.9
500 and under 1,000	1,046.5	1,281.6	122	2,460	100.0
1,000 and over	1,328.8	1,626.8	122	897	100.0
Total	22,263.8	19,935.7	90	61,951	1.6

tax liability would have been the lot of all income classes $100,000 and over. (Between $50,000 and under $100,000 the tax liability would have been about the same under either system.) Another way of putting it is this: Had the partnership method replaced the existing system of taxing corporate earnings, but with the corporate tax retained as a withholding measure, in the aggregate stockholders in the imputed gross income classes up to $50,000, would have received refunds; those in the section of the income array over $100,000 would have owed more. Also, as we can see in column 4 of Table 31, for classes under $50,000, the lower the income class, the more pronounced the excess of the corporate-personal tax liability over the partnership method, while for classes over $100,000, generally the higher the income class, the higher the partnership method liability tended to be in relation to the corporate-personal income tax.

In the aggregate, then, comparison of the two tax systems suggests that in 1950 the existence of income taxes at both the corporate and personal level led to a differential *against* stockholders in income classes under $50,000 (with the differential against them higher, the lower the income class), to roughly neutral taxation of those in the $50,000 and under $100,000 class, and to a differential *in favor of* stockholders in the income classes $100,000 and over (with the differential in their favor increasing with the level of income). With reference to our benchmark, the personal income tax as indicative of the community's consensus on how heavily income of a given size should be taxed, it is apparent that under the corporate-personal tax system, on the whole, "overtaxation" prevailed in the case of stockholders with incomes under $50,000, equal taxation characterized those falling between $50,000 and $100,000, while "undertaxation" ruled for those in the higher income classes.

While in 1950 the amount of "overtaxation" at lower income levels and of "undertaxation" at upper levels was almost the same, the overwhelming majority of stockholders were "overtaxed." Only 130,000— some 4.0 per cent of the total—fell in the undertaxed group (column 5). This, of course, merely reflects the high degree of concentration of dividends and claims to corporate earnings. Small in numbers, the undertaxed group was rich in corporate earnings; about 44 per cent of all corporate earnings of taxable stockholders was accounted for by the undertaxed returns.

The findings for the other three years—1947, 1949, and 1952—are very similar to those reported for 1950.

Rather dramatic is the conclusion that in 1947 from the corpus of taxable stockholders the partnership method would have extracted close to $2 billion more than did the existing two taxes on corporate earnings (the corporate tax on all earnings, the personal tax on the distributed portion). But this is not inconsistent with our finding that no appreciable current revenue gain would have accompanied a switch to the partnership method in this year. For taxable stockholders, the corporate and partnership method bases were the same, but for all stockholders the latter was only 82 per cent as large as the former. Hence, it is reasonable that the partnership method would have involved a decidedly higher liability on taxable stockholders but a total liability about the same as the corporate-personal income tax system.

Comparing 1947, 1949, and 1952 with 1950 highlights some of the determining factors. In 1947, we find a greater degree of undertaxation, more than twice as many undertaxed stockholders (280,000 as against 130,000), and a higher proportion of corporate earnings falling in the undertaxed category (68 per cent compared with 44 per cent). For 1949 we get a higher degree of overtaxation in the aggregate, fewer undertaxed stockholders (79,000 as against 1950's 130,000), and a smaller fraction of all corporate earnings going to undertaxed stockholders (40 per cent compared with 44 per cent). Finally, for 1952 we also get fewer undertaxed stockholders (62,000 as against 130,000), and a smaller fraction of all corporate earnings going to undertaxed stockholders (39 per cent compared with 44 per cent). Variations among these four years in the extent of over- and undertaxation depend on the spread between the corporate and personal income tax rates, a relation commented upon earlier in this chapter in connection with revenue loss estimates. In the four years analyzed, this spread was largest in 1947, smallest in 1952. The large number of undertaxed returns found for 1947 may be explained by an additional factor: prior to the introduction of income-splitting in 1948, some married couples probably divided their dividend receipts to minimize tax liability; such returns, heavily weighted with dividends, would on imputation of corporate earnings fall in a much higher income class and would tend, therefore, to swell the ranks of the undertaxed.

EFFECT OF TAXATION ON THE DISTRIBUTION OF STOCKHOLDERS' INCOME

One of the most pertinent considerations in evaluating both the equity and economic effects of an income tax system is its effect on the distribution of income. The marked differences noted above in the occurrence of over- and undertaxation among income classes under the partnership method of taxation and under the combined corporate-personal tax system suggest different effects for each system on the distribution of stockholders' income. This section is given to a comparative analysis of this matter. (A reminder: both tax systems are interpreted as levies on the income of stockholders including their pro rata share of all corporate earnings—dividends, retentions, and corporate income taxes). The effect of each system is measured by comparing the degree of concentration in the distribution of stockholders' income on a pre-tax and post-tax basis.

On Chart 8 are plotted three Lorenz curves for each of the years 1947, 1949, 1950, and 1952. The solid line traces out the distribution

CHART 8—Comparison of the Equalization Effect of the Partnership Method and the Corporate-Personal Income Tax System on the Distribution of Stockholder Income, 1947, 1949, 1950, and 1952

——————— Pre-tax imputed gross income
·················· Imputed gross income after corporate-personal tax liability
— — — — — Imputed gross income after partnership method tax liability

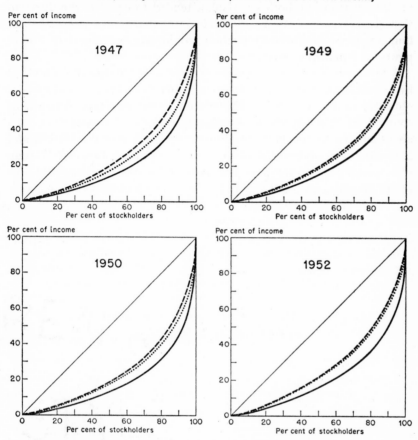

of stockholders' imputed gross income, which includes their full pro rata share of net corporate earnings before being reduced by taxation. The other two lines on the chart, both of which lie closer to the diagonal which theoretically denotes complete "equality,"[31] show the distribution of stockholders' income after taxes. The dotted line plots

[31] The quotes (later omitted) emphasize the purely mathematical nature of this definition of equality. For an interesting analysis of some realistic qualifications that attach to this benchmark see George Garvy, "Inequality of Income: Causes and Measurements," *Studies in Income and Wealth, Volume Fifteen,* National Bureau of Economic Research, 1952.

the distribution of stockholders' income after taxes as levied by the existing corporate-personal income tax system; the dashed line, the distribution net of the tax liability associated with the partnership method.

Since both these lines bend away less from the diagonal than the pre-tax distribution, both tax systems tended to equalize the distribution of stockholders' income. It is apparent that in every one of these four years the partnership method would have exercised the more powerful equalizing effect.

A more precise indication of the degree of equalization is provided by use of Gini's ratio of concentration, which is a measure of inequality obtained by dividing the area between a Lorenz curve and the line of complete equality by the area denoting complete inequality, i.e., the area bounded by the 45 degree line on the chart and the vertical and horizontal axes. The value of this coefficient ranges between 1 (complete inequality) and 0 (complete equality).[32] The relevant values of the Gini coefficient are listed in Table 32. From them we can measure

TABLE 32

The Relative "Push toward Equality" of the Corporate-Personal Income T System and the Partnership Method, 1947, 1949, 1950, and 1952

	Gini coefficient for distribution of imputed gross income			Push toward equality	
YEAR	Before taxes (1)	After corporate-personal tax liability (2)	After partner-ship method tax liability (3)	Corporate-personal income tax (4)	partnership method (5)
1947	0.6084	0.5330	0.4686	12.4%	23.0%
1949	0.5683	0.4966	0.4730	12.6	16.8
1950	0.6131	0.5288	0.4961	13.7	19.1
1952	0.5575	0.4477	0.4333	19.7	22.3

the push toward equality exercised by each of the tax systems under analysis. In 1950, for example, by cutting the area of inequality from 61.31 per cent of the graph to 52.88 per cent the corporate-personal tax pushed the distribution of stockholders' income almost 14 per cent toward complete equality. The partnership method would have exercised a noticeably more powerful effect; the area of inequality would have been cut to 49.61 per cent of the graph, and the push toward

[32] Dwight B. Yntema, "Measures of the Inequality in the Personal Distribution of Wealth and Income," *Journal of the American Statistical Association*, December 1933, pp. 427-428.

equality would have been over 19 per cent. Similar results were obtained for the other three years (columns 4 and 5, Table 32).

This evidence also tells us something about the relative progressivity of these two tax systems. Musgrave and Thin have suggested that one of the more useful ways of defining progressivity is by reference to the degree to which taxation has equalized the distribution of income.[33] Since our calculations measured the degree to which two different tax systems equalized the same before-tax distribution of income, we may say that, according to Musgrave and Thin's definition of progressivity, in all four years we find that the combined corporate-personal income tax was *less* progressive than the tax that would have been levied on stockholders if corporate earnings had been currently and fully reached by the personal income tax alone. This conclusion tends to contradict the frequently voiced claim that the corporation income tax, whatever its merits or demerits on other grounds, does make the tax system more progressive. This analysis illuminates only one facet of the complex subject of progressivity, other aspects of which are dealt with in Chapter 5.

[33] R. A. Musgrave and Tun Thin, "Income Tax Progression, 1929-48," *Journal of Political Economy*, December 1948, pp. 498-514. The particular measure they suggest, effective progression, is defined as the ratio of the after-tax to the before-tax coefficient of equality. The coefficient of equality is the complement of the measure we have been using—the Gini concentration ratio.

ADDENDUM

THE PARTNERSHIP METHOD WITH CORPORATE LOSSES

Within the whole span of our income tax experience, the years for which revenue estimates are presented in this chapter were all "prosperous" years. The choice was in part dictated by limitation of suitable data; even semireliable estimates of this kind are impossible for the earlier period up to the mid-thirties. The choice of years was made also with sights trained on the goal of contributing something to our understanding of the outcome, in terms of federal revenue and individual income tax liabilities, of a possible alternative method of taxing corporate earnings. To this end the more immediate experience of the forties and early fifties seems more relevant. In the present political and institutional climate, these years are widely regarded as probably more likely to characterize our economic future.

The possibility, however, of a severe depression can never safely be ignored. It would be interesting, therefore, to examine the implications of the partnership method of taxing corporate earnings against the backdrop of experience in 1932. It must be emphasized that estimates for this year are necessarily rough and of a lower quality than those presented in the body of this chapter. The data do not permit a full-dress analysis in terms of rearraying stockholders into imputed gross income classes, but are treated more simply as averages derived by imputing corporate earnings to the average stockholder income in each of the adjusted gross income classes, with no attempt to work with an income class, dividend size cross-classification. Returns of individuals and fiducial institutions could not be treated separately.

Ours is a profit and loss system. Too frequently discussions of alternative methods of taxing corporate earnings, including the partnership method, concentrate on positive corporate earnings, often ignoring the reverse possibility. Since, under the partnership method positive corporate earnings would be fully attributed to individuals for personal income tax purposes, considerations of both logic and equity would call for the same treatment for losses. In 1932, in the aggregate, corporations experienced a net loss. The data for this year, therefore, indicate some of the revenue implications of large net corporate losses for the partnership method.

Use of the average stockholder experience in this analysis injects an element of unreality and, hence, inaccuracy. With 1932 corporate earnings negative on net balance, a negative amount of corporate earnings is imputed to the average stockholder in each income class.

162

In reality, varying degrees of positive corporate earnings were imputable to some stockholders, and greater than average negative corporate earnings were imputable to others. This existing diversity is obscured by use of a simple average for each income class. However, because losses in 1932 were generally sweeping they probably dominated the experience of the majority of stockholders.

If the partnership method of taxing corporate earnings had been instituted in 1932, what would have been the change in federal revenue?

The repeal of the corporate income tax would have meant a loss of revenue from this source of about $286 million.[34] In addition, permitted deduction of negative net corporate earnings from personal income would have caused less revenue from the personal income tax. Actual personal income tax liability was $330 million[35] after imputation of corporate losses to individuals, aggregate personal income tax liability would have been about $233 million less. Thus, while corporate and personal income tax assessments totalled about $616 million, under the partnership method the income tax in 1932 would have come to under $100 million, less than 20 per cent of the actual total.

In recent years, in addition to an economic climate very different from that of the early thirties, basic changes in the structure of the income tax have led to a distinctly different picture. The personal income tax now reaches far down the income pyramid, with a consequent decline in importance of dividends and in potential importance of corporate earnings as components of taxable income. But the evidence from the extreme conditions of 1932 serves as an illustration of a general point which emerges: the volatility of corporate earnings would have a stronger effect on the federal revenue under the partnership method than under the combined corporate-personal income tax system. One additional parenthetical observation follows from this material. The sharp annual fluctuations in corporate earnings suggest that the introduction of the partnership method of taxing corporate earnings on a personal basis would require a greater degree of averaging than the personal income tax now permits.

[34] *Statistics of Income for 1932*, p. 136 gives corporate tax liability as $285,576,000.
[35] *Ibid.*, p. 66.

CHAPTER 7

Relief Provisions of the Internal Revenue Code of 1954

THE Internal Revenue Code of 1954 contains two provisions designed to provide stockholders with some, albeit not full, relief from "double taxation." This chapter analyzes these provisions, using the procedures and findings of earlier chapters for this purpose.

In his Budget Message to Congress for the fiscal year 1955, delivered January 21, 1954, President Eisenhower deplored the existence of two sets of taxes on the income of corporations and proposed changes in the tax law that would constitute a step in the direction of removing double taxation. The proposal and the reasons for it are best described in his own words.

"At present, business income is taxed to both the corporation as it is earned and to the millions of stockholders as it is paid out in dividends. This double taxation is bad from two standpoints. It is unfair and it discourages investment. I recommend that a start be made in the removal of this double taxation by allowing stockholders a credit against their own income taxes as a partial offset for the corporation tax previously paid. This will promote investment which in turn means business expansion and more production and jobs.

"Specifically, I recommend that the credit be allowed on an increasing scale over the next three years. For this year, I recommend that a credit of 5 per cent be allowed; for 1955, a credit of 10 per cent; and, in 1956 and later years, 15 per cent. To avoid shifts in the payment dates of corporation dividends, these credits should apply to dividends received after July 31 of each year. To give the full benefit immediately to small stockholders, I recommend that the first $50 of dividends be completely exempted from tax in 1954 and that the first $100 be exempted in 1955 and later years."[1]

This proposal proved to be one of the thorniest and most controversial considered in writing the revenue bill. After hearings and debate, Congress followed the outlines of the President's suggestion

[1] *The Budget of the United States Government for the Fiscal Year Ending June 30, 1955*, Bureau of the Budget, 1954, p. M 18.

164

but set the amounts at a lower level. Marion B. Folsom, then Under Secretary of the Treasury, noted, "Under the new Code each stockholder will be permitted to exclude from his gross income up to $50 of dividends and will be allowed a credit against tax equal to 4 per cent of the dividends in excess of the exclusion. The amount of the credit is limited to 2 per cent of the stockholder's total taxable income in 1954 and to 4 per cent in later years."[2]

The relief provisions of the Revenue Code of 1954 apply only to distributed corporate earnings. At various points in this study reasons have been set forth for holding that double taxation of this portion of corporate earnings is only part of the complex problem of differential taxation of stockholders, solution of which requires also taking account of the tax treatment of retained earnings. But waiving this consideration and restricting the analysis to earnings for distribution still leaves open the question of the appropriateness of these particular relief provisions. This is not in reference to their failure to remove double taxation completely, a fact recognized by the proponents of the exclusion and credit provisions who considered them not a definitive solution but "a significant step in the right direction."[3] The equity of the relief actually conferred is the matter at issue. To examine this question, three aspects of the relief provisions will be investigated:

1. The absolute amount of relief at different stockholder income levels
2. The unequal degree of relief for stockholders at different income levels
3. What would be accomplished by a higher rate of tax credit and amount of exclusion.

In developing these points, the relief provisions are examined within their setting in the code, i.e., as applicable to distributed earnings. The analysis is conducted first in terms of marginal or incremental dollars of earnings for distribution which serves to isolate certain features of the credit and exclusion. Then with the data developed in this study the variations in amount of earnings for distribution at selected average stockholder income levels are utilized to measure the consequently varying weights of the credit and exclusion in the total amount of relief furnished.

[2] Remarks by Marion B. Folsom, Under Secretary of the Treasury, before the American Management Association, New York City, August 19, 1954. The $50 exclusion applies to separate returns. Stockholders filing jointly are permitted an exclusion of $100, if each has at least $50 of dividends. See *Internal Revenue Code of 1954*, Public Law 591, Chapter 736, Sections 34 and 116.

[3] *Ibid.*

THE EXTRA BURDEN ON EARNINGS FOR DISTRIBUTION

Dividends paid out are not a deductible expense under the corporation income tax. A dollar of earnings devoted to distribution as dividends is assessed for corporate income tax at a rate of 52 per cent, and the remainder when received as dividends, is subject to personal income tax at, for a particular example, 40 per cent. The total tax on the distributed earnings dollar is therefore 71 cents (52 cents of corporate tax and 19 cents of personal income tax on the remaining 48 cents paid out as dividends), a rate of 71 per cent. On a dollar of income from other sources the tax would be only 40 cents. Out of the corporate earnings dollar only 29 cents is left to the dividend recipient after income taxation; from a dollar of income from other sources 60 cents is left after income tax. The extra tax burden equals 31 cents or 31 per cent of earnings made for distribution.

But notice that, since the degree of over-taxation is a function of the personal rate that would have been applicable had there been no corporation income tax to choke off a portion of the earnings made for distribution to stockholders, the corporation income tax does not constitute the same net burden at every income level. One dollar of corporate tax represents a subtraction of less than one dollar from personal income, for, if the money taken by the corporate tax had been paid out to stockholders, something less than one dollar would have been left to them, unless their total income were below the taxable minimum. The higher the stockholder's income, the higher the relevant marginal rate of personal income tax, and hence the lower the net excess burden of the corporation income tax.[4] (Of course, so

---

[4] This point has been clearly and expertly developed by Richard B. Goode (*The Corporation Income Tax*, Wiley, 1951, p. 90.) Failure to recognize this relation is evident in some of the arguments in support of the relief provisions of the Internal Revenue Code of 1954. Representative is the following statement which deals with a 10 per cent credit, but the same argument applies no matter what the percentage value of the credit may be. "The method of adjustment affords greater relief for the low-income investor than for those at higher income levels. The percentage reduction of tax under the combined dividend exclusion and credit is greatest in the lowest bracket and declines progressively as the income level rises. For example, in the case of a married couple filing a joint return, the 10 per cent credit alone will reduce existing tax liabilities on dividend income in the $4,000 first bracket (subject to a 20 per cent rate) by 50 per cent; on dividend income in the $12,000 to $16,000 bracket (subject to a 30 per cent rate) by 33 per cent; and on dividend income in the $32,000 to $36,000 bracket (subject to a 50 per cent rate) by 20 per cent. At very high income levels, the percentage reduction in tax on dividend income will be about 11 per cent." (Marion B. Folsom, "Summary of 27 Principal Provisions of H.R. 8300," in *Hearings before the Senate Committee on Finance on H.R. 8300*, 83rd Cong., 2d sess., Part 1, 1954, pp. 101-102.) This analysis is confined to dividends. It is my opinion that it is more appro-

long as the relevant personal income tax rates fall short of 100 per cent, the corporate income tax will constitute an extra burden to some degree.)

In Table 33 by way of specific illustration are tabulated, for selected marginal rate brackets, the extra burden on a dollar of earnings made for distribution to stockholders, assuming the corporate rate to be 52 per cent.

TABLE 33

Net Extra Burden on a Dollar of Earnings Made for Distribution at Selected Personal Income Tax Marginal Rate Levels with a Corporate Income Tax Rate of 52 Per Cent

MARGINAL RATE OF PERSONAL INCOME TAX (1)	Corporate tax (rate 52%) (2)	Personal tax on dividends $0.48 × (1) (3)	Total tax on a dollar of earnings for distribution (2) + (3) (4)	Personal tax on a dollar of income from other sources $1.00 × (1) (5)	Extra burden on a dollar of earnings for distribution (4) − (5) (6)
20%	$0.520	$0.096	$0.616	$0.200	$0.4160
30	.520	.144	.664	.300	.3640
40	.520	.192	.712	.400	.3120
50	.520	.240	.760	.500	.2600
60	.520	.288	.808	.600	.2080
70	.520	.336	.856	.700	.1560
80	.520	.384	.904	.800	.1040
90	.520	.432	.952	.900	.0520

The conceptual scheme for measuring the differential against earnings for distribution, presented in Chapter 1, may be recalled briefly: where C_e denotes the rate of corporate tax, E the amount of earnings for distribution, and P the applicable marginal rate of personal income tax, the extra burden is equal to $C_e E (1 - P)$. The differential is the extra burden computed as a fraction (or per cent) of earnings for distribution and is equal, therefore, to $C_e (1 - P)$. Since P rises with stockholder income, the differential against earnings for distribution declines with rising levels of stockholder income. Computed by the 1955 corporate and personal rate schedule, for example, the differential on an incremental dollar of earnings for distribution ranges from 42 per cent at the lowest personal marginal rate (20 per cent) to 5 per cent at the highest (91 per cent).[5]

priate to analyze the problem in terms of earnings for distribution and to take account of the fact that the extra burden is inversely related to the stockholder's taxable income level.

[5] This top marginal rate is not applicable to the highest stockholder incomes because of the limitation of effective rates to 87 per cent. It should be noted also

DIVIDEND TAX RELIEF PROVISIONS

Against this background what is the nature of the relief provided in the Internal Revenue Code of 1954? For convenience in exposition the tax credit is discussed first, then the exclusion is analyzed, and finally the two in combination are examined.

Tax Credit Relief per Dollar of Earnings for Distribution

The tax credit feature permits stockholders a personal income tax credit equal to 4 per cent of their dividend receipts. After the corporate tax of 52 per cent, dividends paid amount to 48 cents of every dollar of earnings made for distribution. Therefore the tax credit reckoned per dollar of earnings for distribution is about 2 cents.[6] This amount of tax relief, 2 cents, is obtained at every income level regardless of the marginal rate of personal income tax the stockholder is subject to; or in terms of one dollar of earnings for distribution, the same number of percentage points of relief, 2 per cent, is afforded all stockholders. Thus, for stockholders at the bottom of the taxable income scale, subject to a 20 per cent marginal rate of personal income tax, the extra burden on earnings for distribution is reduced from 42 to 40 cents, or from 42 to 40 per cent; for stockholders subject to the highest marginal rate of personal income tax, the extra burden is reduced from 5 cents to 3 cents, or from 5 to 3 per cent. The relative reduction of the extra burden at the lowest bracket is slight—about 5 per cent—but it is much greater at the highest bracket, some 40 per cent.

Because the provisions of the 1954 Code admittedly go only part of the way in relieving stockholders, and because the levels finally set were lower than those initially suggested, it is instructive to analyze, in addition to the provisions incorporated in the Code, the effects of a higher level of credit and exclusion. Therefore, in this chapter estimates are presented based on the 15 per cent credit and the exclusion of $100 for separate returns and (presumably) $200 for joint returns which would have been in effect in 1956 had the original recommendations been adopted.

Table 34 summarizes the relief from "overtaxation" granted a dollar of earnings made for distribution to stockholders in selected marginal

---

that for stockholders not subject to the personal income tax, the extra burden is the full amount of the corporate tax, there being no offset via a potential personal income tax liability.

6 For simplicity here and in most of what follows, 2 cents, 2 per cent, or 0.02 are used instead of the more accurate 1.96 cents, 1.96 per cent, or 0.0196.

TABLE 34

Relief from Overtaxation Afforded a Dollar of Earnings Made for Distribution to Stockholders in Selected Marginal Rate Brackets by the 4 Per Cent Tax Credit of the Internal Revenue Code of 1954 and by the 15 Per Cent Tax Credit Originally Proposed

MARGINAL RATE OF PERSONAL INCOME TAX (1)	Extra burden on a dollar of earnings for distribution (2)	AFTER 4 PER CENT CREDIT			AFTER 15 PER CENT CREDIT		
		Net extra burden on earnings for distribution (3)	Absolute reduction in extra burden (2) — (3) (4)	Relative reduction in extra burden (4) ÷ (2) (5)	Net extra burden on earnings for distribution (6)	Absolute reduction in extra burden (2) — (6) (7)	Relative reduction in extra burden (7) ÷ (2) (8)
20%	$0.4160	$0.3968	$0.0192	4.6%	$0.3440	$0.0720	17.3%
30	.3640	.3448	.0192	5.3	.2920	.0720	19.8
40	.3120	.2928	.0192	6.2	.2400	.0720	23.1
50	.2600	.2408	.0192	7.4	.1880	.0720	27.7
60	.2080	.1888	.0192	9.2	.1360	.0720	34.6
70	.1560	.1368	.0192	12.3	.0840	.0720	46.2
80	.1040	.0848	.0192	18.5	.0320	.0720	69.2
90	.0520	.0328	.0192	36.9	—.0200	.0720	138.5

rate brackets by the 4 per cent credit incorporated in the Internal Revenue Code of 1954 and by the 15 per cent credit originally proposed. This much may be granted for the existing credit—the extra burden is moderated for all dividend recipients. As between stockholders and other taxpayers, the equity of the income tax structure is improved. But within the stockholder group alone this is not the case, for the credit is a constant absolute amount at all income (marginal rate) levels making the relief afforded of varying relative effectiveness. At the lower income levels only a small fraction of the "discrimination" against stockholders is removed; at the highest income levels, the "extra" burden is significantly ameliorated (column 5). This effect would have been even more pronounced had the 15 per cent credit been adopted (column 8). The tax credit based on dividends received is too blunt a device. To ameliorate an extra burden that varies in intensity with the level of stockholders income, it applies the same rate of credit at all income levels. (It is also worth noting that for nontaxable stockholders the extra burden is not lowered at all by either the credit or the exclusion.)

Exclusion Relief per Dollar of Earnings for Distribution

The exclusion feature of the relief incorporated in the Internal Revenue Code of 1954, translated into relief per incremental dollar of earnings for distribution, gives a picture substantially similar. Stockholders filing separately and with dividend receipts of $50 or less and stockholders filing jointly and with no more than $100 in dividend receipts, would be affected only by the exclusion. Their relief would range from 20 per cent to 91 per cent of their dividends, i.e., from about 10 cents to 44 cents per dollar of earnings for distribution. For stockholders subject to the lowest marginal rate, the extra burden would be reduced from 42 cents to 32 cents, while stockholders at the top of the marginal rate scale would enjoy a tax advantage on corporate earnings made for distribution to them, since the extra burden would fall from 5 cents to —39 cents. Once again we find much greater relative relief at the top of the income scale than at the bottom. Moreover, the exclusion also provides, especially at higher incomes, relief in much higher proportion than the credit does for each dollar of corporate earnings. But, as we shall see, there are generally many more dollars affected by the credit than by the exclusion.

In Table 35 we find measured the degree of relief per dollar of earnings for distribution accomplished by the exclusion. These results must be interpreted in the light of the fact that this relief applies in

TABLE 35

Relief Provided by the Exclusion per Dollar of
Earnings for Distribution Subject to It

MARGINAL RATE OF PERSONAL INCOME TAX (1)	Extra burden on a dollar of earnings for distribution (2)	Net extra burden on a dollar of earnings for distribution after exclusion (3)	Absolute reduction in extra burden due to exclusion (2) — (3) (4)	Relative reduction in extra burden due to exclusion (4) ÷ (2) (5)
20%	$0.4160	$0.3200	$0.0960	23.1%
30	.3640	.2200	.1440	39.6
40	.3120	.1200	.1920	61.5
50	.2600	.0200	.2400	92.3
60	.2080	—.0800	.2880	138.5
70	.1560	—.1800	.3360	215.4
80	.1040	—.2800	.3840	369.2
90	.0520	—.3800	.4320	830.8

most cases to only a proportion of the dividend receipts of stockholders
(dealt with more directly below).

Combined Effect of Credit and Exclusion

With the corporate tax at 52 per cent, earnings for distribution would
be slightly more than twice as great as dividends, and the exclusion
limits would then be $104 (i.e. the pre-tax equivalent of $50) for
separate and $208 (i.e. the pre-tax equivalent of $100) for joint returns.
For brevity only joint returns (the majority) will be considered. The
maximum relief afforded by the exclusion varies from $20 to $91, or
from 20 to 91 per cent of the excluded amount. With the corporate
tax at 52 per cent and dividends equal to 48 per cent of earnings for
distribution (designated as E), the relief provided by the tax credit
equals 0.04 (0.48 E — $100) for all stockholders. Hence the combined
relief, i.e. the sum of the credit and exclusion, will cover a span from
0.02 E + $16 for stockholders in the 20 per cent rate bracket, to
0.02 E + $87 for those subject to a marginal rate of 91 per cent; or,
measured as a differential relative to E, from 0.02 + $16/E$ to 0.02
+ $87/E$. When E is small, say $250 (i.e., when dividends are $120),
the fractions $16/E$ and $87/E$ will be considerably larger than 0.02
and noticeably different from each other. The exclusion feature will
outweigh the credit. When E is large, say $100,000, the two fractions
and the differences between them become insignificant. The credit
predominates; the relief is very close to 2 per cent of earnings for
distribution. We cannot, therefore, simply conclude that the same

patterns of relief as described for the credit and exclusion separately will characterize their combination. The degree of relief will vary with the amount of earnings for distribution.

Net Tax Relief Dependent on Relative Weights of Credit and Exclusion

This directs attention to a consideration hitherto neglected in our discussion, which up to this point has run in terms of a marginal dollar of earnings for distribution. With the exclusion and the credit providing different absolute amounts of relief per dollar of dividends and, consequently, per dollar of earnings for distribution, the net degree of relief will be related to the total amount of earnings for distribution. For this will determine the relative weights of each type of relief in the net total. Hence any assessment of the income class pattern of the degree of relief provided by the Internal Revenue Code of 1954 calls for some specific reference to the proportionate importance of earnings for distribution at each income level. Here the possibilities are legion. Three illustrative types of distribution have been chosen, and another analysis utilizes "typical" distributions based on the "average" stockholder data for 1950 and 1952. In both procedures, results were calculated for the provisions of the 1954 Code and for those of the original proposal.

Table 36 summarizes results for the three illustrative distributions. Consider first the data of section A for which it is assumed that 10 per cent of each stockholder's taxable income comes from corporate earnings for distribution.[7] The degree of relief afforded by the Internal Revenue Code of 1954 (i.e., the relief relative to the extra burden at each income level) traces a U-shaped pattern, falling from its initial level at the bottom of the income scale, reaching a low point in the middle range of incomes, and rising after that point to a high at the top incomes. Close to 25 per cent of the extra burden would be wiped out for stockholders with $1,000 of taxable income, $100 of which came from pre-tax distributed corporate earnings. Relief equal to only 10 per cent of the extra burden would accrue to stockholders with $15,000 of income of which $1,500 represents earnings made for distribution. While close to 45 per cent of the differential against the $500,000 stockholder (with $50,000 from earnings for distribution) would be removed.

Why the U-shaped pattern, when our analysis of relief in terms of a

---

[7] Corporate earnings for distribution equal the pre-corporate tax equivalent of dividends received. Since the corporate tax is 52 per cent, it was assumed that close to 5 per cent of stockholder income, at all income levels, consisted of dividends.

TABLE 36

Degree of Relief Afforded Married Taxpayers by the Exclusion and Credit of the Internal Revenue Code of 1954 and of the Original Proposal

TAXABLE INCOME	Earnings for distribution	PERCENTAGE REDUCTION IN EXTRA BURDEN ON STOCKHOLDERS	
		Internal revenue code of 1954a	Original proposalb
A. Earnings for distribution equal 10% of taxable income			
$1,000	$ 100	23.8	23.8
3,000	300	17.6	23.2
5,000	500	13.8	24.6
10,000	1,000	10.6	24.4
15,000	1,500	10.1	25.3
25,000	2,500	10.8	29.9
50,000	5,000	10.4	42.0
100,000	10,000	17.9	57.3
250,000	25,000	39.5	136.2
500,000	50,000	44.7	160.3
1,000,000	100,000	42.9	157.1
5,000,000	500,000	29.1c	106.9c
B. Earnings for distribution equal 100% of taxable income			
$1,000	$1,000	8.4	19.7
3,000	3,000	5.9	18.1
5,000	5,000	5.4	18.0
10,000	10,000	5.3	18.5
15,000	15,000	5.4	19.2
25,000	25,000	5.9	21.5
50,000	50,000	8.0	29.2
100,000	100,000	11.3	41.7
250,000	250,000	25.0	92.9
500,000	500,000	37.8	141.2
1,000,000	1,000,000	41.2	154.2
5,000,000	5,000,000	28.9c	108.3c
C. Earnings for distribution range from 10% to 90% of taxable income			
$1,000	$ 100	23.8	23.8
3,000	600	11.2	21.2
5,000	1,500	7.7	20.1
10,000	4,000	6.2	19.6
15,000	7,500	6.0	20.3
25,000	15,000	6.5	22.8
50,000	35,000	8.7	31.5
100,000	80,000	11.9	43.7
250,000	225,000	26.4	98.1
500,000	450,000	38.4	143.2
1,000,000	900,000	41.2	154.2
5,000,000	4,500,000	28.4c	106.6c

a $100 exclusion and 4 per cent tax credit.
b $200 exclusion and 15 per cent tax credit.
c Taking account of effective rate limitation of 87 per cent.

marginal dollar for both the exclusion and the credit showed a degree of relief rising steadily with stockholder income? This is a matter of weighting. At the lower stockholder incomes where the absolute amount of earnings for distribution is small, the exclusion, which gives more relief per dollar, far outweighs the credit in importance; hence the relatively high degree of relief. Near the top of the income scale, earnings for distribution are large absolutely, and the weight of the exclusion is negligible. Here the strength of the relief is explained by the fact that the differential, being inversely related to the applicable marginal rate of personal income tax, declines as stockholder income rises, while the proportion of relief afforded by the credit is constant.

The initial proposal of a 15 per cent tax credit and an exclusion twice as large as that finally set would have meant more relief for stockholders (see last column of Table 36); so much so, as a matter of fact, that those near the top of the income scale would end up "undertaxed." However, little additional relief would be provided at the lowest income levels where, under our assumption that earnings for distribution are 10 per cent of taxable income, the higher exclusion would have little or no effect. In effect, then, the pattern would be a steady increase in the percentage of relief, compared with the U-shape noted in the case of the relief provisions that were finally incorporated in the law.

Turning now to the illustrative distribution in which, at every income level, all of taxable income is composed of earnings for distribution (section B), we find different magnitudes, particularly at the lower income levels, but the same general pattern of relief with the left-hand side of the U (reading from low to high incomes) much lower. At the lower income levels, the decline in relative importance of the exclusion explains the results, since the absolute amount of corporate earnings at each income level is ten times that in our first example. At the higher income levels, the lesser degree of relief compared with that of section A is due to the higher differential caused by the fact that the marginal personal rate that would have applied to the corporate tax payment was lower.[8]

The income pattern assumed for section C is probably the most realistic of the three, for it is generally true that the proportion of earnings for distribution rises with stockholder income. As in section A, the degree of relief afforded by the two provisions traces a U-shaped pattern, for the same reasons cited above. Once more, also, for the

---

[8] In other words, computing the section B differential involved dipping lower down the marginal rate scale, since all stockholder income, not just the top layer, came from corporate earnings.

original proposal we find that undertaxation would have resulted near the top of the income scale.

To determine how much relief, in terms more representative of actual experience, may be expected from the Internal Revenue Code of 1954, its provisions have been applied to our average stockholder data for 1950 and 1952.[9] The extra burden has been measured as it was then and as affected by the new code. The results are shown in Table 37.

In columns 6 and 9, tabulating the number of percentage points by which the differential against earnings for distribution is lowered, we find that under either the Code or the original proposal the absolute reduction is greatest in the lower income classes and falls steadily as income rises. This is only an apparent contradiction of our earlier point that relief afforded by the credit is the same at all income levels, while relief traceable to the exclusion rises with stockholder income levels. For the proportion of total relief accounted for by the exclusion, which gives a greater amount of relief at all income levels than the tax credit, declines as the amount of earnings for distribution rises. From the $50,000 level up the relief obtained is virtually constant. (The exception—$5,000,000 in both years, and $1,000,000 as well in 1952—is explained in footnote c of the table.)

But if we appraise the relief relative to the severity of the condition it is designed to ameliorate, the picture that emerges resembles the pattern observed in the illustrative cases of Table 36. Proportionately the greatest relief (1954 Code) occurs at the bottom and top of the income scale, with a lesser degree of easing the extra burden in between (column 7). This was explained above as having a dual cause: At the lower income levels the exclusion has a substantial effect, accounting for the high degree of relief there. Moving up the income scale, the exclusion fades rapidly in importance, and the absolute amount of relief provided tends to be constant. With the differential declining as income rises, after a point the higher the income class the greater the degree of relief provided.

The emphasis on the varying degree of relief afforded at different income levels should not obscure the fact that the Internal Revenue

[9] These data are limited to the "average" experience, and this is both their strength and their weakness for this purpose: they furnish a "typical" amount of earnings for distribution at each income level and hence permit some evaluation of how stockholders at different income levels are affected; but they cloak the diversity at a given income level in the proportion of total income represented by earnings for distribution which is suggested by the illustrative material in Table 36. The reader is reminded that the stockholder income data for 1950 and 1952 include earnings for retention.

175

TABLE 37

Effect on the Differential Against Earnings for Distribution of Relief Provisions of the Internal Revenue Code of 1954 and as Originally Proposed, Estimated from 1950 and 1952 Data

(weighted average of joint and separate returns)

AVERAGE STOCKHOLDER IMPUTED GROSS INCOME ($000's) (1)	EARNINGS FOR DISTRIBUTION		Differential against earnings for distribution (4)	Differential after relief (5)	INTERNAL REVENUE CODE OF 1954a		ORIGINAL PROPOSALb		
	Amount (2)	Per cent of stockholders income (2)÷(1) (3)			Absolute reduction in differential (4)−(5) (6)	Relative reduction in differential (6)÷(4) (7)	Differential after relief (8)	Absolute reduction in differential (4)−(8) (9)	Relative reduction in differential (9)÷(4) (10)
				1950					
1	$ 70	7	34.3	24.3	10.0	29.2%	24.3	10.0	29.2%
3	242	8	34.3	27.8	6.5	19.0	24.4	9.9	28.9
5	376	8	33.8	28.3	5.5	16.3	23.7	10.1	29.9
10	1,343	13	32.9	29.3	3.6	10.9	23.3	9.6	29.2
15	2,176	15	32.1	29.1	3.0	9.3	22.9	9.2	28.7
25	4,458	18	29.2	26.4	2.8	9.6	19.9	9.3	31.8
50	11,519	23	24.9	22.3	2.6	10.4	15.8	9.1	36.5
100	27,013	27	19.1	16.6	2.5	13.1	10.1	9.0	47.1
250	73,418	29	13.2	10.8	2.4	18.2	4.3	8.9	67.4
500	169,989	34	10.0	7.6	2.4	24.0	1.1	8.9	89.0
1,000	358,502	36	7.2	4.9	2.3	31.9	−1.3	8.5	118.1
5,000	2,002,824	40	7.2	6.0	1.2c	16.7c	3.1	4.1c	56.9c

(continued on next page)

Table 37, concluded

AVERAGE STOCKHOLDER IMPUTED GROSS INCOME ($000's) (1)	EARNINGS FOR DISTRIBUTION			INTERNAL REVENUE CODE OF 1954a			ORIGINAL PROPOSALb		
	Amount (2)	Per cent of stockholders income (2) ÷ (1) (3)	Differential against earnings for distribution (4)	Differential after relief (5)	Absolute reduction in differential (4) − (5) (6)	Relative reduction in differential (6) ÷ (4) (7)	Differential after relief (8)	Absolute reduction in differential (4) − (8) (9)	Relative reduction in differential (9) ÷ (4) (10)
				1952					
1	$ 94	9	39.4	28.7	10.7	27.2%	28.7	10.7	27.2%
3	332	11	38.9	33.0	5.9	15.2	28.6	10.3	26.5
5	382	8	38.3	32.4	5.9	15.4	27.9	10.4	27.2
10	1,396	14	37.2	33.8	3.4	9.1	28.3	8.9	23.9
15	2,146	14	34.9	31.7	3.2	9.2	26.1	8.8	25.2
25	5,413	22	31.9	29.4	2.5	7.8	23.7	8.2	25.7
50	14,648	29	25.0	22.8	2.2	8.8	17.2	7.8	31.2
100	32,947	33	16.6	14.4	2.2	13.3	8.8	7.8	47.0
250	94,451	38	11.0	9.0	2.0	18.2	3.4	7.6	69.1
500	220,219	44	6.9	4.9	2.0	29.0	−0.7	7.6	110.1
1,000	468,561	47	4.6	3.0	1.6c	34.8c	−1.3	5.9c	128.3c
5,000	2,500,638	50	6.0d	5.0	1.0c	16.7c	+2.1	3.9c	65.0c

a Exclusion of $50 for separate and $100 for joint returns plus tax credit of 4 per cent of dividends in excess of excluded amount, but not to exceed 4 per cent of taxable income.

b Exclusion of $100 for separate and $200 for joint returns plus tax credit of 15 per cent of dividends in excess of excluded amount, but not to exceed 15 per cent of taxable income.

c Relatively slight reduction in the differential is due to the fact that dividends exceed normal and surtaxable income by a considerable margin, so the credit, limited to 4 or 15 per cent of taxable income, comprised less than these percentages of dividends.

d Differential higher than at $1,000,000 because ceiling rate limitation leads to lower effective marginal rate of personal income tax.

Code of 1954 provides substantial relief—running between 20 and 30 per cent of the extra burden—at the bottom and top of the income scale and moderate relief of about 10 per cent in between. The $100 exclusion (for joint returns) and 4 per cent tax credit were not represented by their proponents as a complete cure, as noted earlier, but rather as a step in the right direction. In this context, the $200 exclusion and 15 per cent tax credit can be considered a further step in the same direction. What would they accomplish?

It is obvious that the relief would be much more significant (columns 9 and 10). The extra burden would be practically wiped out near the top of the income scale (more than wiped out for very high incomes), and more moderately cut over the rest of the income range.[10] But for stockholders in the lower section of the income scale, the original proposal would not have afforded much more relief than the provisions finally adopted. Therefore, under the higher credit and exclusion, the U-shape of the pattern of relative relief would tend to disappear; over the lower range of incomes the degree of relief would be much the same, and after a point it would rise steadily with income (except at the very top of the range).

This points to a basic difficulty in the present exclusion-tax credit method. It is inflexible, in the sense that any combination of a flat exclusion and constant proportionate credit which provided complete relief at a particular income level, would leave stockholders above and below this level differentially taxed—some would still be overtaxed (primarily those below this point), while others (in the main those with higher incomes) would be undertaxed.[11] While this difficulty is inherent in any credit-exclusion scheme of the type instituted in 1954, it follows from this analysis that a goodly portion of the inequality in the relief granted stockholders at different income levels could be removed by switching from a flat-rate credit to one with rates varying inversely with stockholder income. The credit would then be more directly geared to the extra burden.

Finally, returning to the analysis developed in the earlier chapters of this investigation, the double taxation of distributed earnings is only part of the broader problem of the differential taxation of corporate earnings. Viewed in this context, the features of the relief

10 Except, of course, for those stockholders whose incomes are so low relative to their exemptions, credits, and deductions that they pay no personal income tax. No relief is provided them by the credit and exclusion.

11 It must be recognized as a corollary point that if the results achieved by a particular credit-exclusion combination is deemed satisfactory and "just," any change in either the corporate rate or personal income tax rate schedule would disturb this equilibrium and necessitate a readjustment in the relief provisions.

provisions of the Internal Revenue Code of 1954, discussed above, stand out even more sharply. Relief is granted to those who need it and also to those who do not. This feature is highlighted by the data of Table 38.

It is apparent that the differential against stockholders (taking account both of distributed and retained earnings), where it exists, is moderated but slightly, something on the order of 5 to 10 per cent for most of them. On the other hand, existing undertaxation is made more pronounced. Compare, for example, the entries in columns 5 and 9 for the $500,000 average income classes. Had the original proposal been adopted by Congress, this effect would have been still stronger (Table 39). Overtaxation would have been alleviated by between 12 and 15 per cent over the lower part of the income range, and more heavily for stockholders at the higher income levels, while at the top of the income scale undertaxation would have been noticeably accentuated.

Aggregate Relief

Up to this point the discussion of the dividend exclusion and tax credit provisions has run in terms of average or representative stockholders at selected income levels, and the relief they afford has been analyzed in terms of the conceptual scheme and methods developed and applied in Chapters 1 and 2. We turn now to the aggregate experience and consider both the amount and degree of relief provided for all stockholders in relation to the total extra burden. For this analysis the conceptual framework and the magnitudes associated with it, as set forth in Chapter 6, are used.

Two purposes are served by the findings to be presented in this section. First, of course, they indicate in the aggregate, for all stockholders as a single group and also for stockholder income classes, the significance of the relief provided in the Internal Revenue Code of 1954. Secondly, they give an idea of how the picture of differential taxation, developed in connection with the data for years prior to 1954, is modified by the relief provisions. While the data presented earlier for 1950, for example, portray correctly what took place in that year, what they signify for the present status of stockholders will be qualified by these subsequent changes in income tax provisions. Both purposes are conveniently served by use of the material in Chapter 6 that sets out the net extra burden (taking account of both retained and distributed earnings) for all double-taxed stockholders arrayed by income classes.

With regard to data for 1950 and 1952 two questions are raised: What proportion of the extra burden would have been removed if

TABLE 38

Estimated Reduction in Differentials against Net Corporate Earnings and Stockholders due to Relief Provisions of the Internal Revenue Code of 1954,ᵃ Using Data for 1950 and 1952

(weighted average of joint and separate returns)

AVERAGE STOCKHOLDER IMPUTED GROSS INCOME ($000's) (1)	DIFFERENTIAL AGAINST NET CORPORATE EARNINGS				DIFFERENTIAL AGAINST STOCKHOLDER INCOME			
	Before relief (2)	After relief (3)	Absolute reduction (2) − (3) (4)	Relative reduction (4) ÷ (2) (5)	Before relief (6)	After relief (7)	Absolute reduction (6) − (7) (8)	Relative reduction (8) ÷ (6) (9)
	1950							
1	31.7	27.8	3.9	12.3%	5.7	5.0	0.7	12.3%
3	31.1	28.6	2.5	8.0	6.5	6.0	0.5	7.7
5	30.7	28.6	2.1	6.8	6.0	5.6	0.4	6.7
10	28.6	27.2	1.4	4.9	9.9	9.5	0.4	4.0
15	25.9	24.7	1.2	4.6	9.7	9.3	0.4	4.1
25	20.1	19.5	1.1	5.3	9.5	9.0	0.5	5.6
50	10.0	8.8	1.2	12.0	5.9	5.3	0.6	10.2
100	0.4	−0.6	1.0	250.0	0.3	−0.4	0.7	233.3
250	−11.4	−12.3	0.9	7.9ᶜ	−8.7	−9.4	0.7	8.0ᶜ
500	−16.3	−17.2	0.9	5.5ᶜ	−14.3	−15.1	0.8	5.6ᶜ
1,000	−17.6	−18.5	0.9	5.1ᶜ	−16.4	−17.2	0.8	4.9ᶜ
5,000	−17.3	−17.7	0.4ᵇ	2.3ᵇ ᶜ	−17.9	−18.4	0.5ᵇ	2.8ᵇ ᶜ

(continued on next page)

Table 38, *concluded*

AVERAGE STOCKHOLDER IMPUTED GROSS INCOME ($000's) (1)	DIFFERENTIAL AGAINST NET CORPORATE EARNINGS				DIFFERENTIAL AGAINST STOCKHOLDER INCOME			
	Before relief (2)	*After relief* (3)	*Absolute reduction* (2) − (3) (4)	*Relative reduction* (4) ÷ (2) (5)	*Before relief* (6)	*After relief* (7)	*Absolute reduction* (6) − (7) (8)	*Relative reduction* (8) ÷ (6) (9)
				1952				
1	37.9	32.6	5.3	14.0%	7.2	6.2	1.0	13.9%
3	37.4	34.5	2.9	7.8	8.4	7.7	0.7	8.3
5	36.9	33.7	3.2	8.7	5.7	5.3	0.4	7.0
10	34.7	33.0	1.7	4.9	9.9	9.4	0.5	5.1
15	31.3	29.8	1.5	4.8	9.1	8.6	0.5	5.5
25	24.9	23.6	1.3	5.2	10.9	10.4	0.5	4.6
50	12.3	11.2	1.1	8.9	7.4	6.7	0.7	9.5
100	2.8	1.7	1.1	39.3	1.8	1.1	0.7	38.9
250	−7.7	−8.8	1.1	14.3c	−5.9	−6.7	0.8	13.6c
500	−12.0	−13.0	1.0	8.3c	−10.8	−11.7	0.9	8.3c
1,000	−13.2	−14.0	0.8b	6.1b c	−12.5	−13.2	0.7b	5.3b c
5,000	−10.9	−11.4	0.5b	4.6b c	−11.1d	−11.6	0.5b	4.5b c

a Exclusion of $50 for separate and $100 for joint returns plus tax credit of 4 per cent of dividends in excess of excluded amount, but not to exceed 4 per cent of taxable income.

b Relatively slight reduction in the differentials is due to the fact that dividends exceeded normal and surtaxable income by a considerable margin, so the credit, limited to 4 per cent of taxable income, comprised less than 4 per cent of dividends.

c Denotes increase in differentials in favor of net corporate earnings and stockholders.

d Differential in favor of stockholders exceeds differential against net corporate earnings because the latter is more than 100 per cent of stockholders imputed gross income.

TABLE 39

Estimated Reduction in Differentials against Net Corporate Earnings and Stockholder Income due to Relief Provisions Originally Proposed,ᵃ Using Data for 1950 and 1952

(weighted average of joint and separate returns)

AVERAGE STOCKHOLDER IMPUTED GROSS INCOME ($000's)	DIFFERENTIAL AGAINST NET CORPORATE EARNINGS				DIFFERENTIAL AGAINST STOCKHOLDER INCOME			
(1)	Before relief (2)	After relief (3)	Absolute reduction (2) — (3) (4)	Relative reduction (4) ÷ (2) (5)	Before relief (6)	After relief (7)	Absolute reduction (6) — (7) (8)	Relative reduction (8) ÷ (6) (9)
				1950				
1	31.7	27.8	3.9	12.3%	5.7	5.0	0.7	12.3%
3	31.1	27.3	3.8	12.2	6.5	5.7	0.8	12.3
5	30.7	26.8	3.9	12.7	6.0	5.2	0.8	13.3
10	28.6	24.9	3.7	12.9	9.9	8.7	1.2	12.1
15	25.9	22.2	3.7	14.3	9.7	8.4	1.3	13.4
25	20.1	17.0	3.6	17.5	9.5	7.9	1.6	16.8
50	10.0	6.3	3.7	37.0	5.9	3.8	2.1	35.6
100	0.4	—3.1	3.5	875.0	0.3	—2.2	2.5	833.3
250	—11.4	—14.8	3.4	29.8ᶜ	—8.7	—11.3	2.6	29.9ᶜ
500	—16.3	—19.6	3.3	20.2ᶜ	—14.3	—17.3	3.0	21.0ᶜ
1,000	—17.6	—20.9	3.3	18.8ᶜ	—16.4	—19.5	3.1	18.9ᶜ
5,000	—17.3	—18.9	1.6ᵇ	9.2ᶜ	—17.9	—19.5ᵇ	1.6ᵇ	8.9ᶜ

(continued on next page)

Table 39, *concluded*

AVERAGE STOCKHOLDER IMPUTED GROSS INCOME ($000's) (1)	DIFFERENTIAL AGAINST NET CORPORATE EARNINGS				DIFFERENTIAL AGAINST STOCKHOLDER INCOME			
	Before relief (2)	*After relief* (3)	*Absolute reduction* (2) − (3) (4)	*Relative reduction* (4) ÷ (2) (5)	*Before relief* (6)	*After relief* (7)	*Absolute reduction* (6) − (7) (8)	*Relative reduction* (8) ÷ (6) (9)
				1952				
1	37.9	32.6	5.3	14.0%	7.2	6.2	1.0	13.9%
3	37.4	32.3	5.1	13.6	8.4	7.2	1.2	14.3
5	36.9	31.6	5.3	14.4	5.7	4.9	0.8	14.0
10	34.7	30.4	4.3	12.4	9.9	8.6	1.3	13.1
15	31.3	27.0	4.3	13.7	9.1	7.8	1.3	14.3
25	24.9	20.8	4.1	16.5	10.9	9.1	1.8	16.5
50	12.3	8.4	3.9	31.7	7.4	5.1	2.3	31.1
100	2.8	−1.0	3.8	135.7	1.8	−0.7	2.5	138.9
250	−7.7	−11.5	3.8	49.4c	−5.9	−8.8	2.9	49.2c
500	−12.0	−15.8	3.8	31.7c	−10.8	−14.1	3.3	30.6c
1,000	−13.2	−16.1	2.9b	22.0b c	−12.5	−15.3	2.8b	22.4b c
5,000	−10.9	−12.8	1.9b	17.4b c	−11.1d	−13.0	1.9b	17.1b c

a Exclusion of $100 for separate and $200 for joint returns plus tax credit of 15 per cent of dividends in excess of excluded amount, but not to exceed 15 per cent of taxable income.
b Relatively slight reduction in the differentials is due to the fact that dividends exceeded normal and surtaxable income by a considerable margin, so the credit limited to 15 per cent of taxable income comprised less than 15 per cent of dividends.
c Denotes increase in differentials in favor of net corporate earnings and stockholders.
d Differential in favor of stockholders exceeds differential against net corporate earnings because the latter is more than 100 per cent of stockholders' imputed gross income.

the relief provisions of the Internal Revenue Code of 1954 had been in effect at an earlier date? By how much would the overtaxation of stockholders have been ameliorated by the combination of a credit and exclusion of the size originally proposed in the Budget Message to Congress for the fiscal year 1955 (submitted in January of 1954)? Answers to both questions are given with data for 1950 and 1952 and, therefore, serve to illustrate the current picture rather than to define it precisely. In this connection the 1952 data are probably the more pertinent.

In brief recapitulation: in 1950 and 1952 (as well as in all other years covered by this study except 1940 and 1941) and certainly also since 1952, overtaxation was the lot of most stockholders, but undertaxation was the portion of those near the top of the income array. Thus, after imputation of their full pro rata share of corporate earnings in both 1950 and 1952, on net balance an extra burden prevailed in all imputed gross income classes under $100,000, while undertaxation resulted over the rest of the income range. With stockholders arrayed on the basis of adjusted gross income—i.e. income before imputation of the excess of corporate earnings over dividends—the division between under- and overtaxation occurred at a lower point on the income scale, below $25,000 in 1950 and under $50,000 in 1952.

How effective would the 1954 provisions have been in relieving the extra burden? The answer is summarized by the data of Table 40. While the findings are presented on both an adjusted and an imputed gross income basis, the discussion will follow the procedure used throughout this study and concentrate on the imputed gross income array. Much the same story, but with differences in levels of income, is told by the adjusted gross income tabulations.

If the dividend exclusion and credit of the Internal Revenue Code of 1954 had been in effect in 1950, they would have led to a tax abatement of about $270 million for double-taxed stockholders. Slightly less than 63 per cent of this relief would have gone to those overtaxed; the rest would have been provided for stockholders in the income classes that were undertaxed.[12] In 1952 about $281 million of relief

12 It may be helpful at this point to remind the reader once again of the sense in which the words "overtaxation" and "undertaxation" are used. When the personal income tax that would have been due had stockholders been taxed in full on their pro rata share of net corporate earnings exceeded the combination of corporate and personal tax they actually were liable for, undertaxation prevailed. We use overtaxation to describe those instances where the corporate-personal tax liability was higher than the personal levy that would have applied had corporate earnings been subject to this latter tax alone. Thus, under- and overtaxation are here measured in the same way as the current revenue gain or loss are under the

would have been provided, over 25 per cent of which would have fallen in the income classes where, on net balance, stockholders were undertaxed.[13] Looking more closely at the income class distribution, we find the relief to be moderate over most of the income range. In 1950 it ran from just under 3 to 7 per cent of the extra burden for the imputed gross income classes under $50,000. In the class $50,000 and under $100,000, however, nearly half of the overtaxation would have been removed; while for the already undertaxed income classes above this level, relief would still be provided, accentuating the degree of their undertaxation. In 1952, approximately the same pattern of relief would have prevailed, with these modifications: over 73 per cent of the relief would have gone to the overtaxed income classes, an increased degree for the two lowest income classes and a decreased degree for the $50,000 and under $100,000 group; above this level, the relief would have increased undertaxation proportionately more than in 1950.

Compared with these findings for the relief provisions of the 1954 Code, those for the originally proposed 15 per cent credit and $100 exclusion ($200 for joint returns) indicate in both years increased degrees of relief from overtaxation. As to the pattern of relief among income classes, we find that in both years the higher provisions would have moderated overtaxation by between 10 and 15 per cent for stockholders in the imputed income classes under $25,000, and much more significantly from this level to under $100,000; for the $50,000 and under $100,000 class in 1950, the extra burden would have been wiped out. Above the $100,000 point, relief higher, of course, than under the 1954 Code, would have been accorded income classes already, in the aggregate, undertaxed. In all, over 41 per cent of the total of relief would have gone to the undertaxed income classes in 1950, and almost 33 per cent in 1952.

While it is true that the main matter of interest here is what would tend to happen as among income classes, nevertheless, to point up the net result of income class disparities (some overtaxed, others undertaxed), a quick summary is given of the findings for all stockholders taken as a single group. In 1950, over- and undertaxation by income classes netted out to an extra burden of $604 million. Thus, the $270

---

partnership method. No account is taken of the capital gains tax that might in the future be due from stockholders because of the reinvested earnings of a given year.

[13] As a matter of general interest we note our estimate (based on *Statistics of Income for 1955* preliminary data, made available late in 1957) that in 1955 the credit and exclusion brought $300 million of tax relief.

TABLE 40
Relief as a Per Cent of Extra Burden, 1950 and 1952
(dollar amounts in thousands)

DATA ARRAYED BY IMPUTED GROSS INCOME CLASSES, 1950

IMPUTED GROSS INCOME CLASS	Extra burden	RELIEF PROVIDED BY INTERNAL REVENUE CODE OF 1954a		RELIEF PROVIDED BY ORIGINAL PROPOSALb	
		Amount	As a per cent of extra burden	Amount	As a per cent of extra burden
$ 0.6 and under 1	$ 512	$ 15	2.9	$ 15	2.9
1 and under 1.5	2,218	144	6.5	181	8.2
1.5 and under 2	7,144	457	6.4	668	9.4
2 and under 2.5	13,713	928	6.8	1,572	11.5
2.5 and under 3	24,698	1,411	5.7	2,518	10.2
3 and under 4	70,993	3,896	5.5	6,668	9.4
4 and under 5	96,925	7,087	7.3	13,060	13.5
5 and under 7	256,656	13,717	5.3	28,274	11.0
7 and under 10	314,503	13,552	4.3	35,874	11.4
10 and under 25	1,044,297	49,352	4.7	150,105	14.4
25 and under 50	579,963	40,545	7.0	137,580	23.7
50 and under 100	86,756	39,433	45.5	138,182	159.3
100 and under 500	—918,027	74,259	—8.1	272,096	—29.6
500 and under 1,000	—443,428	14,380	—3.2	53,573	—12.1
1,000 and over	—533,030	10,491	—2.0	40,097	—7.5
Total	603,893	269,667	44.7	880,463	145.8

DATA ARRAYED BY IMPUTED GROSS INCOME CLASSES, 1952

IMPUTED GROSS INCOME CLASS	Extra burden	Amount	As a per cent of extra burden	Amount	As a per cent of extra burden
$ 0.6 and under 1	$ 610	$ 90	14.8	$ 90	14.8
1 and under 1.5	2,911	341	11.7	420	14.4
1.5 and under 2	11,946	967	8.1	1,521	12.7
2 and under 2.5	18,741	1,394	7.4	2,322	12.4
2.5 and under 3	28,983	1,927	6.6	3,155	10.9
3 and under 4	87,676	5,891	6.7	10,312	11.8
4 and under 5	119,013	8,145	6.8	14,906	12.5
5 and under 7	299,491	19,254	6.4	35,831	12.0
7 and under 10	448,263	20,453	4.6	50,817	11.3
10 and under 25	1,201,953	56,023	4.7	155,071	12.9
25 and under 50	807,901	43,670	5.4	147,393	18.2
50 and under 100	316,574	45,898	14.5	161,873	51.1
100 and under 500	—482,621	57,259	—11.9	209,028	—43.3
500 and under 1,000	—235,124	10,654	—4.5	39,645	—16.9
1,000 and over	—298,015	9,062	—3.0	33,859	—11.4
Total	2,328,302	281,028	12.1	866,243	37.2

Table 40, *concluded*

DATA ARRAYED BY ADJUSTED GROSS INCOME CLASSES, 1950

ADJUSTED GROSS INCOME CLASS	Extra burden	RELIEF PROVIDED BY INTERNAL REVENUE CODE OF 1954[a]		RELIEF PROVIDED BY ORIGINAL PROPOSAL[b]	
		Amount	As a per cent of extra burden	Amount	As a per cent of extra burden
$ 0.6 and under 1	$ 13,325	$ 338	2.5	$ 539	4.0
1 and under 1.5	41,360	1,315	3.2	3,175	7.7
1.5 and under 2	74,166	2,623	3.5	6,668	9.0
2 and under 2.5	101,909	3,544	3.5	8,963	8.8
2.5 and under 3	122,273	4,432	3.6	11,171	9.1
3 and under 4	260,349	10,545	4.1	26,537	10.2
4 and under 5	251,501	11,196	4.5	28,296	11.3
5 and under 8	615,017	27,495	4.5	75,722	12.3
8 and under 10	284,655	14,704	5.1	44,472	15.6
10 and under 25	752,538	61,316	8.1	201,396	26.8
25 and under 50	—119,206	49,732	—41.7	172,873	—145.0
50 and under 100	—504,062	38,486	—7.6	137,014	—27.2
100 and under 500	—978,955	36,381	—3.7	134,485	—13.7
500 and under 1,000	—173,340	4,825	—2.8	18,020	—10.4
1,000 and over	—137,637	2,735	—2.0	11,132	—8.1
Total	603,893	269,667	44.7	880,463	145.8

DATA ARRAYED BY ADJUSTED GROSS INCOME CLASSES, 1952

ADJUSTED GROSS INCOME CLASS	Extra burden	Amount	As a per cent of extra burden	Amount	As a per cent of extra burden
$ 0.6 and under 1	$ 15,766	$ 491	3.1	$ 1,058	6.7
1 and under 1.5	41,438	1,464	3.5	3,416	8.2
1.5 and under 2	84,894	2,987	3.5	7,277	8.6
2 and under 2.5	104,345	3,876	3.7	9,483	9.1
2.5 and under 3	120,953	4,761	3.9	11,192	9.3
3 and under 4	278,264	11,311	4.1	27,565	9.9
4 and under 5	255,415	12,306	4.8	27,816	10.9
5 and under 8	783,747	35,939	4.6	89,030	11.4
8 and under 10	359,088	17,556	4.9	45,507	12.7
10 and under 30	1,237,638	80,593	6.5	253,356	20.5
30 and under 50	7,502	36,730	489.6	125,993	1,679.5
50 and under 100	—221,046	36,860	—16.7	131,308	—59.4
100 and under 500	—563,627	29,261	—5.2	107,482	—19.1
500 and under 1,000	—77,230	3,136	—4.1	11,698	—15.1
1,000 and over	—98,845	3,757	—3.8	14,062	—14.2
Total	2,328,302	281,028	12.1	866,243	37.2

[a] Dividend exclusion of $50 ($100 for joint returns) and a credit against personal income tax equal to 4 per cent of dividends in excess of the excluded amount.

[b] Dividend exclusion of $100 ($200 for joint returns) and a credit against personal income tax equal to 15 per cent of dividends in excess of the excluded amount.

million of relief would have removed nearly 45 per cent of aggregate overtaxation. In 1952 when the aggregate extra burden was much heavier—$2.3 billion—the relief of $281 million would have cut it by only 12 per cent. Under the higher relief measures originally proposed, substantially greater relief, of course, would have resulted. For 1950 it would have totaled an estimated $880 million, more than enough to wipe out overtaxation in the aggregate, while in 1952 the relief of $866 million would have cut the extra burden totaled (algebraically) for all stockholders by 37 per cent.[14]

14 There is an apparent discrepancy in these results, viz., that under the provisions of the Internal Revenue Code of 1954 slightly greater relief would have been forthcoming in 1952 than in 1950, while the opposite would have been the case with the higher credit and exclusion initially proposed. This is explained by the fact that under the original proposal, because of the much higher credit, the relief going to the top income classes would have been over three and a half times greater than under the credit and exclusion actually adopted, whereas, near the bottom of the income scale, the proposal's relief would have been less than twice as great. A higher fraction of total relief would have gone to those near the top of the income scale in 1950 than in 1952.

CHAPTER 8

Summary of Findings

It is necessary at this point, before summarizing the findings, to repeat the caution that in their derivation a number of particular assumptions were used. Resulting qualifications of the findings, set forth in detail (especially in Chapters 1, 2, and 4 and Appendix B), serve to warn the reader of reservations to be kept in mind in reviewing the following statements. The brief summary given here is intended only to underline the major points that emerge either as facts relevant to tax equity or as conclusions about the significance of the findings. Each must be interpreted with reference to the foregoing presentations of the underlying conceptual structure and the interrelations of factors affecting the income tax burden on stockholders. The findings, therefore, are more equivocal than their bald presentation here may suggest.

This brief review begins with a recapitulation of the answers, developed in the course of the study, to the two questions which marked its starting point: How heavy has been the extra tax burden on stockholders' pro rata share of net corporate earnings? How heavy has been the extra burden, measured in terms of effective rates on all of stockholders' income, compared with that for other taxpayers?

In arriving at an answer to the first question, net corporate earnings was broken down into two components—earnings for distribution and earnings for retention. *Earnings for distribution,* taxed at the corporate level when earned and the personal level when distributed, is the segment of net corporate earnings directly involved in the charge of double taxation. No surprise attaches to the finding that the earnings for distribution component was subject to heavier taxation in all years studied and at all income levels than it would have been if reached in full by the personal income tax alone. But there existed in every year consistent variations in the height of the extra tax load by income levels. For the differential against earnings for distribution (i.e., the net extra burden computed as a per cent of earnings for distribution) is an inverse function of the marginal rate of personal income tax to which a stockholder was liable. Therefore, in general, the higher the level of stockholder income, the lower the differential against earnings for distribution. At any given income level significant variations were found from year to year in the relative heaviness of the extra burden on earnings for distribution, variations determined by the gap between the corporate and personal rate which changed from year to year. For reference at various points in the summary, Table 41 gives the numerical results for 1950. (The reader is referred to Appendix A for summary data on the range of the value of the differentials over the period 1940 to 1952.)

TABLE 41

Differentials, 1950, Variant 2

(*weighted average of joint and separate returns*)

AVERAGE STOCKHOLDER IMPUTED GROSS INCOME ($000's)	DIFFERENTIAL AGAINST:			
	Earnings for distribution	Earnings for retention	Net corporate earnings	Stockholder income
1	34.3	30.0	31.7	5.7
3	34.3	29.1	31.1	6.5
5	33.8	28.8	30.7	6.0
10	32.9	26.0	28.6	9.9
15	32.1	22.0	25.9	9.7
25	29.2	15.2	20.6	9.5
50	24.9	0.4	10.0	5.9
100	19.1	—11.4	0.4	0.3
250	13.2	—26.9	—11.4	—8.7
500	10.0	—32.9	—16.3	—14.3

For the undistributed segment of net corporate earnings—*earnings for retention*—the results are more complex. At the lower stockholder income levels, earnings for retention were found to be overtaxed, while at the higher income levels they were shown to be undertaxed in comparison with the potential tax liability on this income segment had it been subject, in full, to the personal income tax alone[1] (except in 1940 when overtaxation prevailed at all income levels). The differential against earnings for retention, being a function of the potentially applicable rate of personal income tax, varied inversely with the size of stockholder income, and was positive or negative depending on whether the applicable personal rate fell short of or exceeded the corporate tax. Evidence on the degree of over- and undertaxation of this component of net corporate earnings for 1950 appears in Table 41, and for all years in Appendix A.

The degree of differential taxation of stockholders and the direction

[1] Low and high income levels are purely relative in this connection. The dividing line between them, which varied from year to year, occurred at a point in the income scale usually associated with the upper tail of the distribution. However, because stockholder income is more highly concentrated than the income of all taxpayers, the area of undertaxation was not limited to a minute segment of the distribution either in terms of number of stockholders involved or, more particularly, in terms of the fraction of earnings for retention falling in the undertaxed portion of the array.

190

of the differentials on the *net corporate earnings component* (i.e., whether it was overtaxed or undertaxed) depended on the stockholder income level. Net corporate earnings is the sum of earnings for distribution and earnings for retention, and the differential against it is a weighted average of the differential against each of its components. It was found, like the differentials on both components, to decline as stockholder income rose, in every year covered by the study. Moreover, in all but the first two years investigated (1940 and 1941) at some point on the income scale, the negative differential on earnings for retention outweighed the differential against earnings for distribution, causing a shift from over- to undertaxation of net corporate earnings. Thus it may be concluded that, while in all years of the decade of the forties and of the early fifties over most of the income scale the net corporate earnings component of stockholder income was overtaxed, in most years and for stockholders in the upper reaches of the income scale, undertaxation was the result.

These findings for the net corporate earnings component apply also to the *total of stockholder income from all sources.* But here the value of the differential is lower since the relationship is between the same absolute extra burden noted above and a base of income from all sources of which stockholders' pro rata share of net corporate earnings is only one component. In all years covered, over most of the income range, stockholders were subject to a significantly higher rate of income taxation than would have applied if all their income including their full pro rata share of net corporate earnings had been subject to the personal income tax alone. For stockholders near the top of the income array, however, the outcome was reversed; despite the corporation income tax, a lower tax liability actually occurred than would have been due on all their income including their pro rata share of net corporate earnings under the personal income tax alone. Unlike the other differentials which followed a smooth pattern of decline reading up the stockholder income scale, the pattern of the differential against stockholders starting from the lowest income level, rose to a peak typically around the $10,000 income level.[2] Then it declined continuously to a cross-over point after which it became negative and ran increasingly in favor of stockholders as their income rose. The results emphasize two problems raised in every year of the study except 1940 and 1941 by the existing method of taxing net corporate earnings: the overtaxation to which most stockholders were subject; and the undertaxation afforded stockholders at the upper income levels.

[2] This is explained by the varying proportion of corporate earnings to the total of stockholder income (see Chapter 2).

191

How are the results modified by alternative assumptions and definitions?

Under an assumption differing from that used in the standard method, e.g., the assumption that *part of the corporate tax is shifted* rather than that it all rests on corporate earnings, the results summarized above would follow the same general pattern with modification of the specific values of the differentials. The extra burden on corporate earnings (both segments) and stockholders would be lighter; the positive differentials at applicable income levels would be less onerous; the negative differentials at income levels above the cross-over would run more heavily in favor of earnings for retention, net corporate earnings, and stockholders. The cross-over from burden to benefit would occur lower down the stockholder income scale. The larger the proportion of corporate income tax assumed to be shifted, the more pronounced the difference between the results under the shifting assumption and the standard method.

Use of a definition of *corporate earnings as net of current costs of maintaining inventory and replacing depreciable assets* would lead to larger extra burdens compared with those summarized above for the standard method of this study, which accepts the Internal Revenue Service definition of corporate earnings as, in general, net of historical costs. In most years covered, especially those characterized by rising price levels, current cost adjustments for inventory and depreciation would result in higher differentials against corporate earnings and stockholders, lower differentials in their favor, and the occurrence of cross-over points higher up the income scale.

If the *shifting assumption and the current costs adjustment* were combined and differentials computed on this basis, the general pattern resulting would, on net balance, be the same as the standard method's, but undertaxation would appear further up the income scale, and the degree of overtaxation would be heavier.

Consideration of *only corporate earnings for distribution* in analyzing the differential burden on stockholders led to differentials against net corporate earnings and stockholders lower at all income levels than those obtained by the standard procedures in which retained as well as distributed earnings were imputed to stockholders. The differentials against stockholders in the lower brackets were shown to be lower, and in the higher brackets to be higher. No cross-over occurred in this test from extra tax burden to tax benefit at any level of stockholders income.

How would federal revenue be affected by the abolition of differential taxation of stockholders?

All differential taxation of stockholders would be removed if the corporate tax were abolished and their tax liability were computed by the same method that now applies to partnerships, i.e., by taxing their full pro rata share of corporate earnings fully and promptly as part of personal income. Without judging the desirability or practicability of this method, estimates were made of the effects of such a change on the federal government's revenue. (The difference in revenue yield may also be construed as the net revenue contribution of the separate and distinct corporate levy as compared with the alternative possibility of taxing corporate earnings fully and promptly under the personal income tax.) By a related set of computations the aggregate extra burden on stockholders was measured.

Detailed estimates were made for 1947, 1949, 1950, and 1952. For 1947, it was found that, given the assumption that the corporate income tax is not shifted, abolition of this tax coupled with the prompt and full taxation of stockholders' pro rata share of net corporate earnings would have resulted in no immediate loss of revenue to the Treasury. If anything, there might have been a slight revenue gain in that year. However, because the basis of valuation of stock for computing capital gains in the future would have been raised by the amount of imputed undistributed earnings, capital gains tax collections in the future would have fallen one billion or so short of what they otherwise would have been. For 1949, the total revenue loss was found to be heavier. Current revenues would have been lower by about $2 billion, with an additional $1 billion revenue shortfall showing up in later years. For 1950 the estimated current decline in revenues would have been on the order of $3 billion plus a future revenue loss from a lower capital gains tax liability of about $1.5 billion. For 1952 a heavier current revenue loss was estimated, $5.7 billion, plus a future revenue loss of $1 billion. Of greatest contemporary interest is the finding for 1955. (The estimate in this case is less accurate than for the four years just mentioned.) In 1955 itself the change in the tax treatment of corporate earnings called for by the partnership method would have cost the Treasury some $5 billion, with an additional billion and a quarter of revenue loss via lowered capital gains tax liability showing up later. To recoup the immediate revenue loss, a rise would have been required in personal income tax rates of about 3.3 percentage points applied to all taxpayers. An analysis limited to taxable stockholders (those who were reached by the personal income tax) resulted in a somewhat different picture. In 1950, for example, their current tax liability would have been only about $600 million lower under the partnership method. Under this aggregate, however, lay great diversity in income class experience; the partnership method would have yielded a lower tax liability, in the aggregate, for stockholders in the imputed gross income classes up to $100,000 and a higher tax liability in the classes over this level.

Does the corporation income tax increase or decrease the progressivity of the income tax structure?

Investigation of the effect of the corporation income tax on the progressivity of the income tax structure was necessarily restricted to stockholders since, under the standard assumption, they are the only personal income taxpayers affected by the corporation income tax. Extreme examples found of differential rates of income tax on stockholders with the same taxable imputed income led to the conclusion that, at best, the progressivity effect is very crude because it affects only stockholders, and it affects unevenly stockholders with similar total incomes. A further examination restricted to average stockholders in which this unevenness was averaged out, showed the progressivity effect to be different under each of two definitions. Under one, the effect was only partial, greater progressivity over the lower and, in some years, the middle span of incomes, with the rest of the income range less progressively taxed than it would have been under the personal income tax alone. Under the other, there was virtually no progressivity effect; on the contrary, in almost all cases stockholders were taxed less progressively than they would have been without the corporate tax and with their corporate earnings subject in full to the personal tax.

How do the relief provisions of 1954 affect the income tax burden of stockholders?

Finally, the stockholder relief provisions of the Internal Revenue Code of 1954 were investigated. The two applicable features of the revised code are the exclusion of the first $50 ($100 for joint returns) of dividend receipts from taxable income, and a credit against personal income tax equal to 4 per cent of dividends over the excluded amount. These provisions were examined first within the context of their avowed purpose, to alleviate to some extent the double-taxation of dividends. They were found subject to criticism on the grounds that they take account only incidentally of the fact that, because personal income tax rates are progressive, the weight of double-taxation declines as stockholder income rises. The relief behaves capriciously. Detailed analysis at selected average stockholder income levels showed the greatest degree of relief at the bottom and top of the income scale. In perspective against the background of retained as well as distributed earnings, the relief provisions moderated overtaxation only slightly (and after a point inversely to the rate of overtaxation) while undertaxation was made more pronounced.

194

Appendix A

THIS appendix presents tabulations of the differentials, variants 1, 2, and 3, annually from 1940 through 1952 with 1942 and 1943 omitted (Table A-1), and for each of the seven alternative tests conducted with the 1947 data (Table A-2).

TABLE A-1

Annual Measures of the Differentials, 1940-1941; 1944-1952

(per cent)

1940

AVERAGE STOCK-HOLDER IMPUTED GROSS INCOME ($000's)	Earnings for distribution Variants 1, 2, 3	DIFFERENTIAL AGAINST:								
		Earnings for retention			Net corporate earnings			Stockholder imputed gross income		
		Variant			Variant			Variant		
		1	2	3	1	2	3	1	2	3
1	25.9									
2	26.0	75.2	76.2	81.0	35.3	35.4	36.3	9.8	9.8	10.1
3	26.1	74.2	75.0	80.0	35.4	35.6	36.5	7.4	7.4	7.6
4	26.0	74.1	74.8	79.9	35.3	35.4	36.4	6.4	6.4	6.6
5	26.0	74.7	75.7	81.1	35.2	35.4	36.5	10.9	11.0	11.3
6	25.4	74.5	75.5	80.6	35.3	35.5	36.5	10.1	10.2	10.5
8	25.2	70.4	71.3	76.5	34.0	34.2	35.2	12.0	12.1	12.4
10	24.5	67.7	68.8	74.0	33.3	33.5	34.5	12.6	12.7	13.0
12	24.1	66.7	68.2	73.3	32.6	32.8	33.8	8.8	8.9	9.1
15	22.6	62.9	64.4	69.6	31.5	31.8	32.8	12.3	12.4	12.8
20	21.3	59.3	61.2	66.4	29.6	30.0	31.0	14.9	15.1	15.6
25	16.9	53.2	55.2	60.4	27.4	27.8	28.7	13.7	13.8	14.3
50	14.5	39.5	41.7	46.9	21.2	21.6	22.6	12.0	12.2	12.8
75	12.9	27.2	29.4	34.6	16.9	17.3	18.3	12.1	12.4	13.1
100	10.8	20.7	23.0	28.2	14.4	14.8	15.8	10.8	11.1	11.9
150	10.0	16.1	18.4	23.6	11.8	12.2	13.2	9.0	9.3	10.1
200	10.0	16.9	19.1	24.3	11.3	11.7	12.7	8.4	8.8	9.5
250	10.0	14.0	16.2	21.4	10.7	11.2	12.2	8.0	8.3	9.1
500	8.7	7.8	10.0	15.2	8.5	8.9	9.9	7.6	8.0	8.8

Table A-1, *continued*
(*per cent*)
1941

AVERAGE STOCK-HOLDER IMPUTED GROSS INCOME ($000's)	Earnings for distribution Variants 1, 2, 3	DIFFERENTIAL AGAINST:								
		Earnings for retention			Net corporate earnings			Stockholder imputed gross income		
		Variant 1	2	3	Variant 1	2	3	Variant 1	2	3
1										
2	40.1	48.4	50.0	59.8	43.9	44.6	48.8	12.5	12.7	13.9
3	40.0	48.8	50.4	60.4	43.8	44.5	48.8	12.6	12.8	14.0
4	40.2	48.7	50.5	60.6	43.8	44.5	48.9	12.6	12.8	14.1
5	39.5	45.9	47.8	57.9	42.3	43.1	47.5	14.4	14.7	16.1
6	38.7	45.4	47.4	57.4	41.5	42.4	46.7	15.0	15.4	16.9
8	37.7	40.8	42.8	52.8	39.1	39.9	44.3	14.6	14.9	16.6
10	36.8	38.4	40.8	50.8	37.5	38.5	42.8	14.5	14.9	16.6
12	35.4	34.6	37.4	47.5	35.1	36.3	40.6	14.0	14.4	16.2
15	33.2	29.1	32.1	42.1	31.4	32.7	37.1	12.9	13.5	15.3
20	31.1	21.5	24.9	34.9	27.0	28.4	32.8	12.5	13.2	15.2
25	28.4	15.2	19.0	29.0	22.7	24.3	28.7	11.6	12.4	14.6
50	22.0	2.2	6.5	16.5	13.5	15.3	19.6	8.4	9.6	12.3
75	19.8	-3.8	0.6	10.6	9.7	11.5	15.8	7.2	8.6	11.9
100	17.7	-7.0	-2.7	7.3	7.0	8.9	13.2	5.4	6.8	10.1
150	15.4	-10.1	-5.8	4.3	4.4	6.2	10.6	3.4	4.9	8.3
200	14.6	-11.2	-6.9	3.2	3.5	5.3	9.6	2.8	4.3	7.8
250	14.0	-11.4	-7.1	3.0	3.1	4.9	9.2	2.5	4.1	7.7
500	13.0	-16.5	-12.2	-2.1	0.2	2.1	6.4	0.2	1.9	5.9

Table A-1, *continued*
(*per cent*)
1944

AVERAGE STOCK-HOLDER IMPUTED GROSS INCOME ($000's)	Earnings for distribution Variants 1, 2, 3	DIFFERENTIAL AGAINST:								
		Earnings for retention			Net corporate earnings			Stockholder imputed gross income		
		Variant			Variant			Variant		
		1	2	3	1	2	3	1	2	3
1	44.0	38.6	40.2	49.4	41.1	41.9	47.1	9.0	9.2	10.4
2	44.1	38.4	40.0	49.4	40.9	41.8	47.1	9.3	9.5	10.7
3	44.4	37.6	39.0	48.4	40.6	41.3	46.6	10.6	10.8	12.1
4	43.8	36.6	38.1	47.4	39.8	40.6	45.8	13.6	13.9	15.7
5	43.1	36.6	38.2	47.6	39.5	40.4	45.6	14.4	14.8	16.7
6	43.1	33.2	34.9	44.1	37.6	38.5	43.7	19.1	19.6	22.2
8	41.1	29.9	31.5	40.8	34.8	35.7	41.0	17.5	17.9	20.6
10	40.0	26.4	28.3	37.6	32.3	33.4	38.6	16.1	16.6	19.2
12	37.6	20.7	22.8	32.1	28.1	29.3	34.5	13.8	14.4	17.0
15	34.3	12.0	14.4	23.7	21.8	23.1	28.3	11.1	11.8	14.5
20	30.1	5.5	8.5	17.8	16.3	18.0	23.2	8.6	9.5	12.3
25										
50	20.8	−8.6	−5.1	4.2	4.3	6.3	11.5	2.4	3.5	6.5
75	17.5	−16.7	−12.9	−3.6	−1.7	0.4	5.6	−1.1	0.2	3.6
100	15.1	−22.1	−18.2	−8.9	−5.8	−3.6	1.6	−4.2	−2.6	1.2
150	12.5	−28.5	−24.5	−15.2	−10.5	−8.3	−3.1	−8.9	−7.0	−2.6
200	9.5	−30.7	−26.7	−17.4	−13.1	−10.9	−5.6	−11.2	−9.3	−4.8
250	7.0	−31.4	−27.4	−18.1	−14.6	−12.3	−7.1	−12.6	−10.7	−6.1
500	4.1	−32.4	−28.4	−19.1	−16.4	−14.1	−8.9	−14.6	−12.6	−7.9

Table A-1, *continued*
(per cent)
1945

AVERAGE STOCK-HOLDER IMPUTED GROSS INCOME ($000's)	Earnings for distribution Variants 1, 2, 3	DIFFERENTIAL AGAINST:								
		Earnings for retention Variant			Net corporate earnings Variant			Stockholder imputed gross income Variant		
		1	2	3	1	2	3	1	2	3
1	39.4	34.9	36.8	47.2	37.1	38.0	43.4	7.6	7.8	8.9
2	39.2	35.3	36.9	46.9	37.2	38.0	43.2	8.7	8.9	10.1
3	39.6	35.3	36.8	46.9	37.4	38.1	43.3	9.6	9.8	11.1
4	39.5	34.3	35.9	46.1	36.8	37.7	42.9	9.0	9.2	10.4
5	38.4	33.1	34.7	44.9	35.7	36.5	41.7	9.4	9.6	11.0
6	38.4	33.0	34.6	44.8	35.6	36.4	41.7	10.7	10.9	12.5
8	36.8	29.1	30.8	41.0	32.8	33.7	38.9	11.3	11.6	13.4
10	36.3	25.0	27.0	37.1	30.5	31.5	36.7	11.1	11.4	13.3
12	34.3	21.7	23.8	34.0	27.8	28.9	34.1	10.4	10.8	12.7
15	32.3	15.8	18.2	28.4	23.8	25.0	30.3	9.1	9.5	11.5
20	28.4	7.3	9.9	20.0	17.5	18.9	24.1	7.4	7.9	10.1
25	25.3	1.1	4.1	14.3	12.8	14.4	19.6	5.8	6.5	8.8
50	18.4	−12.1	−8.4	1.8	2.7	4.6	9.8	1.5	2.6	5.6
75	15.4	−20.3	−16.2	−6.0	−3.0	−0.9	4.4	−1.9	−0.6	2.8
100	12.3	−25.8	−21.4	−11.2	−7.3	−5.0	0.2	−4.8	−3.3	0.1
150	8.7	−33.0	−28.6	−18.4	−12.8	−10.5	−5.3	−8.5	−7.0	−3.5
200	6.0	−34.4	−30.0	−19.8	−14.8	−12.5	−7.3	−10.1	−8.6	−5.0
250	4.6	−35.0	−30.6	−20.4	−15.8	−13.5	−8.3	−11.3	−9.7	−5.9
500	3.6	−36.0	−31.6	−21.4	−16.8	−14.5	−9.3	−13.8	−11.9	−7.6

Table A-1, *continued*
(*per cent*)
1946

	Earnings for distribution	DIFFERENTIAL AGAINST:								
AVERAGE STOCK-HOLDER IMPUTED GROSS INCOME ($000's)		Earnings for retention			Net corporate earnings			Stockholder imputed gross income		
		Variant			Variant			Variant		
	Variants 1, 2, 3	1	2	3	1	2	3	1	2	3
1	26.7	21.5	24.3	38.9	23.5	25.2	34.3	5.4	5.8	7.9
2	27.7	21.0	23.0	37.5	23.5	24.8	33.8	5.5	5.8	7.9
3	27.4	21.1	23.4	38.0	23.5	24.9	34.0	4.4	4.7	6.4
4	27.5	20.2	22.5	36.9	22.9	24.3	33.4	5.2	5.6	7.6
5	27.0	19.2	21.8	36.3	22.1	23.7	32.8	5.2	5.6	7.7
6	27.0	19.2	21.7	36.2	22.1	23.7	32.8	6.2	7.0	9.7
8	26.1	15.3	17.8	32.4	19.4	20.9	30.0	6.4	7.0	10.0
10	25.6	11.4	14.3	28.9	16.7	18.5	27.7	5.9	6.5	9.7
12	24.3	9.0	12.3	26.9	14.7	16.8	25.9	5.4	6.2	9.5
15	23.1	3.7	7.6	22.1	11.0	13.4	22.5	4.2	5.1	8.6
20	20.9	−4.5	−0.3	14.3	5.0	7.7	16.8	2.1	3.2	7.0
25	18.8	−10.3	−5.1	9.4	0.6	3.8	13.0	0.3	1.7	5.8
50	14.5	−23.0	−16.9	−2.3	−9.0	−5.2	4.0	−5.2	−3.0	2.3
75	12.9	−30.5	−24.3	−9.7	−14.3	−10.4	−1.3	−9.3	−6.8	−0.8
100	11.1	−35.7	−29.5	−14.9	−18.3	−14.3	−5.2	−12.2	−9.6	−3.5
150	8.9	−42.5	−36.2	−21.6	−23.3	−19.4	−10.2	−16.0	−13.3	−7.1
200	7.3	−44.6	−38.3	−23.8	−25.2	−21.3	−12.2	−17.8	−15.1	−8.6
250	6.1	−45.3	−39.0	−24.5	−26.1	−22.2	−13.1	−19.3	−16.4	−9.7
500	4.9	−46.3	−40.1	−25.5	−27.1	−23.3	−14.1	−23.0	−19.7	−12.0

Table A-1, *continued*
(*per cent*)
1947

AVERAGE STOCK-HOLDER IMPUTED GROSS INCOME ($000's)	Earnings for distribution Variants 1, 2, 3	DIFFERENTIAL AGAINST:								
		Earnings for retention			Net corporate earnings			Stockholder imputed gross income		
		Variant			Variant			Variant		
		1	2	3	1	2	3	1	2	3
1	28.4	20.1	22.6	37.7	22.9	24.6	34.6	5.5	5.9	8.3
2	27.5	19.5	21.9	36.7	22.2	23.8	33.6	5.0	5.3	7.5
3	27.9	19.5	21.7	36.5	22.3	23.8	33.7	4.5	4.8	6.8
4	27.8	19.6	21.9	36.8	22.3	23.9	33.7	5.0	5.3	7.5
5	27.2	17.6	20.1	35.0	20.8	22.5	32.5	4.8	5.2	7.4
6	27.3	17.6	20.1	35.0	20.9	22.5	32.4	6.3	6.8	9.8
8	26.7	13.9	16.3	31.2	18.1	19.8	29.7	6.0	6.6	9.8
10	25.9	10.8	13.6	28.5	15.8	17.7	27.6	5.4	6.0	9.4
12	24.7	7.8	10.7	25.6	13.5	15.4	25.3	5.1	5.9	9.6
15	23.5	2.9	5.8	20.7	9.8	11.7	21.6	4.0	4.8	8.8
20	20.4	—5.0	—1.6	13.3	3.5	5.8	15.7	1.6	2.6	7.2
25	20.1	—11.1	—7.1	7.8	—0.6	2.0	11.9	—0.3	1.0	5.9
50	15.3	—24.0	—19.0	—4.1	—10.8	—7.6	2.4	—6.8	—4.8	1.5
75	13.8	—31.2	—25.3	—10.4	—16.1	—12.2	—2.3	—11.5	—8.7	—1.6
100	12.1	—36.7	—30.4	—15.5	—20.3	—16.2	—6.3	—14.9	—11.9	—4.6
150	9.6	—43.4	—36.9	—22.0	—25.6	—21.3	—11.4	—19.3	—16.1	—8.6
200	8.1	—45.8	—39.3	—24.4	—27.8	—23.5	—13.6	—21.2	—18.0	—10.4
250	6.8	—46.8	—40.3	—25.4	—28.8	—24.5	—14.6	—22.8	—19.4	—11.6
500	5.2	—47.8	—41.3	—26.4	—30.0	—25.7	—15.8	—26.4	—22.7	—13.9

Table A-1, *continued*
(*per cent*)
1948

| AVERAGE STOCKHOLDER IMPUTED GROSS INCOME ($000's) | Earnings for distribution Variants 1,2,3 | DIFFERENTIAL AGAINST: | | | | | | | | |
| | | Earnings for retention | | | Net corporate earnings | | | Stockholder imputed gross income | | |
		Variant 1	Variant 2	Variant 3	Variant 1	Variant 2	Variant 3	Variant 1	Variant 2	Variant 3
1	28.8	21.7	24.3	39.3	24.1	25.9	35.7	4.9	5.2	7.3
2	28.9	21.6	24.1	39.2	24.1	25.8	35.7	4.5	4.8	6.6
3	28.6	20.7	23.5	38.5	23.4	25.2	35.2	4.7	5.1	7.1
4	28.7	20.9	23.5	38.5	23.5	25.3	35.2	4.9	5.3	7.3
5	28.7	21.0	23.7	38.6	23.6	25.4	35.2	5.1	5.4	7.5
6	28.6	18.4	21.1	36.1	21.9	23.7	33.6	6.0	6.5	9.2
8	27.8	17.7	20.7	35.7	21.2	23.1	32.9	6.6	7.2	10.3
10	27.5	16.4	19.4	34.4	20.2	22.2	32.0	6.9	7.5	10.9
12	27.5	13.7	16.8	31.7	18.4	20.4	30.3	6.9	7.7	11.4
15	26.1	9.8	13.5	28.4	15.4	17.8	27.7	6.5	7.5	11.7
20	24.8	6.2	10.3	25.3	12.5	15.3	25.2	5.8	7.1	11.7
25	21.3	-8.8	-3.7	11.3	1.5	4.9	14.8	0.9	2.9	8.7
50	18.9	-16.5	-10.4	4.6	-4.4	-0.4	9.5	-3.0	-0.3	6.4
75	16.6	-21.4	-14.8	0.2	-8.4	-4.1	5.8	-5.9	-2.9	4.0
100	14.7	-28.3	-21.7	-6.8	-13.6	-9.3	0.6	-9.8	-6.7	0.4
150	13.1	-32.9	-26.3	-11.3	-17.1	-12.8	-2.9	-12.5	-9.4	-2.1
200	12.0	-36.1	-29.6	-14.6	-19.7	-15.4	-5.5	-15.1	-11.8	-4.2
500	9.5	-41.6	-35.1	-20.4	-24.2	-19.9	-10.0	-21.3	-17.4	-8.8

Table A-1, *continued*
(*per cent*)
1949

AVERAGE STOCK-HOLDER IMPUTED GROSS INCOME ($000's)	Earnings for distribution Variants 1, 2, 3	DIFFERENTIAL AGAINST:								
		Earnings for retention			Net corporate earnings			Stockholder imputed gross income		
		Variant			Variant			Variant		
		1	2	3	1	2	3	1	2	3
1	28.0	23.9	26.6	41.3	25.7	27.2	35.6	4.9	5.2	6.8
2	28.5	23.9	26.3	40.8	25.9	27.2	35.5	5.8	6.1	8.0
3	28.6	23.8	26.4	40.7	25.9	27.3	35.4	5.3	5.6	7.3
4	28.0	23.1	25.6	39.9	25.3	26.7	34.8	5.1	5.4	7.0
5	28.1	23.3	25.8	40.1	25.4	26.8	34.9	5.5	5.8	7.6
6	28.3	23.1	25.6	40.0	25.3	26.7	34.9	6.1	6.4	8.4
8	28.1	20.8	23.4	37.9	23.9	25.4	33.6	7.0	7.5	10.0
10	27.2	20.0	22.9	37.4	23.2	24.8	33.0	7.4	8.0	10.6
12	27.2	18.7	21.6	36.0	22.3	23.9	32.2	7.4	7.9	10.7
15	26.2	16.0	19.1	33.5	20.4	22.1	30.3	7.1	7.8	10.7
20	25.6	11.8	15.4	29.8	17.7	19.9	28.1	7.0	7.8	11.1
25	24.4	8.2	12.4	26.8	15.3	17.5	25.7	6.6	7.6	11.1
50	20.1	−7.4	−1.7	12.8	4.6	7.7	15.9	2.6	4.3	8.9
75	17.5	−15.1	−8.9	5.6	−1.0	2.5	10.7	−0.7	2.4	6.7
100	15.6	−19.7	−13.3	1.1	−4.4	−0.8	7.4	−2.9	−0.5	4.9
150	13.9	−26.7	−20.4	−6.0	−9.2	−5.6	2.6	−6.4	−3.9	1.8
200	12.2	−31.0	−24.7	−10.2	−12.3	−8.7	−0.5	−9.1	−6.4	−0.4
250	11.2	−34.4	−28.1	−13.7	−14.7	−11.1	−2.9	−11.4	−8.6	−2.2
500	8.5	−39.6	−33.3	−18.8	−18.8	−15.2	−7.0	−16.8	−13.6	−6.3

Table A-1, *continued*
(*per cent*)
1950

AVERAGE STOCK-HOLDER IMPUTED GROSS INCOME ($000's)	Earnings for distribution Variants 1, 2, 3	DIFFERENTIAL AGAINST:								
		Earnings for retention			Net corporate earnings			Stockholder imputed gross income		
		Variant			Variant			Variant		
		1	2	3	1	2	3	1	2	3
1	34.3	27.3	30.0	43.6	30.0	31.7	40.0	5.4	5.7	7.2
2	34.2	26.9	29.3	43.0	29.7	31.2	39.6	6.0	6.3	8.0
3	34.3	26.8	29.1	42.6	29.7	31.1	39.4	6.2	6.5	8.2
4	33.9	26.1	28.7	42.3	29.1	30.7	39.1	5.5	5.8	7.4
5	33.8	26.3	28.8	42.3	29.1	30.7	39.0	5.7	6.0	7.6
6	34.0	26.2	28.7	42.3	29.2	30.8	39.1	5.7	6.0	7.6
8	33.7	24.0	26.5	40.0	27.7	29.3	37.6	8.6	9.0	11.6
10	32.9	23.1	26.0	39.5	26.8	28.6	36.9	9.3	9.9	12.8
12	32.7	21.7	24.6	38.2	25.9	27.7	36.0	9.4	10.0	13.0
15	32.1	19.2	22.0	35.5	24.0	25.9	34.2	9.1	9.7	12.8
20	30.8	15.2	18.5	32.0	21.2	23.3	31.6	9.0	9.8	13.4
25	29.2	11.3	15.2	28.7	18.2	20.6	28.9	8.4	9.5	13.4
50	24.9	—4.4	0.4	13.9	6.9	10.0	18.2	4.2	5.9	10.8
75	21.7	—12.4	—6.7	6.8	0.7	4.2	12.5	0.5	2.9	8.5
100	19.1	—17.3	—11.4	2.1	—3.3	0.4	8.7	—2.3	0.3	6.1
150	16.7	—24.6	—18.7	—5.1	—8.7	—5.0	3.3	—6.2	—3.6	2.3
200	14.6	—29.3	—23.4	—9.9	—12.4	—8.7	—0.4	—9.0	—6.3	—0.3
250	13.2	—32.8	—26.9	—13.5	—15.0	—11.4	—3.1	—11.5	—8.7	—2.4
500	10.0	—38.8	—32.9	—19.3	—19.9	—16.3	—8.0	—17.5	—14.3	—7.0

Table A-1, *continued*
(*per cent*)
1951

AVERAGE STOCK-HOLDER IMPUTED GROSS INCOME ($000's)	Earnings for distribution Variants 1, 2, 3	DIFFERENTIAL AGAINST:									
		Earnings for retention			Net corporate earnings			Stockholder imputed gross income		
		Variant			Variant			Variant		
		1	2	3	1	2	3	1	2	3
1										
2	40.8	35.3	37.1	47.8	37.7	38.7	44.7	7.9	8.0	9.3
3	40.7	35.1	37.1	47.9	37.6	38.7	44.7	7.9	8.2	9.4
4	40.3	34.4	36.4	47.1	37.0	38.1	44.1	7.1	7.4	8.5
5	40.5	34.8	36.6	47.4	37.3	38.3	44.3	6.8	7.0	8.1
6	40.4	34.7	36.7	47.5	37.3	38.4	44.4	6.4	6.6	7.6
8	40.2	32.7	34.7	45.4	36.0	37.2	43.2	10.0	10.3	12.0
10	39.4	32.3	34.5	45.3	35.4	36.6	42.6	11.0	11.4	13.2
12	39.2	30.2	32.5	43.2	34.1	35.4	41.4	11.0	11.4	13.3
15	37.2	27.0	29.5	40.2	31.6	32.9	38.9	10.7	11.2	13.2
20	36.4	22.9	25.6	36.3	28.9	30.4	36.4	11.7	12.3	14.7
25	34.8	18.3	21.4	32.2	25.7	27.3	33.3	12.1	13.0	15.9
50	28.7	0.9	4.7	15.4	13.2	15.4	21.3	8.0	9.3	13.0
75	22.7	−8.3	−3.6	7.1	5.4	8.0	14.0	3.3	4.9	8.6
100	19.6	−13.1	−8.4	2.4	1.4	4.0	10.0	1.0	2.7	6.6
150	16.9	−20.6	−15.9	−5.1	−3.9	−1.3	4.7	−2.8	−0.9	3.4
200	14.7	−25.7	−20.9	−10.2	−7.8	−5.2	0.8	−5.9	−3.9	0.6
250	12.9	−29.5	−24.8	−14.1	−10.7	−8.0	−2.1	−8.5	−6.4	−1.7
500	8.1	−34.5	−29.7	−19.0	−15.6	−12.9	−6.9	−13.8	−11.5	−6.2

Table A-1, *concluded*
(*per cent*)
1952

AVERAGE STOCK-HOLDER IMPUTED GROSS INCOME ($000's)	Earnings for distribution Variants 1, 2, 3	DIFFERENTIAL AGAINST:									
		Earnings for retention			Net corporate earnings			Stockholder imputed gross income		
		Variant			Variant			Variant		
		1	2	3	1	2	3	1	2	3
1	39.4	34.4	36.5	46.9	36.8	37.9	43.2	7.0	7.2	8.2
2	38.9	33.8	35.6	46.4	36.3	37.2	42.7	8.0	8.2	9.4
3	38.9	34.1	35.9	46.5	36.5	37.4	42.7	8.2	8.4	9.6
4	38.3	32.8	34.8	45.6	35.5	36.5	42.0	6.3	6.5	7.5
5	38.7	33.2	35.0	45.7	35.9	36.9	42.3	5.5	5.7	6.5
6	38.6	33.0	34.9	45.5	35.7	36.7	42.1	5.5	5.7	6.5
8	38.2	30.8	32.7	43.3	34.5	35.4	40.8	8.8	9.1	10.4
10	37.2	30.3	32.4	43.0	33.7	34.7	40.2	9.6	9.9	11.4
12	37.1	28.0	30.2	40.9	32.5	33.6	39.0	9.3	9.6	11.1
15	34.9	25.3	27.8	38.5	30.0	31.3	36.7	8.7	9.1	10.7
20	33.5	19.3	21.9	32.6	26.2	27.6	33.0	9.6	10.2	12.2
25	31.9	15.0	18.0	28.7	23.3	24.9	30.3	10.3	10.9	13.3
50	25.0	—3.4	—0.1	10.6	10.4	12.3	17.7	6.2	7.4	10.6
75	19.9	—12.0	—7.2	3.3	3.7	6.1	11.5	2.4	3.9	7.4
100	16.6	—15.3	—10.7	—0.1	0.5	2.8	8.2	0.3	1.8	5.5
150	14.8	—22.5	—17.8	—7.2	—4.2	—1.8	3.6	—2.9	—1.2	2.5
200	12.5	—26.8	—22.2	—11.5	—7.4	—5.1	0.3	—5.4	—3.7	0.3
250	11.0	—30.6	—25.9	—15.3	—10.1	—7.7	—2.3	—7.7	—5.9	—1.8
500	6.9	—35.1	—30.5	—19.8	—14.4	—12.0	—6.6	—12.9	—10.8	—6.0

TABLE A-2
Differentials as Measured under Alternative Tests, 1947
ALTERNATIVE A, FIFTY PER CENT SHIFTING
(per cent)

DIFFERENTIAL AGAINST:

AVERAGE STOCK-HOLDER IMPUTED GROSS INCOME ($000's)	Earnings for distribution Variants 1, 2, 3	Earnings for retention			Net corporate earnings			Stockholder imputed gross income		
		Variant			Variant			Variant		
		1	2	3	1	2	3	1	2	3
1	16.9	5.1	8.1	26.5	9.2	11.1	23.2	1.9	2.3	4.8
2	16.7	5.0	7.9	26.4	9.0	10.8	23.1	1.9	2.3	4.9
3	16.6	4.7	7.7	26.1	8.8	10.7	22.9	2.1	2.5	5.4
4	16.9	4.0	7.1	25.5	8.4	10.4	22.6	1.9	2.4	5.1
5	16.3	2.9	5.9	24.4	7.5	9.4	21.7	1.9	2.4	5.5
6	16.5	3.0	6.0	24.5	7.6	9.6	21.8	2.0	2.5	5.8
8	16.4	-0.8	2.3	20.7	5.1	7.1	19.3	1.6	2.2	5.9
10	15.7	-4.0	-0.6	17.9	2.7	5.0	17.2	0.9	1.6	5.6
12	14.9	-7.2	-3.6	14.8	0.3	2.7	14.9	0.1	0.9	5.0
15	14.1	-12.3	-8.1	10.4	-3.3	-5.4	11.6	-1.2	-0.2	4.1
20	12.7	-20.5	-16.2	2.2	-9.2	-6.4	5.8	-3.7	-2.6	2.3
25	11.5	-26.0	-21.1	-2.6	-13.3	-10.0	2.2	-5.9	-4.5	1.0
50	9.1	-38.8	-32.1	-13.7	-22.5	-18.1	-5.9	-13.5	-10.9	-3.6
75	8.0	-46.0	-38.4	-20.0	-27.6	-22.6	-10.5	-18.9	-15.5	-7.1
100	6.9	-51.4	-43.4	-25.0	-31.5	-26.3	-14.1	-22.0	-18.4	-9.9
150	5.6	-58.0	-50.0	-31.5	-36.4	-31.1	-18.9	-26.2	-22.4	-13.6
200	4.7	-60.4	-52.4	-34.0	-38.3	-33.0	-20.8	-28.6	-24.7	-15.6
250	3.9	-61.4	-53.4	-34.9	-39.2	-33.9	-21.7	-30.7	-26.6	-17.0
500	3.2	-62.4	-54.4	-36.0	-40.1	-34.8	-22.6	-35.9	-31.1	-20.2

Table A-2, *continued*
ALTERNATIVE B, REPLACEMENT COST DEFINITION
(*per cent*)

AVERAGE STOCK-HOLDER IMPUTED GROSS INCOME ($000's)	Earnings for distribution Variants 1, 2, 3	Earnings for retention			Net corporate earnings			Stockholder imputed gross income		
		Variant 1	2	3	Variant 1	2	3	Variant 1	2	3
1	28.0	48.6	49.5	57.0	39.0	39.5	43.5	7.8	7.9	8.7
2	28.0	47.7	49.2	57.1	38.6	39.4	43.6	9.6	9.8	10.8
3	27.9	48.0	49.5	57.4	38.6	39.5	43.6	8.0	8.2	9.0
4	27.8	47.1	48.5	56.6	38.1	38.1	43.1	7.8	7.8	8.8
5	27.2	46.2	47.6	55.5	37.3	38.1	42.3	9.2	9.4	10.4
6	27.3	46.3	47.6	55.6	37.4	38.1	42.4	9.4	9.6	10.6
8	26.0	42.5	43.9	51.9	34.8	35.5	39.8	10.9	11.2	12.5
10	25.8	38.6	40.1	48.1	32.6	33.4	37.7	10.8	11.1	12.5
12	24.6	35.5	37.0	45.0	30.4	31.2	35.5	10.2	10.5	11.9
15	23.3	30.0	31.8	39.8	26.9	27.9	32.1	9.2	9.5	11.0
20	20.4	21.6	23.7	31.7	21.0	22.2	26.4	7.9	8.3	9.9
25	18.5	16.1	18.2	26.2	17.2	18.3	22.6	6.9	7.4	9.1
50	14.2	3.5	6.4	14.4	8.5	10.1	14.3	4.8	5.7	8.1
75	12.4	-0.4	-0.8	7.1	3.6	5.4	9.6	2.4	3.5	6.3
100	10.4	-9.3	-5.9	2.1	-0.1	1.7	6.0	-0.1	1.2	4.0
150	8.4	-16.2	-12.7	-4.8	-4.7	-2.9	1.4	-3.3	-2.0	0.9
200	6.7	-17.8	-14.3	-6.3	-6.3	-4.5	-0.3	-4.7	-3.3	-0.2
250	5.7	-18.3	-14.9	-6.9	-7.1	-5.3	-1.0	-5.6	-4.1	-0.8
500	5.1	-19.3	-15.9	-7.9	-7.9	-6.1	-1.8	-7.3	-5.6	-1.7

DIFFERENTIAL AGAINST:

Table A-2, *continued*

ALTERNATIVE C, FIFTY PER CENT SHIFTING AND REPLACEMENT COST COMBINED

(*per cent*)

DIFFERENTIAL AGAINST:

AVERAGE STOCK-HOLDER IMPUTED GROSS INCOME ($000's)	Earnings for distribution Variants 1,2,3	Earnings for retention			Net corporate earnings			Stockholder imputed gross income		
		Variant			Variant			Variant		
		1	2	3	1	2	3	1	2	3
1	16.7	31.2	33.0	45.0	23.6	24.5	30.1	5.4	5.6	6.9
2	17.0	31.6	33.6	45.5	24.0	24.9	30.6	6.4	6.6	8.1
3	16.8	31.5	33.5	45.5	23.8	24.8	30.5	4.3	4.4	5.5
4	16.8	30.5	32.4	44.5	23.4	24.2	30.0	4.6	4.8	6.0
5	16.5	30.0	31.6	43.6	22.7	23.7	29.4	4.8	5.0	6.2
6	16.5	29.7	31.7	43.7	22.8	23.7	29.5	5.2	5.4	6.8
8	15.7	25.8	28.2	40.1	20.5	21.6	27.4	5.1	5.4	6.8
10	14.9	22.0	24.3	36.4	18.3	19.4	25.1	4.8	5.1	6.6
12	14.6	18.3	20.5	32.5	16.3	17.4	23.2	4.5	4.8	6.4
15	13.3	12.9	15.7	27.7	13.1	14.4	20.2	3.8	4.2	5.9
20	12.2	4.6	7.7	19.7	8.6	10.1	15.8	3.1	3.6	5.7
25	10.9	—0.6	2.9	14.9	5.4	7.1	12.8	2.3	3.0	5.4
50	8.4	—13.6	—8.8	3.2	—2.1	0.2	5.9	—1.1	0.1	3.0
75	6.7	—21.4	—16.2	—4.2	—6.7	—4.2	1.5	—3.6	—2.3	0.8
100	5.9	—26.4	—21.2	—9.2	—9.6	—7.1	—1.3	—5.5	—4.1	—0.8
150	4.5	—33.1	—27.9	—15.9	—13.4	—10.9	—5.2	—8.6	—7.0	—3.3
200	3.4	—34.3	—29.1	—17.1	—14.6	—12.1	—6.4	—9.9	—8.2	—4.3
250	3.2	—34.9	—29.7	—17.7	—15.0	—12.5	—6.8	—10.6	—8.9	—4.8
500	2.9	—35.9	—30.7	—18.7	—15.6	—13.2	—7.4	—12.9	—10.9	—6.1

Table A-2, *continued*
ALTERNATIVE D, SAVING THROUGH CORPORATIONS
(per cent)

AVERAGE STOCK-HOLDER IMPUTED GROSS INCOME ($000's)	Earnings for distribution Variants 1, 2, 3	DIFFERENTIAL AGAINST:								
		Earnings for retention Variant			Net corporate earnings Variant			Stockholder imputed gross income Variant		
		1	2	3	1	2	3	1	2	3
1	30.7	18.2	20.5	35.6	23.2	24.5	33.6	5.1	5.4	7.4
2	30.0	18.2	20.8	36.1	22.9	24.4	33.7	5.2	5.6	7.6
3	30.0	17.9	20.3	35.5	22.7	24.1	33.3	4.2	4.5	6.2
4	30.0	17.0	19.5	34.8	22.1	23.6	32.9	4.8	5.2	7.2
5	29.4	16.3	18.8	34.0	21.5	23.0	32.2	5.2	5.5	7.7
6	29.4	16.3	18.8	34.0	21.5	23.0	32.2	6.1	6.5	9.1
8	28.4	12.4	14.9	30.1	18.8	20.2	29.5	6.3	6.8	9.8
10	28.0	9.2	12.1	27.3	16.6	18.4	27.6	5.9	6.5	9.7
12	26.6	6.0	9.0	24.3	14.1	15.9	25.2	5.1	5.7	9.0
15	25.2	0.9	4.4	19.6	10.5	12.5	21.8	3.8	4.6	8.0
20	23.0	−7.4	−3.9	11.2	4.4	6.5	15.8	1.9	2.8	6.7
25	20.9	−13.1	−9.1	6.1	−0.0	2.4	11.8	−0.0	1.2	5.5
50	16.2	−25.8	−20.8	−5.6	−10.2	−7.0	2.5	−6.3	−4.3	1.6
75	14.6	−32.8	−26.7	−11.4	−15.5	−11.6	−1.9	−11.0	−8.2	−1.4
100	12.8	−38.2	−31.7	−16.5	−20.3	−16.1	−6.2	−14.8	−11.8	−4.5
150	10.4	−44.6	−38.0	−22.7	−26.3	−21.9	−11.7	−20.0	−16.6	−8.9
200	9.1	−47.1	−40.5	−25.3	−29.2	−24.7	−14.3	−22.7	−19.2	−11.2
250	7.7	−48.0	−41.4	−26.1	−30.6	−26.1	−15.6	−24.4	−20.8	−12.4
500	5.7	−49.2	−42.6	−27.4	−33.1	−28.5	−17.7	−29.2	−25.1	−15.6

Table A-2, *continued*

ALTERNATIVE E, EARNINGS FOR DISTRIBUTION ONLY

(per cent)

AVERAGE STOCKHOLDER IMPUTED GROSS INCOME ($000's)	DIFFERENTIAL AGAINST:	
	Earnings for distribution	Stockholder imputed gross income[a]
1	27.9	7.3
2	27.8	5.8
3	27.9	4.9
4	27.5	4.2
5	27.3	4.2
6	27.3	4.4
8	26.0	4.5
10	24.7	5.2
12	23.3	5.7
15	21.3	6.2
20	18.5	5.2
25	16.4	4.2
50	11.9	3.6
75	9.5	3.7
100	7.9	3.5
150	5.5	2.9
200	5.4	3.0
250	5.0	2.7
500	4.7	2.2

[a] Only earnings for distribution imputed.

Note: The conceptual framework of Alternative E admits of only one set of differentials.

Table A-2, *continued*

ALTERNATIVE F, IMPUTING ONLY A FRACTION OF RETAINED EARNINGS

(per cent)

AVERAGE STOCKHOLDER IMPUTED GROSS INCOME ($000's)	DIFFERENTIAL AGAINST:	
	Net corporate earnings	*Stockholder imputed gross income*
1	27.7	6.0
2	27.7	6.3
3	27.7	5.2
4	27.0	5.9
5	26.3	6.3
6	26.3	7.4
8	23.6	8.0
10	21.5	7.7
12	19.0	6.9
15	15.2	5.6
20	9.4	3.9
25	5.1	2.4
50	—4.5	—2.8
75	—9.7	—6.8
100	—13.8	—9.8
150	—18.9	—13.9
200	—20.8	—15.7
250	—21.8	—17.1
500	—22.8	—20.3

Note: The conceptual framework of Alternative F admits of only one set of differentials.

Table A-2, *concluded*

ALTERNATIVE G, CORRECTION FOR UNDERREPORTING OF DIVIDENDS

(*per cent*)

DIFFERENTIAL AGAINST:

AVERAGE STOCK-HOLDER IMPUTED GROSS INCOME ($000's)	Earnings for distribution Variants 1, 2, 3	Earnings for retention			Net corporate earnings			Stockholder imputed gross income		
		Variant			Variant			Variant		
		1	2	3	1	2	3	1	2	3
1	27.1	19.5	21.9	36.7	22.0	23.6	33.5	5.6	6.0	8.5
2	27.9	19.2	21.4	36.4	22.1	23.6	33.5	5.1	5.4	7.8
3	28.2	19.7	21.9	36.9	22.6	24.0	34.0	4.5	4.8	6.8
4	28.1	18.6	21.1	36.0	21.8	23.5	33.4	5.3	5.7	8.1
5	27.1	17.5	20.0	35.0	20.8	22.4	32.3	5.5	5.9	8.5
6	27.2	17.7	20.2	35.0	20.8	22.5	32.4	6.0	6.5	9.3
8	27.1	13.8	16.3	31.2	18.3	19.9	29.8	6.3	6.8	10.3
10	26.0	11.0	13.9	28.8	16.1	17.9	27.9	6.0	6.7	10.4
12	24.6	7.8	10.7	25.6	13.5	15.4	25.3	5.3	6.1	10.0
15	23.7	3.0	5.9	20.8	9.9	11.9	21.8	4.2	5.0	9.1
20	22.0	−4.7	−1.3	13.6	4.2	6.5	16.5	2.0	3.1	7.8
25	20.3	−11.0	−7.0	7.9	−0.5	2.1	12.0	−0.3	1.1	6.2
50	15.4	−23.9	−18.9	−4.0	−10.7	−7.4	2.5	−6.9	−4.8	1.6
75	13.7	−31.2	−25.5	−10.6	−16.2	−12.4	−2.4	−11.5	−8.8	−1.7
100	12.2	−36.7	−30.6	−15.7	−20.3	−16.3	−6.4	−15.1	−12.1	−4.7
150	9.6	−43.3	−38.1	−23.2	−25.6	−22.2	−12.2	−19.4	−16.8	−9.3
200	8.1	−45.8	−40.6	−25.7	−27.8	−24.3	−14.4	−21.3	−18.6	−11.0
250	6.8	−46.8	−41.6	−26.7	−28.8	−25.4	−15.5	−22.9	−20.1	−12.3
500	5.2	−47.8	−42.6	−27.7	−30.0	−26.6	−16.7	−26.7	−23.6	−14.8

Appendix B. Notes on Methods

DERIVATION OF THE DIFFERENTIALS

THE investigation is limited to the differential taxation of stockholders under the federal government's income tax structure without consideration of state corporation and personal income taxes. The source of the data, unless otherwise specified, was tabulations published annually in *Statistics of Income* by the Internal Revenue Service (Bureau of Internal Revenue prior to 1948), Part 1 covering the personal income tax, Part 2 corporate taxes.[1]

Net Corporate Earnings Component of Stockholder Income

To derive stockholders' pro rata share of all of net corporate earnings (i.e. dividends, retained earnings, plus corporate normal and surtax, and excess profits tax payments), the aggregate of net corporate earnings was computed by deducting intercorporate dividends (i.e., dividends received by corporations from domestic corporations) from the tabulated total of net income for all corporations (both income and deficit).[2] This is the total net income generated by corporate activity. Then it was determined by how much net corporate earnings exceeded net corporate dividends (the latter obtained by subtracting domestic intercorporate dividends from the reported total of dividends paid out in cash and assets other than own stock), and the ratio of dividends to the excess of corporate earnings over dividends was computed.[3] Application of this ratio gave the amount to be added to stockholders' dividend receipts to obtain their pro rata share of net corporate earnings. Behind the use of this ratio, derived from the data for all corporations, lies the assumption that the stockholders used here to represent the average experience at selected income levels have portfolios which show the same ratio of dividends to earnings as is derived from the

[1] Example of abbreviated form to be used hereafter: *SI*, 1950, Part 1, p. 38; Part 2, p. 42.

[2] In effect, then, because the data for income and deficit corporations are combined, the pro rata share of corporate earnings imputed to stockholders included deficits as well as earnings.

[3] No distinction was made in the study between common and preferred dividends. The available data would permit only the crudest of breakdowns, and the wide variety of priority and cumulative provisions attaching to preferred stock would constitute a further conceptual difficulty. Moreover, dividends on both types of stock are paid out of income that is taxed when earned at the corporate level and when distributed at the personal level. Some may prefer to view it this way: the method used in this study implicitly assumes that the proportion of preferred dividends to all dividends and of preferred stockholdings to all stockholdings that applied for all stockholders, taken as a whole, applied also to each average stockholder's portfolio.

aggregate corporate experience. (See Chapter 2 for an explanation of why this assumption appears reasonable.) A tabular summary of the steps just outlined appears in Table B-1.

TABLE B-1

Derivation of the Imputation Ratio, 1950
(*dollar amounts in thousands*)

(1) Net income of all corporations	$42,613,304
(2) Dividends received from domestic corporations	2,459,921
(3) Net corporate earnings = (1) — (2)	40,153,383
(4) Dividends paid (other than in own stock)	11,552,963
(5) Net corporate dividends = (4) — (2)	9,093,042
(6) Excess of net corporate earnings over dividends = (3) — (5)	31,060,341
(7) Ratio of excess of net corporate earnings over dividends to dividends = (6) ÷ (5)	*3.416*

Source: For (1), (2), and (4), *S.I.*, 1950, Part 2, p. 90.

To impute their full pro rata share of net corporate earnings to stockholders, their dividend receipts were multiplied by 3.416, and the product was added to their income. Before this ratio could be applied, however, a number of computational steps were necessary. Our study is limited to those stockholders who were "double-taxed," and stockholders are simply taken to be dividend recipients. Starting with the number of dividend recipients and the amounts of dividends they reported arrayed by adjusted gross income classes, estimates were obtained to be used as a check and correction factor for the more refined breakdown to be described. These tabulations provided the number of personal income taxpayers who reported dividends as one of the components of their income. This number constituted the main body of stockholders, but in addition there were those taxpayers who received income from estates and trusts, derived in part, at least, from dividends. The number of such stockholders was estimated using, first, a ratio based on a special tabulation for 1936 to determine how many of the recipients of income from estates and trusts did not report dividends as well.[4] From these data, for each income class, the percentage of those who received income from estates and trusts but did

---

[4] *Statistics of Income Supplement Compiled from Income Tax Returns for 1936*, Individual Incomes, Section III, Patterns of Income, Treasury Dept., Division of Tax Research with the W.P.A., June 1940. This special study provides elaborate detail on the income patterns of taxpayers, arrayed by total income classes—a definition close enough to adjusted gross (the basis of tabulation of the annual data used in this study) to be usable. (For 1940 and 1941 for which the basis of classification was net income rather than adjusted gross, a cross-classification in the special supplement was used to get the data on a net income basis.)

not receive dividends per se was calculated; then this percentage was applied to the number of returns in each income class reporting income from estates and trusts in the years covered by the study. But not all estates and trusts had dividends. A further correction, therefore, was made by a percentage representing the portion of taxable estates and trusts reporting dividends. This procedure assumes that each taxpayer with estate and trust income received it from one such entity, and that the data for taxable estates and trusts are representative of all estates and trusts. (This latter assumption appears substantially correct. See the Fiduciary section of *Statistics of Income for 1937, Part 1*).[5] The number of stockholders in each income class, then, equalled the sum of those who reported dividends directly, plus those who received dividends as one of the components of their income from fiduciaries.

The amount of dividends in each income class was obtained as the sum of dividends reported by the class plus an estimated amount of dividends received from fiduciaries (estates and trusts).[6] The estimate was made by multiplying the total of income reported by individuals as received from fiduciaries by the percentage that dividends comprised of total income reported by taxable fiduciaries. These procedures are illustrated by an example, Table B-2.

The next set of computations utilized a distribution of the number of dividend recipients cross-classified by size of dividend receipts and size of adjusted gross income.[7] For each adjusted gross income class, in other words, there was available a dividend size distribution (see, for example, Table 4 in *Statistics of Income for 1950, Part 1*). In all, this distribution consisted of about 225 income-dividend size cells, e.g., dividend recipients with between $100 and under $200 of dividends and $3,000 and under $4,000 of adjusted gross income, etc.

Several adjustments were made in this cross-classification. Since the study covers only double-taxed stockholders, while the cross-classification covered nontaxable as well as taxable dividend recipients, the number of taxable stockholders in each cell was estimated by applying

[5] A long line of assumptions indicates numerous possible sources of error. Since, however, the total of such returns was very small (less than 4 per cent of all dividend returns in 1950) a large error in this item would have a small effect on the figures.

[6] In 1944 and 1945 dividends and interest were reported as a combined total. By assuming that, in each class, the relative weights of dividends and interest were the same as in 1946, an estimate of dividends received by personal income taxpayers was made for these two years.

[7] For 1944 and 1945, the 1946 distribution was used; for 1940 and 1941, the data for the income classes under $5,000 was estimated; for 1950 and 1951, the self-employment-tax-only dividend returns were ignored in obtaining the distribution, since they represented a negligible amount of the total.

TABLE B-2

Derivation of Dividend Returns and Amount of Dividends

ADJUSTED GROSS INCOME CLASS $8,000 AND UNDER $10,000, 1950

(1) Taxable reported individual dividend returns	244,875
(2) Returns with income from estates and trusts:	
Class $8,000 and under $9,000	12,648
Class $9,000 and under $10,000	10,026
(3) With 49.86 per cent (class $8,000 and under $9,000) and 28.35 per cent (class $9,000 and under $10,000) of all returns reporting income from estates and trusts but not reporting dividends,[a] the number of recipients of income from estates and trusts who did not report dividends was estimated at	11,154
(4) Percentage of taxable fiduciary returns (estates and trusts) reporting dividend receipts	73.44%
(5) Assuming this percentage to characterize all income from estates and trusts, and assuming further that every individual who reported income from estates and trusts received this income from only one such entity, there would be a net addition to the number of individual dividend returns (11,154 × 73.44%) of	8,191
(6) Total taxable dividend returns, therefore, would equal (1) + (5)	253,066
(7) Dividends reported on taxable individual returns	$273,814,000
(8) Income from estates and trusts reported on taxable individual returns	65,662,000
(9) Dividends comprised 56.18 per cent of the total income reported by taxable estates and trusts. Assuming this percentage to apply to all income from estates and trusts, the dividend component of income received by individuals from estates and trusts was estimated as an additional	36,889,000
(10) Total estimated dividends of taxable individuals equal (7) + (9)	310,703,000

Source: *S.I.*, 1950, Part 1: for (1), p. 48; for (2), p. 50; for (4), p. 157; for (7), p. 38; for (8), p. 40; for (9), pp. 152 and 154.

[a] *Statistics of Income Supplement for 1936*, Sect. III, Table 3, Bureau of Internal Revenue.

the fraction that taxable returns comprised of total returns in each income class.[8] It was necessary, also, to estimate the number of dividend returns for some cells—those at the extreme bottom of the array —because an entry for these was not published on the grounds that it was considered statistically unreliable.[9] In most cases such items were obtained as residuals from row or column totals. In the cells where this could not be done, i.e. two or more cells for which no entries were published, the aggregate residuals were broken down by proportions based on the totals of the classes concerned.

[8] Obtained from *Statistics of Income*, Part 1 Table 2, for all years.
[9] These figures were used, despite the wide margin of error attached to them, because the insignificant number of returns involved was swamped in the income class averages.

The average dividend receipts for each dividend-income cell were tentatively set at the mid-point of the dividend size class. This average was multiplied by the number of dividend returns, and the total for that adjusted gross income class was compared with the corresponding figure (see above) obtained from tabulations and, therefore, presumably correct. The comparison provided the basis for a proportionate correction of the initially assumed average size of dividend receipt. As corrected, the dividend total derived from the array of dividend-income cells and that tabulated in *Statistics of Income* (and the estimated dividend component of income from estates and trusts) were equal.

Imputed Gross Income

The average dividend amounts in each cell, as corrected, were used to derive what is called in this study imputed gross income. The average dividend figure was multiplied by the imputation ratio—the excess of net corporate earnings over dividends as a proportion of dividends. It was assumed that, in each income class, stockholders' adjusted gross income was the same as the average for all taxpayers. To this average for each class was added the result of multiplying average dividends by the imputation ratio, the resulting figure being the imputed gross income, defined as stockholder income including pro rata shares of net corporate earnings, rather than only dividends, as the measure of personal income from the corporate sector.[10] Then stockholders, their imputed gross income, and their share of net corporate earnings were rearrayed in income classes based on the size of imputed gross income. For every such income class—some fifteen in all—the average amount of imputed gross income and the proportion comprised by corporate earnings were computed. Plotting these two values furnished a chart from which could be read off the corporate earnings percentage of average imputed incomes of selected amounts. This was done for nineteen average imputed income levels—those that appear in the annual tables in Appendix A, and Table 4 in Chapter 2. A specific numerical illustration of the procedures used in imputation and rearraying is given in Table B-3.

Certain Aspects of the Derivation of the Differentials

Derivation of the differentials, explained in detail in Chapter 2, will not be repeated here. Elaboration of some points below will refer to the relevant columns of Table 4 in Chapter 2.

---

[10] Adjusted gross income already included dividends; this explains the addition of the excess of net corporate earnings over dividends to arrive at imputed gross income.

TABLE B-3

Steps in Imputation and Rearraying

ADJUSTED GROSS INCOME CLASS $8,000 AND UNDER $10,000,

AND DIVIDEND SIZE CLASS $1,500 AND UNDER $2,000, 1950

(1) The average adjusted gross income of all taxable returns in this income class was	$8,849
(It was assumed that dividend returns in this class, on average, also had this income.)	
(2) The number of returns reporting dividends in income class $8,000 and under $10,000, and dividend class $1,500 and under $2,000	*10,751*
(3) But, because of adjustments summarized in Table B-2, (3) to (5), this number must be increased by 3.345 per cent, making the estimate for the number of returns	*11,111*
(4) In the absence of any other information the average size of dividends was tentatively set at the mid-point of the class, at	$ 1,750
(5) But for the whole class $8,000 and under $10,000, use of this mid-point assumption yielded a dividend total of $294,914,000, while our figure from Table B-2 (10) is $310,703,000. Therefore the average size of dividends was raised [$1,750 × ($310,703/$294,914)] to	1,844
(6) With the imputation ratio, Table B-1 (7), at 3.416, this meant an addition to the average stockholder's income of ($1,844 × 3.416), equal to	6,299
(7) Therefore, the average imputed gross income equalled $6,299 +$8,849 [from (1) above],	15,148
(8) Total imputed income = (7) × (3)	168,309,000
(9) Of this total the net corporate earnings component was	90,478,000
[This equals average dividends plus the average imputation multiplied by the number of returns ($1,844 + $6,299) × 11,111]	
(10) Items (3), (8), and (9) were rearrayed into the imputed gross income class $10,000 and under $25,000, because average imputed gross income was	15,148

Note: For every adjusted gross income—dividend class cell (225 in all) a similar calculation was made. The data were rearrayed by size of imputed gross income, the average imputed gross income was computed, and the total item (9) for each class as a per cent of item (8) for each class was plotted against it. From this plot was read off the percentage that corporate earnings comprised of imputed gross income for a number of selected income levels ranging from $1,000 to $500,000, to be used in the computation of the differentials.

Source: *S.I.*, 1950, Part 1: for (1), pp. 38, 42; for (2), pp. 56-57.

In column 7, taxable income equivalent, the initial taxable income at each imputed income level was obtained by interpolation from values shown by plotting size of adjusted gross income against taxable income as obtained from the data for all taxpayers. This procedure which saved more complicated computation appears rough and ready, but its results are very close to those obtainable by the much more laborious process of striking weighted averages of the taxable income in each of the 225 dividend-income size cells.[11]

Several items in the derivation of column 8, corporation income tax on earnings for distribution, deserve mention. First, the effective rate of corporation income tax on earnings for distribution is slightly less than the effective rate on net income corporations. This is because the corporate tax was allocated between dividends and retentions on the basis of the ratios for net income corporations; but, in obtaining earnings for distribution, dividends of deficit corporations as well as those of income corporations are added to the corporation income tax on distributed earnings. Since the dividends of deficit corporations are small, however, little change occurs. In 1950, for example, whereas the effective rate on income corporations was 41.5 per cent, we found 41.3 as the effective rate on earnings for distribution. The derivation of this rate for 1950, as well as the effective rate on earnings for retention (column 14), is shown in Table B-4, below, lines 20 and 23. Secondly, an additional conceptual difficulty arises from dividends in excess of earnings paid out by income corporations. Such dividends are paid out of earnings made in prior years, yet the rate applied to them in these derivations was the rate ruling in a given year—in Table 4, the 1950 rate. There is no way of estimating dividends in excess of earnings paid by income corporations from the annual tabulations in *Statistics of Income*. But it would be surprising if they were of any substantial magnitude. Some estimate of the relative importance of dividends paid in excess of current earnings can be obtained from a study undertaken by O. J. Curry.[12] From his sample of industrial corporations, it appears that over the three years 1931-1933, for net income corporations, dividends in excess of current earnings (after taxes) accounted for less than 12 per cent of the total of dividends paid out.[13] On the basis of

---

[11] The accuracy of this method was tested with the 1947 data for two selected imputed income levels, by computing the actual taxable income for all the cells used in the derivation of the $5,000 and $250,000 average imputed gross income levels. In both cases, these test figures differed relatively slightly from those of the more summary procedure. While there was some disparity in taxable income under the two methods, it had little effect on the differentials. And this is the important consideration here: at the $250,000 level, for example, where the disparity between taxable income ran at 12 per cent, the differentials would have varied by only 0.5 per cent.

[12] O. J. Curry, "Utilization of Corporate Profits in Prosperity and Depression," *Michigan Business Studies*, Vol. X, No. 4, 1941.

[13] Curry's sample consisted of 72 large corporations which in 1936 accounted for more than 50 per cent of the assets in 10 of the 12 industrial groups into which the sample was divided. While, in general, his figures for dividends in excess of current earnings covered the period 1931-1933, in a few cases data for 1930 and 1934 were used. From Tables 10, 11, and 12 in Curry's study each entry for

this finding for an extremely depressed period, we may safely take it that such dividend payments did not exceed 5 per cent of the total in the years covered by our study. To take some extreme figures, suppose such dividends comprising 5 per cent of the total came out of earnings that were taxed at 30 per cent but that they were paid out in a year when the effective rate of corporate tax was 40 per cent. Our standard method would use 40 per cent; the more correct figure to be applied against earnings for distribution should be 39.5 per cent. The difference is not great. Thirdly, in column 8 and column 14, under the heading of corporation income tax were included the corporation income tax (normal and surtax—all years), the excess profits tax (1940-1941, 1944-1945, and 1950-1952), and the declared value excess profits tax (1940-1941, 1944-1945). Thus we dealt with "double" not "triple" taxation. In other words there was no special allowance for the tax on intercorporate dividends,[14] which entered, however, into the total tax liability used in our computations.

A More Refined Distribution of Dividend Receipts and Imputed Gross Income

A final note on the differentials. In 1951, a more refined dividend size class distribution was published in *Statistics of Income*. The Lorenz curve for the distribution of dividend receipts was found to be very similar in all the years 1946-1952, making reasonable use of the 1951 percentages within certain ranges to break down the 1950 distribution into a larger number of cells. For 1950, the income class $5,000 and under $8,000 was made up of 14 cells from the 1950 data, and 27 cells using the more refined breakdown obtained from the 1951 percentages. Were our standard method results affected by the "lumpiness" of the data? Will this more refined data yield significantly different findings? The answer to both these questions is no. The differentials obtained from the test data varied only slightly from those provided by our standard method. At only two of the nineteen income levels was the difference more than one percentage point. The "lumpiness" of the imputed gross income classes was next tested. Using the 1950 data, 27 income classes rather than 15 were used. The resultant effect on the differentials using these more refined imputed gross income classes turned out to be negligible. Only 9 per cent of all differentials varied by more than one percentage point from the standard method.

---

individual net income corporations where dividends were paid in excess of adjusted earnings was picked out, these entries were totalled, and then this total was computed as a per cent of all dividends paid out by net income corporations.
[14] 15 per cent of such dividends are included in taxable income.

ALTERNATIVE MEASURES OF THE DIFFERENTIALS

The rationale of each alternative of the standard method has been presented in Chapter 4. The derivation of the differentials by these alternatives is that described in Chapters 1 and 2, with variations for each alternative in the imputation ratio and the effective rate of corporation income tax. The relevant data for the standard method and for each of the alternatives (except D and G) are summarized in Tables B-4 through B-9. Under alternative D, saving through corpora-

TABLE B-4

Derivation of Imputation Ratio and Effective Rates of
Corporate Income Tax, Standard Method, 1950

(*dollar amounts in thousands*)

(1) Net income all corporations	$42,613,304
(2) Dividends received from domestic corporations	2,459,921
(3) Net corporate earnings all corporations = (1) — (2)	40,153,383
(4) Dividends (other than own stock) paid out by all corporations	11,552,963
(5) Net dividends all corporations = (4) — (2)	9,093,042
(6) Excess of net corporate earnings over dividends = (3) — (5)	31,060,341
(7) Imputation ratio Standard Method = (6) ÷ (5)	*3.4158*
(8) Net income of income corporations	$44,140,741
(9) Dividends received from domestic corporations	2,440,022
(10) Net corporate earnings income corporations = (8) — (9)	41,700,719
(11) Dividends (other than own stock) paid out by income corporations	11,454,755
(12) Net dividends income corporations = (11) — (9)	9,014,733
(13) Corporation income tax	17,316,932
(14) Dividends plus retained earnings of income corporations = (10) — (13)	24,383,787
(15) Retained earnings of income corporations = (14) — (12)	15,369,054
(16) Retained earnings proportion of after-tax earnings of income corporations	*0.63030*
(17) Corporation income tax allocable to retained earnings = (13) × (16)	$10,914,828
(18) Retained earnings all corporations = (3) — [(5) + (13)]	13,743,409
(19) Earnings for retention = (17) + (18)	24,658,257
(20) Corporation income tax allocable to distributed earnings = (13) — (17)	6,402,104
(21) Earnings for distribution = (5) + (20)	15,495,146
(22) Effective rate of corporation income tax on earnings for retention = (17) ÷ (19)	44.264%
(23) Effective rate of corporation income tax on earnings for distribution = (20) ÷ (21)	41.317%
(24) Effective rate of corporation income tax on net corporate earnings = (13) ÷ (3)	43.127%

Source: *S.I.*, 1950, Part 2, Table 3.
Note: The steps as presented here follow a somewhat different order than in Chapter 2.

TABLE B-5

Alternative A—Fifty Per Cent Shifting, 1947
(dollar amounts in thousands)

(1) Net income all corporations	$31,422,728
(2) Dividends received from domestic corporations	1,882,400
(3) Net corporate earnings all corporations (1) — (3)	29,540,328
(4) Corporation income tax	10,981,482
(5) One-half of (4)	5,490,741
(6) Net corporate earnings, Alternative A = (3) — (5)	24,049,587
(7) Effective rate of corporation income tax, Alternative A = (5) ÷ (6)	22.831%
(8) Dividends (other than own stock) paid out by all corporations	$8,365,046
(9) Net corporate dividends = (8) — (2)	6,482,646
(10) Excess of net corporate earnings over dividends = (6) — (9)	17,566,941
(11) Imputation ratio, Alternative A = (10) ÷ (9)	2.7098

Source: S.I., 1947, Part 2, Table 3.

TABLE B-6

Alternative B—Replacement Cost Definition, 1947
(dollar amounts in thousands)

(1) Net income all corporations	$31,422,728
(2) Dividends received from domestic corporations	1,882,400
(3) Net corporate earnings all corporations = (1) — (2)	29,540,328
From (3) deduct:	
(4) Inventory valuation adjustment[a]	5,757,000
(5) One-half of depreciation all corporations[b]	2,610,045
To get:	
(6) Net corporate earnings, Alternative B	21,173,283
(7) Corporation income tax	10,981,482
(8) Effective rate of corporation income tax, Alternative B = (7) ÷ (6)	51.865%
(9) Dividends (other than own stock) paid out by all corporations	$8,365,046
(10) Net corporate dividends = (9) — (2)	6,482,646
(11) Excess of net corporate earnings over dividends = (6) — (10)	14,690,637
(12) Imputation ratio, Alternative B = (11) ÷ (10)	2.2662

Source: S.I., 1947, Part 2, Table 3, except (4), (5).
[a] Survey of Current Business, July 1953, p. 16.
[b] One-half suggested by E. Cary Brown, Effects of Taxation: Depreciation Adjustments for Price Changes, Harvard University Press, 1952, pp. 28, 151-154.

tions, and alternative G, correction for underreporting of dividends, the corporation tax is the same as by the standard method, but the imputation ratios vary with levels of stockholder income (see Chapter 4).

TABLE B-7

Alternative C—Fifty Per Cent Shifting and Replacement Cost Combined, 1947
(dollar amounts in thousands)

(1) Net income all corporations	$31,422,728
(2) Dividends received from domestic corporations	1,882,400
(3) Net corporate earnings all corporations = (1) — (2)	29,540,328
From (3) deduct:	
(4) One-half of corporation income tax	5,490,741
(5) Inventory valuation adjustment	5,757,000
(6) One-half of depreciation all corporations	2,610,045
To get:	
(7) Net corporate earnings, Alternative C	15,682,542
(8) Effective rate of corporation income tax, Alternative C = (4) ÷ (7)	35.012%
(9) Dividends (other than own stock) paid out by all corporations	$8,365,046
(10) Net corporate dividends = (9) — (2)	6,482,646
(11) Excess of net corporate earnings over dividends = (7) — (10)	9,199,896
(12) Imputation ratio, Alternative C = (11) ÷ (10)	1.4192

Source: *S.I.*, 1947, Part 2, Table 3, except (5) and (6) (see Table B-6).

TABLE B-8

Alternative E—Earnings for Distribution Only, 1947
(dollar amounts in thousands)

(1) Dividends (other than own stock) paid out by all corporations	$8,365,046
(2) Dividends received from domestic corporations	1,882,400
(3) Net dividends all corporations = (1) — (2)	6,482,646
(4) Dividends (other than own stock) paid out by net income corporations	8,222,121
(5) Dividends received from domestic corporations	1,837,581
(6) Net dividends net income corporations	6,384,540
(7) Net income of income corporations	33,381,291
(8) Net corporate earnings of income corporations = (7) — (5)	31,543,710
(9) Corporation income tax	10,981,482
(10) Effective rate of corporation income tax = (9) ÷ (7)	34.184%
(11) Earnings for distribution income corporations = (6) ÷ (1 — 0.34184)	9,794,342
(12) Excess of earnings for distribution over dividends = (11) — (3)	3,311,696
(13) Imputation ratio, Alternative E = (12) ÷ (3)	0.51086

Source: *S.I.*, 1947, Part 2, Table 3.

TABLE B-9

Alternative F—Imputing only a Fraction of Retained Earnings, 1947
(dollar amounts in thousands)

(1) Net income all corporations	$31,422,728
(2) Dividends received from domestic corporations	1,882,400
(3) Net corporate earnings all corporations = (1) — (2)	29,540,328
(4) Corporation income tax	10,981,482
(5) Dividends (other than own stock) paid out by all corporations	8,365,046
(6) Net corporate dividends = (5) — (2)	6,482,646
(7) Retained earnings = (3) — [(4) + (6)]	12,076,200
(8) 72% of retained earnings	8,694,864
(9) Net corporate earnings for stockholders, Alternative F = (4) + (6) + (8)	26,158,992
(10) Effective rate of corporation income tax, Alternative F = (9) ÷ (4)	41.980%
(11) Excess of net corporate earnings over dividends = (4) + (8)	$19,676,346
(12) Imputation ratio, Alternative F = (11) ÷ (6)	3.0352

Source: S.I., 1947, Part 2, Table 3.

The imputation ratios and effective rates of corporation income tax by the standard method and by the alternative from each of the foregoing tables are summarized for comparison in Table B-10.

TABLE B-10

Comparison of Imputation Ratio and Effective Rate of Corporation Income Tax, Standard Method and Alternative Tests, 1947

	Imputation ratio	Effective rate of corporation income tax on net corporate earnings (per cent)
Standard	3.5568	37.175
Alternative A	2.7098	22.831
Alternative B	2.2662	51.865
Alternative C	1.4192	35.012
Alternative E	0.5109	34.184
Alternative F	3.0352	41.980

MEASURING PROGRESSIVITY

The formulas for the average rate progression and the liability progression definitions of progressivity have been given in the text (Chapter 5). The change in the degree of progressivity, measured by average rate progression, is determined by observing whether the differential against stockholders rose (increased progressivity), fell (decreased progressivity), or remained the same as we read up the nineteen income levels for which this differential was measured. Liability progression was determined in essentially the same way, except that the differential was taken as a proportion of the rate applicable under the personal income tax at each income level. If the tax rate was raised by the differential in increasing proportion with income level, progressivity increased; if the tax rate was raised by a decreasing proportion, progressivity declined. A defect was injected into this calculation by use, as the personal income tax rate applicable at each level, of the rate against adjusted gross income based on data for all taxpayers. But adjusted gross income, at about the $25,000 level and above, includes long-term capital gains subject to a flat rate under the alternative tax. However, the indications for liability progression were sufficiently pronounced to stand in the face of this qualification.

PARTNERSHIP METHOD REVENUE ESTIMATES AND RELATED COMPUTATIONS

Careful estimates of the partnership method aggregate revenue loss, which may be construed also as the net revenue contribution of the existing method of taxing corporate earnings, were undertaken for 1947, 1949, 1950 and 1952. The corporation income tax liability of a given year represents the gross revenue loss upon a shift to the partnership method; the increased personal income tax liability constitutes the gross revenue increase that would currently (i.e. in that year) accompany the shift. The difference between the two is a measure of the net revenue loss on a current basis.[15]

The data arranged in the dividend-income size array, derivation of which is described in the first section of this Appendix, were the starting point. For 1949, 1950, and 1952, the array was broken down into joint and separate returns, because different marginal rate schedules have applied to each category since the introduction of income-splitting in 1948. The breakdown was based on the ratios for joint and separate returns derived from data for all taxpayers. For each of these years (and 1947 also) the stockholder return total was also subdivided into: 1. returns subject only to the normal and surtax rates of the personal income tax; and 2. returns subject to the alterna-

[15] To measure the current revenue loss connected with the repeal of the corporate tax, corporation income tax liability as tabulated in *Statistics of Income* was used, net of the credit for foreign income taxes paid by corporations. Cf. the similar procedure followed by the Department of Commerce in its National Income Accounts. (*National Income*, 1954 Edition, a supplement to *Survey of Current Business*, p. 93.)

tive tax, an additional flat rate of 50 or 52 per cent on one-half of realized long-term capital gains includible in taxable income.[16] This separation enabled isolation of normal and surtax income, the appropriate base to which was added the excess of net corporate earnings over dividends (adjusted for foreign tax credit). In summary, for 1952, 1950, and 1949, the dividend-income size array for each year was broken down into four categories of returns—separate normal and surtax, joint normal and surtax, separate alternative tax, and joint alternative tax—amounting to over 560 cells for each year. For 1947, there were only two categories of returns—normal and surtax, and alternative tax—giving a total of 280 cells.

Taxable income for each cell was determined by working back from the normal and surtax liability to the taxable income equivalent. To the taxable income was added the previously computed excess of corporate earnings over dividends (adjusted for foreign tax credit) on which the additional personal income tax was computed, with allowance for that portion of the standard deduction that would be available to some stockholders. The total sum of increased personal income tax liability in each cell provided for individual stockholders the increase in personal income tax liability that would accompany the institution of the partnership method.[17]

Calculations for taxable estates and trusts were less detailed, for no dividend size class data were tabulated for fiduciaries. Therefore, only the average amount of dividends in each income class was used as the base for imputation. The error introduced by this procedure was probably not serious. But even a major error in the taxable estates and trusts estimate would affect the results only slightly, since the aggregate partnership method tax liability for fiduciaries was only about 15 per cent of the aggregate liability for individuals. A summary tabulation outlining the steps just discussed appears in Table B-11.

But, an additional revenue loss would accompany the partnership method, realized only over a number of years, not currently. Under the partnership method, which would follow the procedure for taxing partnership shares, the basis of valuation of stock for capital gains tax

[16] All alternative tax returns were assumed to be divided returns. In the higher income classes subject to the alternative tax, dividend returns predominated, and since capital gains arise primarily from stock sales the assumption appeared reasonable.

[17] For 1947 an estimate, necessarily rough, was made of the increase in personal income tax liability that would occur because imputation of their pro rata share of net corporate earnings would move some previously nontaxable stockholders into the taxable category. This turned out to be so small, about $20 million, that it did not seem necessary to undertake an adjustment on this score in the other years.

TABLE B-11

Partnership Method Revenue Estimate

ADJUSTED GROSS INCOME CLASS $8,000 AND UNDER $10,000;

DIVIDEND SIZE CLASS $1,500 AND UNDER $2,000, 1950

(1) Joint returns equalled 89.60% of all returns in the adjusted gross income class $8,000 and under $10,000		
(2) Assuming this same percentage to characterize each dividend size class, in this income class, gave estimated joint returns (i.e. 11,111 × 89.60%)		9,555
and separate returns (i.e. 11,111 — 9,955)		1,156
(3) The average tax liability per joint return in this income class equalled	$	1,036
Given the rate schedule applicable to joint returns, the taxable income equivalent of this tax liability is		5,698
(4) Similarly, the average tax liability per separate return came to		1,423
the taxable income equivalent of which is		6,738
(5) Under the partnership method, stockholders' pro rata share of net corporate earnings would be reached in full by the personal income tax. So the imputed sum [Table B-3 (6), after adjustment for foreign tax credit]		6,203
would, in the case of joint returns, be subject to the marginal rates applicable to a taxable income of $5,698. The increment to tax liability would be		1,384
With 9,955 such returns, the total increment to personal income tax liability would be		13,777,720
(6) Similarly for separate returns, with the imputed sum of		6,203
reckoned an increment to a taxable income of $6,738, the increase in personal income tax liability would be		2,023
Since there are 1,156 such returns, the total increase in personal income tax liability on separate returns would be		2,338,588
(7) But both (5) and (6) are tentative estimates, for they have failed to take into account the fact that some taxpayers used the standard deduction, and in their case, therefore, a portion of the imputed amount would be excluded from taxable income.		
(8) Returns using the standard deduction were 69.12% of all returns. Therefore, it was estimated that 6,879 joint returns and 799 separate returns used the standard deduction. For joint returns the tax on 10% (the standard deduction) of the average amount imputed came to $27, aggregating for all such returns		186,000
For separate returns the average per return was $45, the aggregate		36,000
In all, the estimate of the increment in personal income tax due to the institution of the partnership method was lowered by		222,000

(continued on next page)

Table B-11, *concluded*

(9) By adding (5) and (6), and subtracting (8), we obtain the net increase in personal income tax under the partnership method—in this case $15,894,308

Similar calculations were made for all the income-dividend size class cells, 563 in all, using a further breakdown in the upper income classes for alternative and for normal and surtax returns. To get the net current revenue loss these increases in personal income tax liability were totaled and subtracted from the actual corporate income tax liability.

purposes would be raised by the amount of retained earnings which would be taxed to stockholders. Because the basis of valuation would be raised, future realized capital gains and capital gains tax liability would be lower than they would otherwise have been. Procedures for measuring this future revenue loss consisted of a number of steps. First, the amount by which the basis of valuation would be raised was estimated by assuming that rescinding the corporation tax would not change the *proportion* of earnings retained.[18] Using the Cowles Commission finding of an increase, on average, over the period 1871-1937 of 72 cents in share prices for every dollar of reinvested earnings, it was assumed that 72 cents of every increased dollar of retained earnings would show up as capital gains.[19] The difference between the amount of retained earnings (the amount by which the basis would be raised making gains in the future lower) and the estimated future increase in capital gains (because of the higher level of retained earnings that would follow the repeal of the corporate tax) constituted the estimated net future decline in capital gains.

Further steps were necessary to arrive at the revenue loss associated with this decline. Not all capital gains are realized by taxable persons; some who realize them fail to report them wholly or in part; still others pass potential capital gains tax-free at death. So it is assumed that only two-thirds of capital gains were realized in taxable form.[20] Since they are long-term gains (i.e. gains from assets held over six months), only half their amount is included in taxable income. This

[18] To put it another way, it was assumed that what formerly went into corporation income tax payments would be divided proportionately between dividends and retained earnings.

[19] Alfred Cowles, 3rd, *et al., Common Stock Indexes, 1871-1937*, Principia, 1938, p. 42.

[20] There was no particular warrant for two-thirds rather than, say, 75 or 50 per cent. The two-thirds was suggested as reasonable by the following considerations: on average, about 80 per cent of dividends are reported; as shown in 1950 data, distribution of capital gains is rather close to that of dividends in general; the option of transferring capital gains income-tax free at death reduces the 80 per cent to something on the order of two-thirds.

half, it was assumed, would have been subject in the future to an effective rate of about 30 per cent. (This is not unduly low, because the alternative tax sets a ceiling rate of 50 or 52 per cent on long-term gains.) All together, this suggests a revenue loss of 10 per cent of the amount by which potential future capital gains would have been reduced by the change in basis because retained earnings would be included in the taxable income of stockholders under the partnership method.[21] But this is a revenue loss that would materialize in the future. Its present value is something else again. It was assumed that the realization would occur at an even rate over the five year period following the year under investigation. With 5 per cent taken as the applicable rate of discount, the present value would equal 86 per cent of the future value, and the present value of the future loss in capital gains tax revenue due to the change in basis would come to 8.6 per cent of the estimated net decline in taxable capital gains. The derivation of the future revenue loss is outlined in Table B-12.

TABLE B-12

Derivation of Future Revenue Loss, 1950

(*dollar amounts in billions*)

(1) Net corporation income tax liability	$16.8
(2) Retained earnings as a per cent of dividends plus retained earnings of net income corporations	63.0%
(3) Assumed increase in retained earnings due to partnership method = (1) × (2)	$10.6
(4) 72 per cent of (3)	7.6
(5) Retained earnings after corporation income tax	13.8
(6) Assumed retained earnings under partnership method = (3) + (5)	24.4
(7) Net decrease in future capital gains = (6) − (4)	16.7
(8) Present value of estimated decrease in future capital gains tax liability = 8.6% of (7)	1.4

Revenue estimates for all other years covered by the study, and for 1953, 1954, and 1955, were carried out by the same procedure but in more summary fashion with less reliable results. This is especially true of 1955, although the broad order of magnitude is probably correct. The data on foregone corporate tax revenue up through 1952 were unquestionable, having been tabulated annually.[22] The offset in terms

[21] 10 per cent is the product of 67 percent × 50 per cent × 30 per cent.

[22] For 1953, 1954, and 1955 all the relevant IRS values used in the estimates were, in turn, estimated from available national income figures of the Department of Commerce. The relations used were those existing between the two sets of data in 1952. A rather stable set of ratios characterizing these relations in this and the several preceding years made their use for the later years a reasonably accurate procedure.

of personal income tax revenue by the partnership method was calculated, with the marginal tax rate for imputations derived from data of years for which detailed estimates were made in Chapter 6—1947, 1949, 1950, and 1952. The 1947 relationship between marginal rate and imputations was used for 1946 (in which the tax structure was the same), and for 1945 and 1944 (in which, while personal income tax rates were higher than in 1947 and exemptions lower, taxable income was lower, thus making reasonable use of the 1947 relationship). Because of unchanged tax rate schedules the 1949 marginal rate on partnership imputations was used for 1948; the 1952 rate for 1953. For 1951, 1954, and 1955, the marginal rate for 1950, 42.2 per cent, was raised to 47.5 per cent in view of the higher personal income tax rates in the three later years.

Table B-13 outlines the derivation of the revenue loss estimates and the percentage point increase in personal income tax rates required to recoup the current partnership method revenue loss for 1944-1955.

The computation of the aggregate differential was straightforward. It involved only one new step—the corporate-personal income tax liability. Here it was assumed for each cell that the personal tax liability was the same as for all taxpayers in the adjusted gross income class in which this cell fell, and it was added to the corporate tax on the stockholders in this cell. Then this personal-corporate tax liability was compared with the partnership method tax liability.

As to the Gini coefficients, the percentile shares of each imputed income class in imputed income before taxes and after deduction of the liabilities associated with each tax system—the corporate-personal and the partnership method—were calculated, and then a formula for the calculation of the Gini coefficient developed by Dwight Yntema was applied.[23]

[23] Dwight B. Yntema, "Measures of the Inequality in the Personal Distribution of Wealth and Income," *Journal of the American Statistical Association*, December 1933, pp. 427-428.

TABLE B-13

Estimate of Partnership Method Revenue Loss, 1944-1955

(dollars in billions)

CURRENT REVENUE LOSS

YEAR	Corporate tax liability (1)	Total increase for individuals and fiduciaries in personal income tax liability, partnership method (2)	Excess of net corporate earnings over dividends[a] (imputations partnership method) (3)	Marginal tax rates on imputations (2) ÷ (3) (4)	Current revenue loss (1) — (2) (5)
1944	$14.8	$ 9.6[b]	$20.1	48.0%[c]	$ 5.2
1945	10.7	7.2[b]	14.9	48.0	3.5
1946	8.7	8.4[b]	17.4	48.0[c]	0.3
1947	10.8	11.0	22.8	48.0	—0.2[d]
1948	11.6	9.7[b]	24.7	39.4[c]	1.9
1949	9.5	7.2	18.4	39.4	2.3
1950	16.8	13.5	30.6	44.2	3.3
1951	21.5	15.0[b]	31.6	47.5[c]	6.5
1952	18.4	12.7	26.5	47.9	5.7
1953[e]	19.8	13.7[b]	28.6	47.9[c]	6.1
1954[e]	15.9	11.4[b]	23.9	47.5[c]	4.5[f]
1955[e]	20.1	15.2[b]	32.0	47.5[c]	4.9[f]

a Excludes credit for foreign corporation income taxes paid.

b Product of columns 3 and 4 for 1944-1945, 1948, 1951, 1953-1955. Derived as described for 1947, 1949, 1950, and 1952.

c Assumed.

d Revenue gain.

e Data for this year estimated from Department of Commerce national income figures on basis of 1952 relation of Internal Revenue Service and Department of Commerce data.

f These estimates take no account of the dividend credit and exclusion, in effect since 1954 Roughly, these two relief provisions lowered the personal income tax burden on stockholders, in the aggregate, by about $200 million in 1954 and $300 million in 1955. These two items might more accurately be, therefore, $4.3 and $4.6 respectively because, with the partnership method in effect, there would be no reason, on equity grounds at least, to keep the exclusion and credit

Table B-13, *continued*

FUTURE REVENUE LOSS

'AR	Assumed retained earnings, partnership methodᵍ (6)	Estimated increase in retained earningsʰ (7)	72% of (7) (8)	Net increase in basis (6) — (8) (9)	Present value of future revenue loss 8.6% of (9) (10)
44	$13.8	$ 8.5	$ 6.1	$ 7.7	$ 0.7
45	10.1	5.9	4.2	5.9	0.5
46	14.5	5.8	4.2	10.3	0.9
47	19.5	7.4	5.3	14.2	1.2
48	21.0	7.9	5.7	15.3	1.3
49	14.6	5.8	4.2	10.4	0.9
50	24.4	10.6	7.6	16.7	1.4
51	22.4	12.3	8.9	13.5	1.2
52	17.9	9.9	7.1	10.8	0.9
53e	18.5	9.7	7.0	11.5	1.0
54e	15.1	7.1	5.1	10.0	0.9
55e	22.3	10.4	7.5	14.8	1.3

e Data for this year estimated from Department of Commerce national income figures on basis 1952 relation of Internal Revenue Service and Department of Commerce data.
ᵍ Obtained by dividing the corporate income tax liability between retained and distributed rnings on the basis of their after-tax weights for net income corporations.
ʰ Difference between column 6 and retained earnings under existing tax structure.

Table B-13, *c o n c l u d e d*

PERSONAL INCOME TAX RATE INCREASE REQUIRED

TO RECOUP CURRENT REVENUE LOSS

YEAR	Total surtax net income[1] (11)	Addition to surtax net income due to partnership method [80% of (3)] (12)	New surtax net income, partnership method (11) + (12) (13)	Percentage point rise in personal rates required to recoup current revenue loss[j] (14)
1944	$ 55.3	$ 16.1	$ 71.4	7.3%
1945	56.7	11.9	68.6	5.1
1946	64.8	13.9	78.7	0.4
1947	75.2	18.3	93.5	—0.2
1948	75.2	19.8	95.0	2.0
1949	72.1	14.7	86.8	2.6
1950	84.9	24.5	109.4	3.0
1951	100.0	25.3	125.3	5.2
1952	108.1	21.2	129.3	4.4
1953e	117.9	22.9	140.8	4.3
1954e	115.7	19.1	134.8	3.3
1955e	125.0	25.6	150.6	3.3

e Data for this year estimated from Department of Commerce national income figures on basis of 1952 relation of Internal Revenue Service and Department of Commerce data.

i Includes taxable fiduciaries. For 1944-1947 see Joseph A. Pechman, "Yield of the Individual Income Tax During a Recession," *National Tax Journal*, March 1954, Vol. VIII, p. 7; worksheets for 1948 on.

j More accurately, this is the increase that would be necessary in the over-all effective rate (i.e. column 15 as a per cent of column 14). Only if the tax bracket distribution of the amount in column 12 is precisely similar to that in column 11 would this be the same as the required percentage point rise in the whole rate schedule. But the imputed amount (column 12) is more concentrated than the rest of surtax net income (column 11). The entries in column 14, therefore, can be construed as very conservative estimates; a lower rate increase than they indicate would probably recoup the current revenue loss.

MEASURING THE EFFECT OF THE RELIEF PROVISIONS

There is no need to elaborate on the procedures used in measuring the effect of the relief provisions—both those incorporated in the Internal Revenue Code of 1954 and those initially proposed by President Eisenhower—because they are simple extensions of some of the methods already discussed.

To determine by how much the relief would moderate the differentials for Tables 37, 38 and 39, data similar to that of Table 4 were used, and the column numbers in what follows refer to this table. To measure the relief afforded by the exclusion at selected stockholder income levels (column 1), the excluded amounts—$50 for separate and $100 for joint returns in the 1954 Code, and twice these amounts under the original proposal—were multiplied by the marginal rates applicable to the taxable incomes in column 7. To get the tax saving due to the credit, all dividends (column 5) above the excluded amount were multiplied by 4 per cent for the actual law and 15 per cent for the original proposal. Then the two types of tax saving were combined, and weighted averages of the joint and separate return totals were computed following the method of Table 5.

In estimating the aggregate relief (Table 40) procedures similar to those just noted were used. But in this case the relief provisions were applied to the data—the dividend-adjusted gross income cells—developed for the partnership method revenue estimates.

Index

NATIONAL BUREAU BOOKS *are available from bookstores or Princeton University Press, Princeton, New Jersey, except that contributors and subscribers to the National Bureau should order directly from the Bureau.* OCCASIONAL *and* TECHNICAL PAPERS, EXPLORATORY REPORTS, *and* ANNUAL REPORTS *are available from the National Bureau of Economic Research, 261 Madison Avenue, New York 16, New York.*

SOME RECENT PUBLICATIONS OF THE
NATIONAL BUREAU OF ECONOMIC RESEARCH

BOOKS

Financial Intermediaries in the American Economy since 1900 (1958) Raymond W. Goldsmith	452 pp.	$ 8.50
Federal Lending and Loan Insurance (1958) R. J. Saulnier, Harold G. Halcrow, and Neil H. Jacoby	596 pp.	12.00
Capital in Agriculture: Its Formation and Financing since 1870 (1957) Alvin S. Tostlebe	260 pp.	6.00
The Demand and Supply of Scientific Personnel (1957) David M. Blank and George J. Stigler	220 pp.	4.00
A Theory of the Consumption Function (1957) Milton Friedman	260 pp.	4.75

OCCASIONAL PAPERS

59. *Corporate Bonds: Quality and Investment Performance* (1957) W. Braddock Hickman	44 pp.	$ .75
58. *Federal Lending: Its Growth and Impact* (1957) A summary, prepared by the National Bureau's editorial staff, of *Federal Lending and Loan Insurance*, by R. J. Saulnier, Harold G. Halcrow, and Neil H. Jacoby	56 pp.	1.00
57. *Electronic Computers and Business Indicators* (1957) Julius Shiskin	56 pp.	1.00
56. *Distribution of Union Membership among the States, 1939 and 1953* (1957) Leo Troy	40 pp.	.75
55. *Some Observations on Soviet Industrial Growth* (1957) G. Warren Nutter	20 pp.	.50
54. *Bank Stock Prices and the Bank Capital Problem* (1957) David Durand	86 pp.	1.00

ANNUAL REPORTS (GRATIS)

By Solomon Fabricant

37th. *Financial Research and the Problems of the Day*	May 1957
36th. *Basic Research and the Analysis of Current Business Conditions*	May 1956